Sovereignties in Question

John D. Caputo, *series editor*

PERSPECTIVES IN
CONTINENTAL
PHILOSOPHY

JACQUES DERRIDA

Sovereignties in Question
The Poetics of Paul Celan

EDITED BY THOMAS DUTOIT AND OUTI PASANEN

FORDHAM UNIVERSITY PRESS
New York ∎ 2005

Texts in this volume were originally published in French as follows: "Shibboleth: For Paul Celan" appeared as *Schibboleth: Pour Paul Celan*, by Jacques Derrida, Copyright © Éditions Galilée 1986; "Poetics and Politics of Witnessing" appeared as "Poétique et politique du témoinage," by Jacques Derrida, Copyright © Éditions Galilée 2004; "Language Is Never Owned: An Interview" appeared as "La langue n'appartient pas," by Jacques Derrida, Copyright © Éditions Galilée 2001; "Rams: Uninterrupted Dialogue—Between Two Infinities, the Poem" appeared as *Béliers: Le dialogue ininterrompu: Entre deux infinis, le poème*, by Jacques Derrida, Copyright © Éditions Galilée 2003; "The Truth That Wounds: From an Interview" translates a portion of "La vérité blessante," by Jacques Derrida, Copyright © Éditions Galilée 2004. "Majesties" has not yet been published in French; it is an excerpt from the seminar "La bête et le souverain," by Jacques Derrida, Copyright © Éditions Galilée 2005. For full bibliographical information, see the editor's preface.

An earlier and shorter version of "Shibboleth: For Paul Celan" was published as "Shibboleth," in *Midrash and Literature*, ed. Geoffrey H. Hartman and Sanford Budick (New Haven: Yale University Press, 1986), 307–47, copyright © 1984 Yale University.

This work has been published with the assistance of the National Center for the Book—French Ministry of Culture.

Ouvrage publié avec le soutien du Centre national du livre——ministère français chargé de la culture.

Perspectives in Continental Philosophy Series, No. 44

Library of Congress Cataloging-in-Publication Data

Derrida, Jacques.
    Sovereignties in question : the poetics of Paul Celan / Jacques Derrida ; edited by Thomas Dutoit and Outi Pasanen.
    v. cm.—(Perspectives in continental philosophy series, ISSN 1089-3938 ; no. 44)
    Essays, except for "Majesties," originally published in French.
    Includes bibliographical references.
    Contents: To receive, to send : a note on the text / by Thomas Dutoit—Shibboleth: for Paul Celan—Poetics and politics of witnessing—Language is never owned : an interview—Majesties—Rams : uninterrupted dialogue—between two infinities, the poem—The truth that wounds : from an interview—Appendix : the meridian / by Paul Celan.
    ISBN 0-8232-2437-6 (hardcover : alk. paper)—ISBN 0-8232-2438-4 (pbk. : alk. paper)
    1. Celan, Paul—Aesthetics. I. Dutoit, Thomas. II. Pasanen, Outi. III. Title. IV. Series: Perspectives in continental philosophy ; no. 44.
PT2605.E4Z5972   2005
831'.914—dc22   2005028307

16 15 14   5 4 3 2

Contents

To Receive, to Send: A Note on the Text

THOMAS DUTOIT

Sovereignties in Question: The Poetics of Paul Celan brings together Jacques Derrida's writings on the work of Paul Celan. Jacques Derrida accepted the idea for this book, conceived in May 2004, and he provided its title in August 2004. All those involved in its preparation for publication had dearly hoped to give it to him, to return to him in English what he had originally delivered in French. Yet death ends not what continues to send, and so, infinitely, to receive will in turn be still to send.

The essays are presented in chronological order. All the translations have been revised by the editors, in view of the coherence of the volume overall. We would like especially to thank Helen Tartar for her wisdom at the helm, Haun Saussy for helpful suggestions concerning idiom, and Michael Naas for final adjudications and polish.

"Shibboleth: For Paul Celan" was published in French as *Schibboleth: Pour Paul Celan* (Paris: Galilée, 1986). The present version, which restores the full French text, as well as the layout of the French publication, was revised by Thomas Dutoit. It is based on the translation by Joshua Wilner that appeared in *Word Traces: Readings of Paul Celan*, ed. Aris Fioretos (Baltimore: The Johns Hopkins University Press, 1994), 3–72. (A shorter version of that translation was earlier published as "Shibboleth," in *Midrash and Literature*, ed.

Geoffrey H. Hartman and Sanford Budick [New Haven: Yale University Press, 1986], 307–47).

"Poetics and Politics of Witnessing" appeared in English in an earlier version as "'A Self-Unsealing Poetic Text': The Poetics and Politics of Witnessing," trans. Rachel Bowlby, in *Revenge of the Aesthetic: The Place of Literature in Theory Today*, ed. Michael Clark (Berkeley: University of California Press, 2000), 180–207, Copyright © 2000 The Regents of the University of California. As published in the present volume, the essay has been newly translated by Outi Pasanen from the expanded French version, "Poétique et politique du témoignage," published in *Derrida*, ed. Marie-Louise Mallet and Ginette Michaud, *Cahiers de l'Herne* (Paris: l'Herne, 2004), 521–39.

"Language Is Never Owned," published in French as "La langue n'appartient pas," in the special issue *Paul Celan* of *Europe*, no. 861–62 (January-February 2001), 81–91, has been translated by Thomas Dutoit and Philippe Romanski for this volume.

"Majesties," translated by Outi Pasanen, is excerpted from the French text of Jacques Derrida's seminar "La bête et le souverain," delivered at the École des Hautes Études en Sciences Sociales, Paris, in 2001–3. It is extracted from the sessions of February 20 and March 6, 2002. A different translation of the same extract, by Alessia Ricciardi and Chris Yu, appeared in *New German Critique*, special issue on Paul Celan, ed. Ulrich Baer and Amir Eshel, Winter 2004.

The essay "Rams: Uninterrupted Dialogue—Between Two Infinities, the Poem," published in French as *Béliers. Le dialogue ininterrompu: Entre deux infinis, le poème* (Paris: Galilée, 2003), has been translated by Thomas Dutoit and Philippe Romanski. The first two parts of the essay were published in slightly different form under the title "Uninterrupted Dialogue: Between Two Infinities, the Poem," *Research in Phenomenology* 34 (2004): 3–20.

"The Truth That Wounds," translated by Thomas Dutoit, is excerpted from "La vérité blessante," in the special issue *Jacques Derrida* of *Europe*, no. 901 (May 2004), 22–27.

The first English translation of Paul Celan's "The Meridian," by Jerry Glenn, which Jacques Derrida used in teaching "Majesties," Stanford University Press, appeared in the *Chicago Review*, ed. Joel Golb, 29, no. 3 (1978): 29–40. It appears here as an appendix courtesy of the *Chicago Review* and Stanford University Press, in light of the latter's planned English translation of the German critical edition (see p. 205, n. 5, below).

Sovereignties in Question

Shibboleth
For Paul Celan

I

Only one time: circumcision takes place only once.[a]

Such, at least, is the appearance given to us, and the tradition of the appearance, let us not say of the simulacrum.

We will have to turn around this appearance. Not so much in order to circumscribe or to circumvent some *truth* of circumcision — that we must renounce for essential reasons. But rather to let ourselves be approached by the resistance that *once* may offer to thought. And this is a question of offering, and of what such resistance *gives* one to think. And resistance will be our theme, too, as it points back to the last war, all wars, clandestine activity, demarcation lines, discrimination, passports, and passwords.

Before we ask ourselves what *one time* [une fois] means, if this *means* something, and the word *time* in *only one time* [*le mot* fois *dans* une seule fois]; before interpreting, as philosophers or philosophers of language, as hermeneuts or poeticians, the meaning of what is said in French *une fois*, we should no doubt make a long and thoughtful stop along the linguistic borders where, as you know, one must pronounce *shibboleth* properly in order to be granted the right to pass, indeed, the right to live. *Une fois* — nothing, one might believe, is easier to translate than that: *einmal, once, one time* [in English in the original], *una volta*. As for the vicissitudes of our Latinity: the Spanish *vez,* the whole syntax of *vicem, vice, vices, vicibus, vicissim, in vicem, vice versa,* and even *vicarius,* its turns, returns, replacements, and supplantings, voltes and revolutions—we will be led back to them more than once. For the moment, a single remark: the semantic registers of all these idioms do not *immediately* translate one another; they appear heterogeneous. The English expression *one time* indicates time [*le temps*], whereas neither *once* nor *einmal,* nor any of the French, Italian, or Spanish locutions does. The Latin idioms resort instead to the turn, the tour or volte. And yet, despite this border, the crossing of ordinary translation takes place every day without the least uncertainty, each time the semantics of the everyday imposes its conventions. Each time that it effaces the idiom.[b]

If a circumcision takes place only one time [*une fois*], this time is therefore, *à la fois,* at the same time [in English in the original], *en même temps,* the first and last time. Such would be the appearance— archaeology and eschatology—around which we will have to turn, as around the ring [*anneau*] that is outlined, carved, or detached in circumcision. This ring or annulus holds together a band, a weddingband [*alliance*],[c] the anniversary date and the return of the year.

I will speak, therefore, at once of circumcision and of the one-and-only time, in other words, of what *comes down to*[d] marking itself as the one-and-only time: what one sometimes [*parfois*] calls a *date.*

My main concern will not be to speak about the date in general. Rather, I will listen to what Celan says about it; better, I will watch him give himself over to the inscription of invisible, perhaps unreadable, dates: anniversaries, rings, constellations, and repetitions of singular, unique, *unrepeatable* events—*unwiederholbar* is his word.

How can one date what does not repeat if dating also calls for some form of return, if it recalls in the readability of a repetition? But how can one date anything other than that which never repeats itself?

Having just named the unrepeatable (*unwiederholbar*) and remarked upon the French language and the borders of translation, I am tempted to cite a poem to which Celan gave a French title, "À la pointe acérée,"* not because it would have some immediate relation to the surgery of circumcision, but because it orients itself, in the night, along the path of questions "Nach / dem Unwiederholbaren," toward the non-repeatable. I will limit myself first to these small pebbles of white chalk on a board, a sort of non-writing in which the concretion of language hardens:

Ungeschriebenes, zu	Unwritten things, hardened
Sprache verhärtet	into language*

Without writing, non-written, the unwritten switches over to this question of reading on a board or tablet that you perhaps are. You are a tablet or a door: much later, we will see how a word can address itself, indeed, confide itself, to a door, hinge on a door opened to the other.

Tür du davor einst, Tafel	Door you in front of it once, tablet

(and in the *einst* it is again "once, only one time")

mit dem getöteten	with the killed
Kreidestern drauf:	chalk star on it:
ihn	that
hat nun ein—lesendes?—Aug.)	has now a—reading?—eye has it now).

We could have followed in this poem the ever discrete, discontinuous, *caesuraed*, naturally elliptical relays of the hour (*Waldstunde*), or of the trace, and of the track of a wheel that turns on itself (*Radspur*). But I rush headlong *toward* the question that seeks its way *toward* or *after* (*nach*) the unrepeatable, through the hedges of beech, among the beechmast (*Buchecker*). These may also be read as the corners of books or the open, gaping angles of a text:

Wege dorthin.	Ways to that place.
Waldstunde an	Forest hour alongside
der blubbernden Radspur entlang.	the spluttering wheeltrack.
Auf-	Sel-
gelesene	lected
kleine, klaffende	small, gaping
Buchecker: schwärzliches	beechnuts: blackish
Offen, von	openness, questioned
Fingergedanken befragt	by fingerthoughts
nach—	after—
wonach?	after what?
Nach	After
dem Unwiederholbaren, nach	the unrepeatable, after
ihm, nach	it, after
allem.	everything.
Blubbernde Wege dorthin.	Spluttering ways to that place.
Etwas, das gehn kann, grußlos	Something that can walk, ungreeting

wie Herzgewordenes,   as all that's become heart,
kommt.   comes.*

Ways (*Wege*): something comes, which can go ("Etwas, das gehn kann, . . . kommt"). What is going, coming, going to come, going and coming? And becoming heart? What coming, what singular event is at issue? What impossible repetition ("Nach / dem Unwiederhol-baren, nach / ihm")?

How to "become heart"? Let us not, for the moment, appeal to Pascal or to Heidegger—who, incidentally, suspects the former of having yielded too much to science and forgotten the original think-ing of the heart. Hearing me speak of the date and of circumcision, some might hasten toward the "circumcised heart" of the Scriptures. That would be going too fast and along a path of too little resistance. Celan's trenchant ellipsis requires more patience, it demands discre-tion. Caesura is the law. Yet it gathers in the discretion of the discon-tinuous, in the severing of the relation to the other or in the interruption of address, as address itself.

It makes no sense, as you may well imagine, to dissociate, on the one hand, Celan's writings *on the subject* of the date, those that name the theme of the date, from, on the other hand, the poetic traces of dating. To trust in the partition [*partage*ᵉ] between a theoretical, phil-osophical, hermeneutic, even poeticist discourse on the phenomenon of the date, on the one hand, and, on the other hand, a poetic imple-mentation of datingᶠ is to no longer read him.

The example of the "Meridian" warns us against such a misunder-standing. It is, as they say, a "speech": an address pronounced on a given occasion and date. Its date is that of the bestowal of a prize ("Rede anläßlich der Verleihung des Georg-Büchner-Preises, am 22. Oktober 1960"). On October 22, 1960, this address, in its manner, treats art, more precisely, the memory of art, perhaps art as a thing from the past, Hegel would have said "art as we already know it,"* but also art as "a problem," "a problem which is hardy, long-lived, and transformable—that is to say, eternal."* The thing from the past: "Meine Damen und Herren! Die Kunst, das ist, Sie erinnern sich . . . ," "Art, you will remember. . . ."* The ironic attack of this first sentence seems to speak of a bygone history, but it does so in order to appeal to the memory of those who have read Büchner. Celan announces that he is going to evoke several appearances of art, in particular in *Woyzeck* and *Leonce and Lena*: you remember. A thing from our past that comes back in memory, but also a problem of the future or the to-come, an eternal problem, and above all a path toward poetry. Not poetry, but a path in view of poetry, one of the paths only, one among others, and not the shortest. "In that case art would be the path [*Weg*] traveled by poetry—nothing more and nothing less. // I know, there are other, shorter paths. But after all poetry, too, often runs ahead of us. *La poésie, elle aussi, brûle nos étapes.*"*

At this crossing of the paths between art and poetry, in this place to which poetry makes its way sometimes without even the patience of a path, lies the enigma of the date.

It seems to resist every question, every form of philosophical questioning, every objectivation, every theoretico-hermeneutic thematization.

Celan shows this poetically: by a *mise-en-oeuvre* of the date. In this speech itself. He begins by citing several dates: 1909, the date of a work devoted to Jakob Michael Lenz by a part-time lecturer in Moscow, M. N. Rosanov; then the night of May 23–24, 1792, the date of Lenz's death in Moscow, itself cited, already mentioned in this work. Then Celan *mentions* the date that appears this time on the first page of Büchner's *Lenz*, "the Lenz who 'walked through the mountains on the 20th of January.'"*

Who walked through the mountains, *on this date*?

He, Lenz, Celan insists, he and not the artist preoccupied with the questions of art. He, as an "I," "he as Me," "lui en tant que Moi," says André du Bouchet's translation,* "er als ein Ich." This *I* who is not the artist obsessed by questions of art, those posed to him by art—Celan does not rule out that this may be the poet, but in any case it is not the artist.

The singular turn of this phrase, "he as an *I*," will support the whole logic of individuation, of the "sign of individuation" that each poem constitutes. The poem is "the language of an individual which has taken on form"* ("gestaltgewordene Sprache eines Einzelnen"). Singularity, but also solitude: the only one, the poem is alone (*einsam*). And from within the most intimate essence of its solitude, it is underway (*unterwegs*), "aspiring to a presence," "aspirant à une présence," following the French translation by du Bouchet* ("und seinem innersten Wesen nach Gegenwart und Präsenz"). Insofar as it is alone, solitary, the poem would stand then, perhaps, within the "secret of encounter."*

The only one: singularity, solitude, the secret of encounter. What assigns the singular to its date?

For example: there was a 20th of January. Such a date will have been able to be written, alone, unique, exempt [*soustraite*] from repetition. Yet this absolute property can also be transcribed, exported, deported, expropriated, reappropriated, repeated in its absolute singularity. Indeed this has to be if the date is to expose itself, to risk losing itself in a readability. As a sign of individuation, this absolute property can announce something like the essence of the poem, the singular. Celan prefers to say of "every poem," better still, of "each poem": "Vielleicht darf man sagen, daß jedem Gedicht sein '20. Jänner' eingeschrieben bleibt?" "Perhaps one can say that in every poem its own '20th of January' remains inscribed."* Here is a generality: to the keeping of each poem, of every poem, the inscription of a date, of this date—for example, a "20th of January"—is entrusted. But despite the generality of the law, the example remains irreplaceable. And what must remain, committed to the keeping, in other words, to the truth of each poem, is this irreplaceable itself: the example offers its example only if it is valid for no other. But precisely in that it offers its example, and the only example possible, the one which it alone offers: the only one.

Today, on this day, at this date. And this marking of today perhaps tells us something about the essence of the poem today, for us now. Not the essence of poetic modernity or postmodernity, not the essence of an epoch or a period in some history of poetry, but what happens "today" "anew" to poetry, to poems, what happens to them at this date.

What happens to them at this date is precisely the date, a certain experience of the date. Very ancient, certainly, without date, but absolutely new as of this date. And new because, for the first time, it is here *borne* or sought after "most clearly" (am *deutlichsten*). Clarity, distinction, sharpness, readability, this is what today would be *new*. Let us not believe that what thus becomes readable would be the date *itself*; rather, it is only the poetic experience of the date, that which a date, *this one*, ordains in our relation to it, a certain poetic seeking. "Perhaps the novelty of poems that are written today is to be found in precisely this point: that here the attempt is most clearly made to remain mindful of such dates?" ("Vielleicht ist das Neue an den Gedichten, die heute geschrieben werden, gerade dies: daß hier am deutlichsten versucht wird, solcher Daten eingedenk zu bleiben?").*

Celan dates this question concerning the date, this hypothesis ("Perhaps . . ."); it concerns *today* every poem of *today*, the newness of each poetic work of our time, each of which, at this date, would have the singularity of dating (transitively), of remaining mindful of dates (*Daten eingedenk zu bleiben*). What would date the poetics of today would perhaps be an inscription of the date or at least a certain coming to clarity, newly, of a poetic necessity that, itself, does not date from today. Granted.

But—the sentences we have just heard are followed three times by "But."

The first, the least energetic and the least oppositional, raises again the same questions about the traces of the other *as I*: how can such an *other* date, irreplaceable and singular, the date of the other, the date for the other, be deciphered, transcribed, or translated? How can I appropriate it for myself? Or, better, how can I transcribe myself into it? And how can the memory of such a date still dispose of a to-come [*avenir*]? What dates to come [*à venir*] do we prepare in such a transcription?ᵍ Here, then, is the first "But." The ellipsis of the sentence is more economical than I can convey, and its gripping sobriety can only sign, which is to say, date itself, from within its idiom, a certain manner of inhabiting the idiom (signed: Celan from a certain place in the German language, which was his property alone). I continue to cite the translation, not having the courage to hazard one myself: "But do we not all circumscribe ourselves in reference to such dates? And to which dates to come do we subscribe ourselves?" ("Aber schreiben wir uns nicht alle von solchen Daten her? Und welchen Daten schreiben wir uns zu?").*

Here resounds the second *But*: after a blank, the mark of a long silence, the time [*le temps*] of a meditation through which the preceding question makes its way. It leaves the trace of an affirmation, against which arises, at least to complicate it, a second affirmation. And the force of this opposition carries the momentum right up to the point of an exclamation. ("Aber das Gedicht spricht ja! Es bleibt seiner Daten eingedenk, aber—es spricht. Gewiß, es spricht immer nur in seiner eigenen, allereigensten Sache.")

What does this *but* mean? No doubt that *despite* the date, in spite of its memory rooted in the singularity of an event, the poem speaks: to all and in general, and first of all to the other. The *but* seems to carry the poem's utterance beyond its date: if the poem recalls a date, calls itself back to its date,ʰ to the date *on which* it writes or *of which* it writes, as of which it writes (to) itself [*il s'écrit*], yet it speaks! to all, to the other, to whoever does not partake in [*partage*] the experience or the knowledge of the singularity thus dated, *as of* or *from* a particular place, day, month, year. In the preceding phrase, the ambiguous force of *von* gathers in advance all of our paradoxes ("Aber schreiben wir uns nicht alle von solchen Daten her?"): we write *of* the date, *about* certain dates, but also *as of* certain dates, *at* or *to* [à] certain dates. The French *à* carries itself, in the ambiguous force of its own idiom, toward a to-come of unknown destination. No particular sentence of Celan says this, but it doubtless corresponds to the general logic of this discourse, as the sentence that follows makes explicit: "Und welchen Daten schreiben wir uns zu?" To which date do we ascribe ourselves, which dates do we appropriate, now, but also, in more ambiguous fashion, turned toward which dates to come do we write ourselves, do we transcribe ourselves? As if writing *at* a certain date meant not only writing on a particular day, at a particular hour, on a particular date, but also writing *to* the date, addressing oneself to it, destining oneself to the date as to the other, the date past as well as the date promised.

What is this *to* of *the to*-come—insofar as it is a date?

Yet the poem speaks. Despite the date, even if it also speaks thanks to it, as of it, of it, toward it, and speaks always of itself on its own, very own behalf, *in seiner eigenen, allereigensten Sache*, in its own name,* without ever compromising the absolute singularity, the inalienable property, of that which convokes it. And yet this inalienable must speak of the other, and to the other; it must speak. The date provokes the poem, but the poem speaks! And it speaks of what provokes it, *to* the date that provokes it, thus convoked from the to-come of the *same* date, in other words, from its return at *another* date.

How are we to hear the exclamation? Why this exclamation point after the *but* of an objection that has no rhetorical pretense about it? One might find it surprising. I think that it confers the accent, it accentuates and marks the tone, of admiration, of astonishment before poetic exclamation itself. The poet exclaims—before the miracle that makes clamor, poetic acclamation, possible: the poem speaks! and it speaks to the date of which it speaks! Instead of walling up the poem and reducing it to the silence of singularity, a date gives it its chance, the chance to speak to the other!

If the poem *owes* a debt to the date, if it owes itself to its date as to its own most proper thing (*Sache*), cause, or signature, if it owes itself to its secret, it speaks only insofar as it acquits itself, so to speak, of such a date—and of a date that is also a gift—in order to release itself from the date without denying it, above all without disavowing it. It absolves itself of the date so that its utterance may resonate and clamor beyond a singularity that might otherwise remain undecipherable, mute, and immured in its date—in the unrepeatable. One must, while preserving its memory, speak of the date that already speaks of itself: the date, by its mere occurrence, by the inscription of a sign "as a memorandum," will have broken the silence of pure singularity. But to speak of it one must also efface it, make it readable, audible, intelligible *beyond the pure singularity* of which it speaks. Now the beyond of absolute singularity, the chance for the poem's exclamation, is not the simple effacement of the date in a generality, but *its effacement in front of* another date, the one *to which* it speaks, the date of an other, masculine or feminine, which is strangely allied in the secret of an *encounter*, a *chance* secret, with the same date. In a moment I will, to clarify, offer some examples.

What takes place in this experience of the date, experience itself? And of a date that must be effaced in order to be preserved, in order to preserve the commemoration of the event, this coming of the unique in thrall to the poem, which must exceed it and which alone, precisely thereby, may transport it, giving it to be understood beyond its unreadable cipher? What takes place is perhaps what Celan calls, a little further on, *Geheimnis der Begegnung*, the secret of encounter.

Encounter—in this word two values without which a date would never take place encounter one another: the encounter as random occurrence, as chance, as luck or coincidence, as the conjuncture that comes to seal one or more than one event *once*, at a particular hour, on a particular day, in a particular month, year, and region; and when the encounter with the other, the ineluctable singularity from which and destined to which a poem speaks.[i] In its otherness and its solitude (which is also that of the poem, "alone," "solitary"), it may inhabit the conjuncture of one and the same date. This is what happens.

What happens, if something happens, is that—and this encounter, in an idiom, of all the meanings of encounter.

But—a third time, a third *but* opens a new paragraph. It begins "But I think . . . ," it closes with "today and here," and it is the signature of an "Aber ich denke . . . heute und hier":

> But I think—and this thought can scarcely come as a surprise to you—I think that it has always belonged to the hopes of the poem, in precisely this manner to speak in the cause of the *strange*—no, I can no longer use this word—in precisely this manner to speak *for the sake of an Other*—who knows, perhaps for the sake of a *wholly Other*.

This "who knows," at which I see I have arrived, is the only thing I can add—on my own, here, today—to the old hopes.*

The *wholly other* thus comes to open the thought of the poem to some thing or sake (*Sache*: "in eines Anderen Sache zu sprechen . . . in eines *ganz Anderen* Sache"), whose otherness must not contradict but ally itself with, by expropriating it, the "ownmost sake" just in question, that due to which the poem speaks to its date, as of its date, and always, in its proper name, "in seiner eigenen, allereigensten Sache." Several singular events may be conjoined, allied, *concentrated* in the same date, which therefore becomes both the same and an other, wholly other as the same, capable of speaking to the other of the other, to the one who cannot decipher such an absolutely closed date, a tomb, closed over the event that it marks. Celan calls this gathered multiplicity by a strong and charged name: *concentration*. A little further on he speaks of the poem's attention (*Aufmerksamkeit*) to all that it encounters. This attention would be, rather, a concentration that remains mindful of "all our dates" ("eine aller unserer Daten eingedenk bleibende Konzentration"). The word *concentration* can become a terrible one for memory. But one can hear it *at once* in the register in which one speaks of the gathering of the soul, of the heart, and of spiritual concentration, for example, in prayer (and Celan cites Benjamin citing Malebranche in his essay on Kafka, "Attention is the natural prayer of the soul")—and in the other sense in which concentration gathers a multiplicity of dates around the same anamnestic center, "all our dates" coming to conjoin or constellate at once, in a single place: in truth, in a single poem, in *the only one*, in the poem that is each time, we have seen, alone, the only one, solitary and singular.

That is perhaps what goes on in the exemplary act of the "Meridian." This speech, this address, this speech act (*Rede*) is not—not only—a treatise or a metadiscourse *about* the date, but rather the habitation, by a poem, of its own date, its poetic *mise-en-œuvre* as well, making a date specific to the poet a date for the other, the date of the other, or, inversely—for this gift returns like an anniversary—a step by which the poet transcribes or promises himself in the date of the other. In the unique ring of its constellation, one and the "same" date commemorates heterogeneous events, suddenly neighbors to one another, even though one knows that they remain, and must remain, strangers, infinitely. It is just this which is called the encounter, the encounter of the other, "the secret of encounter"—and precisely here the meridian is discovered. There was a 20th of January, that of Lenz, who "'walked through the mountains on the 20th of January.'" And then at the *same* date, on *another* 20th of January, Celan encounters, he encounters the other, and he encounters himself at the intersection of this date with itself, with itself as other, as the date of the other. And yet this takes place only once, and always anew, each time only one time, the *each-time-only-one time* constituting a generic law, a law of genre, of that which always confronts genre. One would have to resituate here the question of transcendental schematism, of the imagination and of time [*du temps*], as a question of the date — *of the time* [fois].ʲ And one would have to reread what Celan said earlier about images:

> And what, then, would the images be?
> That which is perceived and to be perceived one time, one time over and over again, and only now and only here. And the poem would then be the place where all tropes and metaphors are developed ad absurdum.*

This radical *ad absurdum* — the impossibility of that which, each time only once, has meaning only by having no meaning, no ideal or general meaning, or has meaning only so as to invoke, in order to betray them, the concept, law, or genre — is the pure poem. Now the pure poem does not exist; better still, it is that "which isn't there!" ("das es nicht gibt!"). To the question "Of what do I speak when I speak not of poems but of the poem?" Celan answers,

> I am speaking of the poem which doesn't exist!
> The absolute poem — no, it doesn't exist, it cannot exist."*

But if the absolute poem does not take place, if there is no such thing ("es gibt nicht"), there is the image, the each time only once, the poetics of the date and the secret of encounter: the other-I, a 20th of January that was also mine after having been that of Lenz. Here:

> A few years ago I wrote a little quatrain which reads:
>
> Voices from the path of the nettles:
> *come on your hands to us.*
> Whoever is alone with the lamp
> has only his palm to read from.

> And last year, in commemoration of a proposed encounter in Engadine which came to naught, I composed a little story in which I had a person walk, "like Lenz," through the mountains.

Both times I started to write from a "20th of January," from my "20th of January."

I encountered . . . myself.*

I encountered myself—myself *as* the other, one 20th of January *like* another, and *like* Lenz, as Lenz *himself*, "wie Lenz": the quotation marks around the expression set off, in the text, what is unusual in the figure.

This *like* is also the signal of another appearance summoned within the same comparison. This man whom I described, wrote, signed, was *just like* Lenz, almost like Lenz himself, *as* Lenz. The *wie* almost has the force of an *als*. But *at the same time*, it is myself, since in this figure of the other, as the other, I encountered myself at this date. The *like* and the co-signature of the date, the very figure or image, each time, of the other, "both times," one time *like* the other time ("das eine wie das andere Mal"). Such would be the anniversary turn of the date. In the "Meridian," it is also the finding, the encounter of the place of encounter, the discovery of the meridian itself:

> I am also seeking the place of my own origin, since I have once again arrived at the point of my own departure.
>
> I am seeking all this on the map with a finger which is uncertain, because it is restless—on a child's map, as I readily confess.
>
> None of these places is to be found, they do not exist, but I know where they would have to exist—above all at the present time—and . . . I find something!
>
> Ladies and gentlemen, I find something which offers me some consolation for having traveled this impossible path, this path of the impossible, in your presence.
>
> I find something which binds and which, like the poem, leads to an encounter.
>
> I find something, like language, immaterial, yet earthly, terrestrial, something circular, which traverses both poles and returns to itself, thereby—I am happy to report—even crossing the tropics and tropes. I find . . . a *meridian*.*

Almost the last word of the text, near the signature. What Celan finds or discovers, on the spur of the moment, invents, if one may say so, more and less than a fiction, is not only a meridian, the Meridian, but the word and the image, the trope *meridian*, which offers the example of the law, in its inexhaustible polytropy, and which *binds* (*das*

Verbindende, "that which binds," "ce qui lie," as André du Bouchet translates; "the intermediary," "l'intermédiare," as Jean Launay translates), which provokes in broad daylight, at noon, *at midday,* the encounter with the other in a single place, at a single point, that of the poem, of this poem: "In the here and now of the poem — and the poem itself, after all, has only this one, unique, punctual present — even in this immediacy and proximity to itself it lets speak what the Other has that is most proper to it: its time."*

II

A date would be like the gnomon of these meridians.

Does one ever speak of a date? But does one ever speak without speaking of a date? Of it and as of it?

Whether one will or not, whether or not one knows it, acknowledges it, or dissembles it, an utterance is always dated. What I am going to hazard now concerning the date in general, concerning what a generality may say or gainsay where the date is concerned, concerning the gnomon of Paul Celan,[k] will all be dated in its turn.

Under certain conditions, at least, dating comes down to signing. To inscribe a date, to consign it, is not only to sign as of a given year, month, day, or hour, all words that punctuate Celan's text, but also to sign at a place. Particular poems are "dated" Zürich, Tübingen, Todtnauberg, Paris, Jerusalem, Lyon, Tel Aviv, Vienna, Assisi, Cologne, Geneva, Brest, and so on. At the beginning or at the end of a letter, the date consigns a "now" of the calendar or of the clock ("alle Uhren und Kalender," on the second page of the "Meridian"), as well as the "here" of a country, of a region, of a house, in their proper names. It marks, in this way, at the point of the gnomon, the provenance of what is *given,* or, in any case, sent; of what is, whether or not it arrives, destined. *Speaking at its date,* what a discourse declares about the date in general, about the concept or the general meaning of the date, is not, by this fact, "dated," as one says of something that it dates in order to imply its age, that it has aged or aged badly; to speak of a discourse as dated is not to disqualify or invalidate it, but rather to signify that it is, at the least, marked by its date, signed by it, re-marked in a singular manner. What is thus remarked is its *departure,* that to which it no doubt belongs but from which it departs in order to address itself to the other: a certain (im)parting [*partage*].

On the subject of this singular remarking, I am going to hazard in my turn some remarks — in memory of some sendings dated *from* Paul Celan.

What is a date? Do we have the right to pose such a question, and in this form? The form of the question "What is . . .?" is not without provenance. It has its place of origin and its language. It dates. That it is dated does not discredit it; if we had the time, we could draw certain philosophical inferences from this, inferences, in truth, *about* its philosophical regime.

Has anyone ever been concerned with the question "What is a date?" The *you* who is told "Nirgends / fragt es nach dir," nowhere is there any asking about you, nowhere any concern for you, is a date, of that we can be certain: *a priori*. This you, who must be an I, like the "Er, als ein Ich" of a moment ago, always figures an irreplaceable singularity. Only another singularity, just as irreplaceable, can take its place without substituting for it. One addresses this *you* as one addresses a date, the here and now of a commemorable provenance.

As it reaches me, at least, the question "What is a date?" presupposes two things.

First, the question "What is . . .?" has a history, a provenance; it is signed, engaged, commanded by a place, a time, a language or a network of languages, in other words, by a date in relation to whose essence this question has only a limited power, a finite claim, its very pertinence contestable. This is not unrelated to what our symposium calls "the philosophical implications" of Celan's work. Perhaps philosophy, as such, and insofar as it makes use of the question "What is . . .?," has nothing essential to say about what dates from Celan or about what Celan says or makes of the date—which might in turn say something to us, perhaps, about philosophy.

Second, in the inscription of a date, in the explicit and coded phenomenon of dating, *what is dated must nonetheless not be dated*. The date: yes and no, Celan would say, as he does more than once.

Sprich	Speak—
Doch scheide das Nein nicht vom Ja.	But keep yes and no unsplit.
Gib deinem Spruch auch den Sinn:	And give your say this meaning:
gib ihm den Schatten.	give it the shade.
Gib ihm Schatten genug,	Give it shade enough
gib ihm so viel,	give it as much
als du um dich verteilt weißt	as you know has been dealt out
zwischen	between
Mitnacht und Mittag und Mitnacht,	midnight and midday and
	midnight.*

Again the meridian. This mark that one calls a date must nonetheless be *marked off*, in a singular fashion, detached from the very thing that it dates, and must, in this demarcation, in this very deportation, become readable, readable as a date, precisely, by wresting itself or subtracting itself from itself, from its immediate adherence, from the here and now, by freeing itself from what it nonetheless remains, a date. It is necessary that in the date the unrepeatable (*das Unwieder-holbare*) repeat itself, effacing in itself the irreducible singularity that it denotes. It is necessary that, in a certain manner, the unrepeatable divide itself in repeating itself, and in the same stroke encipher or encrypt itself. Like *physis*, a date loves to encrypt itself. It must efface itself in order to become readable, to render itself unreadable in its very readability. For if the date does not suspend in itself the unique marking that connects it to an event without witness, without other witness, it remains intact but absolutely indecipherable. It is no longer even what it has to be, what it will have had to be, its essence and its destination; it no longer keeps its promise, that of a date.

How, then, can that which is dated, while marking a date, not date? This question, whether one fears it or hopes for it, cannot be formulated in this way in all languages. It remains barely translatable. I insist on this because what a date, always bound up with some proper name, gives us to think, commemorate, or bless, as well as to cross in a possible-impossible translation, is, each time, an idiom. And if the idiomatic form of my question appears untranslatable, that is because it plays on the double functioning of the verb *to date*. In French or in English. Transitively: I date a poem. Intransitively: a poem dates if it ages, if it has a history and is of a certain age.

To ask "What is a date?" is not to wonder about the meaning of the word *date*. Nor is it to inquire into established or putative etymology, though this may not be without interest. It might, in fact, lead us to think about the gift and literality, even the gift of the letter: *data littera*, the first words of a formula for indicating the date. This would set us on the track of the first word, of the initial or the *incipit* of a letter, of the first letter of a letter—but also of a gift* or sending. The gift or the sending will carry us beyond the question given in the form "What is?" A date is not, since it withdraws in order to appear, but if *there is no* absolute poem ("Das absolute Gedicht—nein, das gibt es gewiß nicht, das kann es nicht geben!"), says Celan, perhaps there is (*es gibt*) something of the date—even if the date does not exist.

I will associate for the moment, in a preliminary and disorderly way, the values of the gift and the proper name (for a date functions like a proper name) with three other essential values:

1. That of what is sent within the strict limits of the epistolary code.

2. The re-marking of place and time, at the point of the here and now.

3. The signature: even if the date is a starting point, it may come at the letter's end and in all cases, whether at the beginning or the end, have the force of a signed commitment, of an obligation, a promise or an oath (*sacramentum*). In essence, a signature is always dated and has value only on this condition. It dates, and it has a date. Prior to being mentioned, the inscription of a date (here, now, this day, etc.) always entails a kind of signature: whoever inscribes the year, the day, the place, in short, the present of a "here and now" attests thereby his or her own presence at the act of inscription.

Celan dated all his poems. I am not thinking here, primarily, of a kind of dating that one might—mistakenly, but conveniently—call *external*, that is, the mention of the date on which a poem was written, begun, or finished. In its conventional form such mention lies in some ways outside the poem "properly speaking." One is certainly not entitled to push to the limit the distinction between such an external notation of the date and a more essential incorporation of the date within a poem whereof it is a part, a poem itself. In a certain manner, as we will see, Celan's poetry aims to displace, even to efface, such a limit. But supposing we maintain for clarity of exposition the provisional hypothesis of such a limit, we will first focus on a dating recorded *in* the body of the poem, *in* one of its parts, and in a form that can be recognized according to traditional codes (e.g., "the 13th of February"), then in a non-conventional, non-calendrical form of dating, one that would merge entirely, without remainder, with the general organization of the poetic text.

In "Eden," that memorable reading of a poem from *Schneepart*, "DU LIEGST im großen Gelausche," Peter Szondi recalls that an indication of date accompanied its first publication: Berlin, 22./23. 12. 1967.* We know how Szondi turned to account these dates and the chance of his having been the intimate witness of, and at times an actor in or party to, the experiences commemorated, displaced, and ciphered by the poem. We also know with what rigor and modesty he posed the problems of this *situation*, both with regard to the poem's genesis and with regard to the competence of its decipherers. With him, we must take into account the following fact: as the intimate and lucid witness of all the random contingencies and all the necessities that intersected in Celan's passing through Berlin *at this date*, Szondi was the only one able to bequeath to us the irreplaceable passwords of access to the poem, a priceless *shibboleth*, a luminous and humming swarm of notes, so many signs of gratitude for deciphering and translating the enigma. And yet, left to itself without witness, without a go-between, without the alerted complicity of a decipherer, without even the "external" knowledge of its date, a certain internal necessity of the poem would nonetheless *speak* to us, in the sense in which Celan says of the poem "But it speaks!" beyond what appears to confine it within the dated singularity of an individual experience.

Szondi was the first to acknowledge this. He set this enigma before himself with an admirable lucidity and prudence. How is one to give an account of this: concerning the circumstances in which the poem was written or, better, concerning those which it names, ciphers, disguises, or dates in its own body, concerning whose secrets it partakes, witnessing is *at once* indispensable, *essential* to the reading of the poem, to the partaking that it becomes in its turn, and, finally, *supplementary, nonessential*, merely the guarantee of an excess of intelligibility, which the poem can also forgo. *At once* essential and inessential. This *at once* stems — this is my hypothesis — from the structure of the date.

(I will not give myself over here to my own commemorations; I will not hand over my dates. Permit me nevertheless to recall that in my encounter with Paul Celan and in the friendship that subsequently bound us, such a short time before his death, Peter Szondi was always the mediator and witness, the mutual friend who introduced us in Paris, although we were already working there at the same institution. This took place a few months after a visit I made to the University of Berlin, at Szondi's invitation, in July 1968, not long after the month of December 1967 of which I spoke a moment ago.)

What does Szondi recall for us, from the outset of his reading? That Celan suppressed the poem's date for the first collection. It does not figure in the *Selected Poems* (*Ausgewählte Gedichte*) edited by Reichert in 1970. This conforms, according to Szondi, to Celan's customary practice: "The poems are dated in the manuscript, but not in the published versions."

But the retraction of the "external" date does not do away with the internal dating. While, as I will try to show, the latter carries within itself, in its turn, a force of self-effacement, what is involved is then another structure, that of the very inscription of the date.

We will therefore focus on the date as a cut[l] or incision that the poem bears in its body like a memory, sometimes several memories in one, the mark of a provenance, of a place and of a time. To speak of an incision or cut is to say that the poem is first cut into there [*s'y entame*]: it begins in the wounding of its date.

If we had the time, we should first patiently analyze the modalities of dating. There are many. In this typology, the most conventional form of dating, dating in the so-called literal or strict sense, consists in marking a sending with coded signs. It entails reference to charts and the utilization of so-called "objective" systems of notation and spatiotemporal plottings: the calendar (year, month, day), the clock (the hours, whether or not they are named—and how many times Celan names them, here or there, but only to restore them to the night of their ciphered silence: "sie werden die Stunde nicht nennen," "they will not call the hour by its name"*), toponomy, and, above all, the names of cities. These coded marks all share a common resource, but also a dramatic, fatal, and fatally equivocal power. Assigning or consigning absolute singularity, they must mark themselves off simultaneously, *at the same time*, and from themselves, by the possibility of commemoration. Indeed, they mark only insofar as their readability announces the possibility of a return. Not the absolute return of precisely what cannot come again: a birth or a circumcision takes place only once, nothing could be more self-evident. But rather the spectral revenance of that which, as a unique event in the world, will never come again.[m] A date is a specter. But this revenance of impossible return is marked *in* the date; it seals or specifies itself in the anniversary ring guaranteed by the code. For example, by the calendar. The anniversary ring inscribes the possibility of repetition, but also the circuit of return to the city whose name a date bears. The first inscription of a date signifies this possibility: that which cannot come back will come back as such, not only in memory, like all remembrance, but also at the same date, at a date in any case analogous, for example, each February 13 . . . And each time, at the same date, what one commemorates will be the date *of* that which could never come back. This date will have signed or sealed the unique, the unrepeatable, but to do so, it must have given itself to be read in a form sufficiently coded, readable, and decipherable for the indecipherable *to* *appear* in the analogy of the anniversary ring (February 13, 1962, is *analogous* to February 13, 1936), even if it appears *as* indecipherable.

One might be tempted to associate here all of Celan's rings with this alliance between the date and itself *as* other. There are so many, and each time they are unique. I will cite only one; it imposes itself here, since it seals in the same beeswax—and the fingers themselves are of wax—the alliance, the letter, the ciphered name, the hive of the hours, and the writing of what is not written:

MIT BRIEF UND UHR	WITH LETTER AND CLOCK
Wachs,	Wax,
Ungeschriebnes zu siegeln,	to seal the unwritten
das deinen Namen	that guessed
erriet,	your name.
das deinen Namen	that enciphers
verschlüsselt.	your name,
Kommst du nun, schwimmendes	Swimming light, will you come
Licht?	now?
Finger, wächsern auch sie,	Fingers, waxen too,
durch fremde,	drawn
schmerzende Ringe gezogen.	through strange, painful rings.
Fortgeschmolzen die Kuppen.	With tips melted away.
Kommst du, schwimmendes Licht?	Swimming light, will you come?
Zeitleer die Waben der Uhr,	Empty of time the honeycomb cells of
	the clock,
bräutlich das Immentausend,	bridal the thousand of bees
reisebereit.	ready to leave.
Komm, schwimmendes Licht.	Swimming light, come.*

Clock and rings are quite close again in "Chymisch." A ring awakens on our finger, and the fingers are the ring itself in "Es war Erde in ihnen. . . ." But above all, since a date is never without a letter to be deciphered, I think of the ring of the carrier pigeon at the center of "La Contrescarpe." The carrier pigeon transports, transfers, or transmits a ciphered message, but this is not a metaphor. It departs at its date, that of its sending, and it must return from the other place to the same one, that from which it came, completing a round trip. Now the question of the cipher is posed by Celan not only with regard to the message but also with regard to the ring itself, sign of belonging,[n] alliance, and condition of return. The cipher of the seal, the imprint of the ring, *counts*, perhaps more than the content of the message. As with *shibboleth*, the meaning of the word matters less than, let us say, its signifying form once it becomes a password, a mark of belonging, the manifestation of an alliance:

Scherte die Brieftaube aus, war ihr Ring	Did the carrier-pigeon sheer off, was its ring
zu entziffern? (All das	decipherable? (All that
Gewölk um sie her—es warr lesbar.) Litt es	cloud around it—it was readable.) Did the
der Schwarm? Und verstand,	flock endure it? And understand,
und flog wie sie fortblieb?	and fly as the other stayed on?*

A date gets carried away, transported; it takes off, takes itself off—and thus effaces itself in its very readability. Effacement is not something that befalls it like an accident; it affects neither its meaning nor its readability; it merges, on the contrary, with reading's very access to that which a date may still signify. But if readability effaces the date, the very thing that it gives to be read, this strange process will have begun with the very inscription of the date. The date must conceal within itself some stigma of singularity if it is to last longer than that which it commemorates—and this lasting is the poem. This is its only chance of assuring its revenance. Effacement or concealment, this annulment proper to the annulation, or ring, of return belongs to the movement of dating. And so what must be commemorated, *at once* gathered and repeated, is therefore, *at the same time*, the date's annihilation, a kind of nothing, or ash.

Ash awaits us.

III

Let us remain for a moment with the dates that we recognize through the language-grid of the calendar: the day, the month, and sometimes the year.

First case: a date relates to an event that, at least *in appearance and outwardly*, is distinct from the actual writing of the poem and the moment of its signing. The metonymy of the date (a date is always also a metonymy) designates part of an event or a sequence of events in order to recall the whole. The mention "13th of February" forms a part of what happened on that day, only a part, but it stands for the whole in a given context. What happened on that day, in the first case we are going to consider, is not, in appearance and outwardly, the advent of the poem.

The example is the first line of "In eins" ("As One"*). It begins with "Dreizehnter Feber," "Thirteenth of February."

What is gathered and commemorated, in a single poetic stroke, in the unique time of this "In eins"? And is it a matter of one commemoration? The "as one," all at once, several times at the same time, seems to constellate in the uniqueness of a date. But this date, in being unique and *the only one*, all alone, the one of its kind—is it one?

And what if there were more than one thirteenth of February?

Not only because the thirteenth of February recurs, becoming each year its own revenant, but above all because a multiplicity of events, in dispersed places—for example, on a political map of Europe, at different epochs, in foreign idioms—may have come together at the heart of the same anniversary.

IN EINS	AS ONE
Dreizehnter Feber. Im Herzmund	Thirteenth of February. In the heart's mouth
erwachtes Schibboleth. Mit dir,	An awakened shibboleth. With you,
Peuple	Peuple
de Paris. *No pasarán.*	de Paris. *No pasarán.*

Like the rest of the poem, and well beyond what I could say concerning them, these first lines seem *evidently* ciphered.

Ciphered, evidently, they are: in several senses and in several languages.

Ciphered, first of all, in that they include a cipher, a number, the cipher of the number thirteen. This is one of those numbers in which randomness and necessity cross, in order to be consigned at a single time. Within its strictures, a ligament holds together, in a manner at once significant and insignificant, fatality and its opposite: chance and coming-due [*chance et échéance*], coincidence in the case, that which *falls*—well or ill—together.

DIE ZAHLEN, im Bund	THE NUMBERS, bonded
mit der Bilder Verhängnis	with the images' doom
und Gegen-	and their counter-
verhängnis.	doom.*
Und Zahlen waren	And numbers were
mitverwoben in das	interwoven into the
Unzählbare. Eins und Tausend	innumerable. One and a thousand*

Even before the number 13, the *one* of the title "In eins" announces the con-signing and co-signing of a multiple singularity. From the title and the incipit onward, the cipher, like the date, is incorporated into the poem. They give access to the poem that they are, but a ciphered access.

These first lines are ciphered in another sense: more than others, they are untranslatable. I am not thinking here of all the poetic challenges with which this great poet-translator confronts poet-translators. No, I will limit myself here to the aporia (to the barred passage, *no pasarán*: this is what *aporia* means). What seems to bar the passage of translation is the multiplicity of languages in the same poem, at once. Four languages, like a series of proper names and dated signatures, like the face of a seal.

Like the title and the date, the *incipit* is read in German. But with the second line, a second language, an apparently Hebrew word, arises in the "heart's mouth": *shibboleth*.

Dreizehnter Feber. Im Herzmund	Thirteenth of February. In the heart's mouth
erwachtes Schibboleth. Mit dir,	an awakened shibboleth. With you,

This second language could well be a first language, the language of the morning, the language of origin speaking of the heart, from the heart, and from the East. "Language" in Hebrew is "lip," rather than "tongue," and does not Celan elsewhere (we will come to it) call words circumcised, as one speaks of the "circumcised heart"? For the moment, let this be. *Shibboleth*, this word I have called Hebrew, is found, as you know, in a whole family of languages: Phoenician, Judeo-Aramaic, Syriac. It is traversed by a multiplicity of meanings: river, stream, ear of grain, olive twig. But beyond these meanings, it has acquired the value of a password. It was used during or after war, at the crossing of a border under watch. The meaning of the word was less important than the way in which it was pronounced. The relation to the meaning or to the thing was suspended, neutralized, bracketed: the opposite, one might say, of a phenomenological *epochē*, which preserves, above all, the meaning. The Ephraimites had been defeated by the army of Jephthah; in order to keep their soldiers from escaping across the river (*shibboleth* also means "river," of course, but that is not necessarily the reason it was chosen), each person was required to say *shibboleth*. Now the Ephraimites were known for their inability to pronounce correctly the *shi* of *shibboleth*, which became for them, in consequence, an *unpronounceable name*. They said *sibboleth*, and, at the invisible border between *shi* and *si*, betrayed themselves to the sentinel at the risk of their life. They betrayed their difference by showing themselves indifferent to the diacritical difference between *shi* and *si*; they marked themselves with their inability to re-mark a mark thus coded.

This came to pass at the border of the Jordan. Another border, another barred passage, in the fourth language of the strophe: *no pasarán*. February 1936: the electoral victory of the *Frente Popular*, the eve of civil war. *No pasarán*: la Pasionaria, the no to Franco, to the Phalange supported by Mussolini's troops and Hitler's Condor Legion. Rallying cry or sign, clamor and banners during the siege of Madrid, three years later, *no pasarán* was a *shibboleth* for the Republican people, for their allies, for the International Brigades. What passed this cry, what came to pass despite it, was the Second World War, with its exterminations. A repetition of the First World War, certainly, but also of the *dress rehearsal* [répétition générale], its own future anterior, that was the Spanish Civil War. Dated structure of the dress rehearsal: everything happens [*se passe*] as if the Second World War had begun in February 1936, in a slaughter at once civil and international, violating or reclosing the borders, leaving ever so many scars in the body of a single country—grievous figure of a metonymy. Spanish is allotted to the central strophe, which transcribes, in sum, a kind of Spanish *shibboleth*, a password, not a word in passing, but a silent word transmitted like a *symbolon* or handclasp, a rallying cipher, a sign of membership and a political watchword.°

er sprach	into our hands
uns das Wort in die Hand, das wir	he spoke the word that we
brauchten, es war	needed, it was
Hirten-Spanisch, darin,	shepherd-Spanish,
im Eislicht des Kreuzers "Aurora"	in icelight of the cruiser "Aurora"*

Amidst the German, the Hebrew, and the Spanish, there is, in French, the Peuple de Paris:

Mit dir,	With you
Peuple	Peuple
de Paris. *No pasarán.*	de Paris. *No pasarán.*

It is not written in italics, no more than is *shibboleth*. The italics are reserved for *No pasarán* and the last line, *Friede den Hütten!*, "Peace to the cottages!," whose terrible irony must surely aim at someone.

The multiplicity of languages may concelebrate, *all at once*, on the same date, the poetic and political anniversary of singular events, spread like stars over the map of Europe, and henceforth conjoined by a secret affinity: the fall of Vienna and the fall of Madrid, for, as we shall see, Vienna and Madrid are associated in one line in another poem, entitled "Schibboleth"; once again memories of February, the beginnings of the October Revolution with the incidents linked to the cruiser *Aurora* and to Petrograd, both named in the poem, and even to the Peter and Paul Fortress. It is the last stanza of "In eins" that recalls other "unforgotten" singularities, that of "Tuscan," for example, which I will not here undertake to decipher.

<table>
<tr><td>"Aurora":</td><td>"Aurora":</td></tr>
<tr><td>die Bruderhand, winkend mit der</td><td>the brotherly hand, waving with</td></tr>
<tr><td>von den wortgroßen Augen</td><td>the blindfold removed from</td></tr>
<tr><td>genommenen Binde — Petropolis, der</td><td>his word-wide eyes — Petropolis, the</td></tr>
<tr><td>Unvergessenen Wanderstadt lag</td><td>roving city of those unforgotten,</td></tr>
<tr><td>auch dir toskanisch zu Herzen.</td><td>was Tuscanly close to your heart also.</td></tr>
</table>

Friede den Hütten!   *Peace to the cottages!*

But already within the hearth of a single language, for example French, a discontinuous swarm of events may be commemorated all at once, *at the same date*, which consequently takes on the strange, coincident, *unheimlich* dimensions of a cryptic predestination.

The date itself resembles a *shibboleth*. It gives ciphered access to this collocation, to this secret configuration of places for memory.

The series thus constellated becomes all the more ample and numerous insofar as the date remains relatively indeterminate. If Celan does not specify the day (13) and says only "February" ("Februar," this time and not *Feber*), as in the poem entitled "Schibboleth,"* memories of the same kind of demonstrations, with the same political significance, multiply: these brought together the People of Paris, that is, the people of the left, in the élan of a single impulse to proclaim, like the Republicans of Madrid, *No pasarán*. A single example: on February 12, 1934, after the failure of the attempt to form a Common Front of the Right, with Doriot, after the riot of February 6, a huge march took place, bringing together the masses and the leadership of the parties of the left. This was the origin of the Popular Front.

But if, in "In eins," Celan specifies the 13th of February (*Dreizehnter Feber*), one may think of February 13, 1962. I hand this hypothesis over to those who may know something about or can bear witness to the "external" date of the poem; I am unaware of it, but should my hypothesis be factually false, it would still designate the power of those dates to come, toward which, Celan says, we transcribe ourselves. A date always remains a sort of *hypothesis*, the support for a by definition unlimited number of projections of memory. The slightest indetermination (the day and the month without the year, for example) increases these chances, and the chances for the future anterior. The date is a future anterior; it gives the time one assigns to anniversaries to come. Thus on the 13th of February 1962 Celan was in Paris. *Die Niemandsrose*, the collection in which "In eins" appears, was not published until 1963. Yet in moving from "Schibboleth," published eight years before, to "In eins," Celan specifies *13th* of February where the earlier poem said only *February*. Thus something must have happened. February 13, 1962, was in Paris the day of the funeral for the victims of the massacre at the métro station Charonne, and of an anti-OAS demonstration at the end of the Algerian war. Several hundred thousand Parisians, the People of Paris, were marching. Two days later, the meetings that led to the Evian accords would begin. These People of Paris remain those of the Commune, with whom one must band together: with you, Peuple de Paris. In the same event, at the same date, national war *and* civil war, the end of one and the beginning—*as* the beginning—of the other.

Like the date, *shibboleth* is marked several times, several times in *en une seule fois*, *in eins*, at once [in English in the original]. A marked but also a marking multiplicity.

On the one hand, indeed, within the poem it names, as is evident, the password or rallying cry, a right of access or sign of membership in all the political situations along the historical borders *configured* by the poem. This *visa*, it will be said, is the *shibboleth*; it determines a theme, a meaning, or a content.

But on the other hand, as cryptic or numerical cipher, *shibboleth* also spells the anniversary date's singular power of gathering together. This anniversary date gives access to the memory of the date, to the to-come of the date, to its proper to-come, but also to the poem—itself. *Shibboleth* is the *shibboleth* for the right to the poem that calls itself a *shibboleth*, its proper *shibboleth* at the very instant that it commemorates others. *Shibboleth* is its title, whether or not it appears in that place, as in one of these two poems.

This does not mean—two things.

On the one hand, this does not mean that the events commemorated in this fantastic constellation are non-poetic events, suddenly transfigured by an incantation. No, I believe that for Celan the signifying conjunction of all these dramas and historical actors will have *constituted* the signature of a poem, its signed dating.

Nor does it mean, on the other hand, that to have the *shibboleth* at one's disposal effaces the cipher, gives the key to the crypt, and ensures the transparency of meaning. The crypt remains, the *shibboleth* remains secret, the passage uncertain, and the poem unveils a secret only to confirm that there is something secret there, withdrawn, forever beyond the reach of hermeneutic exhaustion. A non-hermetic secret, it remains, and the date with it, heterogeneous to all interpretative totalization. Eradication of the hermeneutic principle. There is no one meaning, as soon as there is date and *shibboleth*, no longer a sole originary meaning.

A *shibboleth*, the word *shibboleth*, if it is one, names, in the broadest extension of its generality or its usage, every insignificant, arbitrary mark, for example, the phonemic difference between *shi* and *si* when that difference becomes discriminative, decisive, and divisive. The difference has no meaning in and of itself, but it becomes what one must know how to recognize and above all to mark if one is to make the *step*, to step across the border of a place or the threshold of a poem, to see oneself granted the right of asylum or the legitimate habitation of a language. So as no longer to be outside the law. And to inhabit a language, one must already have a *shibboleth* at one's disposal: not only understand the meaning of the word, not only *know* this meaning or *know* how a word *should be* pronounced (the difference of *h*, or *sh*, between *shi* and *si*: this the Ephraimites knew), but *be able* to say it as one ought, as one must be able to say it. It is not enough to know the difference; one must be capable of it, must be able to do it, or know how to do it—and here doing means *marking*. This differential mark that it is not enough to know like a theorem— that is the secret. A secret without secret. The right to alliance involves no hidden secret, no meaning concealed in a crypt.

In the word, the difference between *shi* and *si* has no meaning. But it is the ciphered mark that one must *be able to partake of* with the other, and this differential capability must be inscribed in oneself, that is, in one's own body as much as in the body of one's own language, the one to the same extent as the other. This inscription of difference in the body (e.g., the phonatory aptitude to pronounce this or that) is, nonetheless, not natural; it is in no way an innate, organic faculty. Its very origin presupposes belonging to a cultural and linguistic community, to a milieu of apprenticeship, in sum, an alliance.

Shibboleth does not cipher something. It is not only a cipher, and the cipher of the poem; it is now, from the outside-of-meaning where it holds itself in reserve, the cipher *of* the cipher, the ciphered manifestation of the cipher as such. And when a cipher shows itself for what it is, that is to say, in encrypting itself, this is not in order to say to us: I am a cipher. It may still conceal from us, without the slightest hidden intention, the secret that it shelters in its readability. It moves, fascinates, and seduces us all the more. The ellipsis and the caesura of discretion are in it; there is nothing it can do about it. This pass is a passion before becoming a calculated risk, prior to any strategy, prior to any poetics of ciphering intended [*destinée*], as in Joyce, to keep the professors busy for generations. Even supposing that this exhausts Joyce's first or true desire, something I do not believe, nothing seems to me more foreign to Celan.

Multiplicity and migration of languages, certainly, and within language itself. Babel: named in "Hinausgekrönt," after the "Ghetto-Rose" and the phallic figure knotted in the heart of the poem (*phallisch gebündelt*), this is also its last word, both its address and its sending.

Und es steigt eine Erde herauf, die unsre, diese.	And an earth rises up, ours, this one.
Und wir schicken	And we'll send
keinen der Unsern hinunter	none of our people down
zu dir,	to you,
Babel.	Babel.*

Address and sending of the poem, yes, but what seems to be said to Babel, addressed to it, is that nothing will be addressed to it. One will send it nothing, nothing from us, none of ours.

Multiplicity and migration of languages, certainly, and within language. Your country, it says, migrates all over, like language. The country itself migrates and transports its borders. It is displaced like the names and the stones that one gives as a pledge, from hand to hand, and the hand is given, too, and what gets carved out, cut off, torn away, can gather itself together anew in the symbol, the pledge, the promise, the alliance, the partaken word, the migration of the partaken word.

—was abriß, wächst wieder zusammen—
da hast du sie, da nimm sie dir, da hast du alle beide,
den Namen, den Namen, die Hand, die Hand,
da nimm sie dir zum Unterpfand,

er nimmt auch das, und du hast
wieder, was dein ist, was sein war,

Windmühlen

stoßen dir Luft in die Lunge.

—what was cut off grows together again—
there you have it, so take it, there you have them both,
the name, the name, the hand, the hand,
so take them, keep them as a pledge,
he takes it too, and you have
again what is yours, what was his,

windmills

push air into your lungs.*

Chance and risk of the windmill—language, which is related as much to wind and mirage as it is to breath and spirit, to the breathing bestowed. We will not recall all the ciphered trails of this immense poem ("Es ist alles anders"), from Russia—"the name of Osip"—to Moravia, to the Prague cemetery ("the pebble from / the Moravian hollow / which your thought carried to Prague, / on to the graves, to the grave, into life") and "near Normandy-Niemen," this French squadron in war exile in Moscow, and so forth. Only this, which speaks of the emigration of the country itself, and of its name. Like language:

wie heißt es, dein Land	what is it called, your country
hinterm Berg, hinterm Jahr?	behind the mountain, behind the year?
Ich weiß, wie es heißt.	I know what it's called.
. . .	. . .
es wandert überallhin, wie die Sprache,	it wanders off everywhere, like language,
wirf sie weg, wirf sie weg,	throw it away, throw it away,
dann hast du sie wieder, wie ihn,	then you'll have it again, like that other thing.
den Kieselstein aus	the pebble from
der Mährischen Senke,	the Moravian hollow
den dein Gedanke nach Prag trug.	which your thought carried to Prague.

Multiplicity and migration of languages, certainly, and within language itself, Babel within *a single* language. *Shibboleth* marks the multiplicity within language, insignificant difference as the condition of meaning. But by the same token, the insignificance of language, of the properly linguistic body: it can take on meaning only in relation to a *place*. By place, I mean just as much the relation to a border, country, house, or threshold as any site, any *situation* in general from within which, practically, pragmatically, alliances are formed, contracts, codes, and conventions established that give meaning to the insignificant, institute passwords, bend language to what exceeds it, make of it a moment of gesture and of step, secondarize or "reject" it in order to find it again.

Multiplicity within language, or rather heterogeneity. One should specify that untranslatability does not stem only from the difficult passage (*no pasarán*), from the aporia or impasse that isolates one poetic language from another. Babel is also this *impossible impasse*, this *impossible pass* [*ce* pas impossible]—and without transaction to come—stemming from the multiplicity of languages within the uniqueness of the poetic inscription: several times at once, several languages within a single poetic act. The uniqueness of the poem, in other words, yet another date and *shibboleth*, forges and seals, in a single idiom, *in eins*, the poetic event, a multiplicity of languages and of equally singular dates. "In eins": within the unity and the uniqueness of this poem, the four languages are certainly not untranslatable, neither among themselves nor into other languages. But what will always remain untranslatable into any *other* language whatsoever is the marked difference of languages in the poem. We spoke of the *doing* that does not reduce to *knowing*, and of the *being able to do the difference* that comes down to *marking*. That is what goes on and what comes about here. Everything seems, in principle, *de jure*, translatable, except for the mark of the difference among the languages within the same poetic event. Let us consider, for example, the excellent French translation of "In eins." It translates German into French, there's nothing more normal than that. *Schibboleth* and *no pasarán* are left untranslated, which respects the foreignness of these words in the principal medium, the German idiom of what one calls the original version. But in keeping, and how could one do otherwise, the French of this version in the translation "Avec toi, / Peuple / de Paris" the translation must efface the very thing it keeps, the foreign effect of the French (unitalicized) in the poem, which puts it in configuration with all the ciphers, passwords, or *shibboleth*s that date and sign the poem, "In eins," in the unity—at once dissociated, torn, and adjoined, rejoined, regathered—of its singularities. There is no remedy to which translation could have recourse here, none, at least, in the body of the poem. No one is to blame; moreover, there is nothing to bring before the bar of translation. The *shibboleth*, here again, does not resist translation by reason of some inaccessibility of its meaning to transference, by reason of some semantic secret, but by virtue of that in it which forms the cut of a non-signifying difference in the body of the mark—written or oral, written in speech as a mark can be within a mark, an incision marking the very mark itself. On both sides of the historical, political, and linguistic border (a border is never natural), the meaning, the different meanings of the word *shibboleth*, are known: river, ear of grain, olive twig. One even knows how it should be pronounced. But a single trial determines that some cannot while others can pronounce it with the heart's mouth. The first will not pass, the others will pass the line—of the place, of the country, of the community, of what takes place in a language, in languages as poems. Every poem has its own language; it is one time alone its own language, even and especially if several languages *are able* to cross there. From this *point of view*, which may become a watchtower, the vigilance of a sentinel, one sees well: the value of the *shibboleth* may always, and tragically, be inverted. Tragically because the inversion sometimes overtakes the initiative of subjects, the goodwill of men, their mastery of language and politics. Watchword or password in a struggle against oppression, exclusion, fascism, and racism, it may also corrupt its differential value, which is the condition of alliance and of the poem, making of it a discriminatory limit, the grillwork of policing, of normalization, and of methodical subjugation.

IV

Inserted in the second line of "In eins," the word *shibboleth* forms the title of a longer and earlier poem, published in 1955 in the collection *Von Schwelle zu Schwelle. Shibboleth* could also serve, by metonymy, as the title of the collection. Indeed, it speaks of the threshold, of the passing of the threshold (*Schwelle*), of that which permits one to pass or to go through, to transfer from one threshold to another: to translate. One finds there more or less the same configuration of events, sealed by the same February anniversary, the linking of the capitals, Vienna and Madrid, substituting perhaps for the linking, in "In eins," of Paris, Madrid, and Petropolis. *No pasarán* is already very close to *shibboleth*. A memory again, no doubt, of February 1936–39, though this time neither the day (13), nor the year appears. Which leads one to think, given that references to France and the French language seem absent, that, in fact, another date is in question this time, in whose otherness other Februaries, and then a certain thirteenth of February, come, and then come together, overdetermining the *Sprachgitter* of the signature. The play of resemblances and differences, the *shibboleth between* the two poems, could occasion an interminable analysis.

Apart from its presence as title, the word *shibboleth* precedes, almost directly, the word *February* and the *no pasarán*, in a strophe that one might call openhearted, opened here again through the heart, through the single word *heart* (in the first line of the poem "In eins," it will also be *Im Herzmund*, in the heart's mouth):

Herz:	Heart:
gib dich auch hier zu erkennen,	make yourself known even here,
hier, in der Mitte des Marktes.	here, in the midst of the market.
Ruf's, das Schibboleth, hinaus	Call it out, the *shibboleth*,
in die Fremde der Heimat:	into the foreign land of the
	homeland:
Februar. No pasarán.	February. No pasarán.*

Strangeness, estrangement in one's own home, not being at home, being called away from one's homeland or away from home in one's homeland, this "not" passage [*ce pas du "ne pas"*], which secures and threatens every border passing in and out of oneself, this moment of the *shibboleth* is re-marked in the date, in the month, and in the word *February*. The difference is hardly translatable: it is *Februar* in "Schibboleth," *Feber* (*Dreizehnter Feber*) in "In eins," which could thus lead back, *shibboleth in February*, through a play of archaism and Austrian,* to some no doubt falsely attributed etymology of *februarius* as the moment of fever, attack, crisis, inflammation.

The two poems beckon to one another, kindred, complicitous, allies, but as different as they can possibly be. They bear and do not bear the same date. A *shibboleth* secures the passage from one to the other, in the difference, in the interior of the selfsame, of the same date, between *Februar* and *Feber*. They speak, in the same language, two different languages. They partake of it.

I will thus use, as does Jean-Luc Nancy in *Le partage des voix*, this word *partage* [partition, partaking], which in French names difference, the line of demarcation or the parting of the waters, scission, caesura, as well as participation, that which is divided because it is shared or held in common, imparted and partaken of.[P]

Fascinated by a resemblance at once semantic and formal, which nonetheless has no linguistico-historical explanation, no etymological necessity, I will hazard a comparison between partaking as *shibboleth* and as *symbolon*: In both cases of S-B-L, one passes a pledge to the other, "er sprach / uns das Wort in die Hand" ("he spoke / the word in our hand"), a word or a piece of a word, the complementary part of a thing parted in two to seal an alliance, a tessera. Moment of engagement, of signature, of the pact or contract, of the promise, of the ring.*

The signature of the date plays this role here. Beyond the singular event that the date marks and of which it would be the detachable proper name, capable of surviving and thus of calling, of recalling, the vanished as vanished, its very ash, it gathers together, like a title (*titulus* includes a sense of gathering), a more or less apparent and secret conjunction of singularities that partake of, and in the future will continue to partake of, the *same* date.

No limit can be assigned to such a conjunction. It is determined from the to-come to which a fracture promises it. No testimony, no knowledge, not even Celan's, could by definition exhaust its decryption. First, because there is no absolute witness for an external deciphering. Celan may always imply [*sous-entendre*] one more *shibboleth*: under cover [*sous*] of a word, a cipher, or a letter. Second, he would not have claimed himself to have totalized the possible and compossible meanings of a constellation. Finally, and above all, the poem is destined to remain *alone*, from its first breath, alone at the vanishing of the witnesses and the witnesses of witnesses. And of the poet.

The date is a witness, but one may very well bless it without knowing all of that for which and of those for whom it bears witness. It is always possible that there may no longer be any witness for this witness. We are slowly approaching this affinity between a date, a name—and ash. The last words of "Aschenglorie" ("Ash-glory"):

Niemand	No one
zeugt für den	bears witness for the
Zeugen.	witness.*

Folded or refolded in the simplicity of a singularity, a certain repetition thus assures the minimal and "internal" readability of the poem, in the absence even of a witness, indeed, of a signatory or of anyone who might have some knowledge concerning the historical reference of the poetic legacy. This, in any case, is what the word or title *shibboleth signifies* (if one can still say this). Not this or that meaning derived from its language of origin: river, ear of grain, olive twig, or, indeed, even the other meanings it takes on in the two poems. It signifies: there is *shibboleth*, there is something of a crypt, one that remains incalculable; it does not conceal a single, determinate secret, a semantic content waiting behind the door for the one who holds a key. If there is indeed a door, we will come to this, it does not present itself in this way. If this crypt is symbolic, that does not, in the final analysis, derive from some tropic or rhetoric. To be sure, the symbolic dimension never disappears, and at times it takes on thematic values. But what the poem marks, what enters and incises language in the form of a date, is that there is a partaking of the *shibboleth*, a partaking at once open and closed. The date (signature, moment, place, gathering of singular marks) always operates as a *shibboleth*. It shows that there is something not shown, that there is ciphered singularity: irreducible to any concept, to any knowledge, even to a history or tradition, be it of a religious kind. A ciphered singularity that gathers a multiplicity *in eins*, and through whose grid a poem remains readable—thus giving multiplicity to be read: "Aber das Gedicht spricht ja!" The poem speaks, even if none of its references is intelligible, none apart from the Other, the one to whom the poem addresses itself and to whom it speaks in saying that it speaks to it. Even if it does not reach the Other, at least it calls to it. Address takes place.

In a language, in the poetic writing of a language, there is nothing but *shibboleth*. Like the date, like a name, it permits anniversary, alliance, return, commemoration—even if there were no more trace, what one commonly calls a trace, the subsistent presence of a remainder, even if there were scarcely an ash of what one thus still dates, celebrates, commemorates, or blesses.

We will content ourselves, for the moment, with conventional dating, as it is coded in a calendar or public toponymy. "Tübingen, Jänner" (*Jänner*, in the old Austrian style, also heralds *Feber*) is at once the title of a poem, a date, and a signature. Like a *shibboleth*, it takes into its consignment enigma and memory, citing the enigma:

Ihre—"ein	Their—"an enigma
Rätsel ist Rein-	is the purely
entsprungenes"—, ihre	originated"—, their
Erinnerung an	memory of
schwimmende Hölderlintürme,	Hölderlin towers afloat, circled
möwen-	
umschwirrt.	by whirring gulls.*

In parentheses, "La Contrescarpe" writes, "(*Quatorze / juillets*)."
Like the title of the poem, the date is in French in the original and
thus untranslatable. Untranslatable first and foremost into French. It
does not suffice to transcribe it in italics.

Moreover, the date, incorporated in the poem, is overdetermined
in multiple ways. For one, it commemorates quite evidently that
which, for two centuries now, every *July 14* may recall. At times, in
many places in Western culture, *July 14* becomes the emblem of the
commemorative ceremony in general. It then figures a political and
revolutionary anniversary in general, whether past or to come: the
anniversary, in other words, the return, by revolution, of the
revolutionary.

What is more, "(*Quatorze / juillets*)" bears an *s*. Disorthography:
this inaudible mark of the plural insists on the plurality of rings [*an-
neaux*]. The anniversaries do not signal only, necessarily, the return
of the same, original July 14. Other events, more or less secret, other
rings, anniversaries, and alliances, other partakings partake, perhaps, of the same date. A parenthesis, as its name indicates, *sets alongside: aside*. The same parenthesis *sets aside*, in reserve, other "quatorze
juillets": "(*Quatorze / juillets. Et plus de neuf autres*)." One may read either *nine other* fourteenths of July or 14 + 9 = 23 July, or 23 months
of July, 23 anniversaries, and so forth. When I say that I do not
know what other anniversaries the poem thus turns itself toward,
this does not, above all, come down to an "I do not want to know,"
"This does not interest me," or that I am forgoing all interpretation,
all use of the resources of hermeneutics, philosophy, historical
knowledge, or biographical testimonies. "I do not know" signals a
situation. In what I have elsewhere called its simple *remaining* [re-
stance], the poem speaks beyond knowledge. It writes, and what it
writes is, above all, precisely this: that it is addressed and destined
beyond knowledge, inscribing dates and signatures that one may encounter, in order to bless them, without knowing everything of what
they date or sign. Blessing beyond knowledge, commemorating
through forgetting or the unimparted secret, partaking, still, in the
unpartakeable. These "Quatorze / juillets" form the cut [*entaille*] of
an unrepeatable (*unwiederholbar*) singularity. But they repeat the
unique in the ring. A tropic sets anniversaries turning around the
same. Moreover, the entire poem multiplies the signs of other events
associated with July 14. One is thus led to think that "(Quatorze /
juillets)" is not a listed date, the date of public and political history,
but perhaps, who knows, a date that signs in secret, the private seal

that at least marks with its initials or flourishes the advent of this particular poem, the sublime tearing open that I prefer to leave intact. Such a signature would make up part of the constellation. Let us merely recall, without further commentary, that "Conversation in the Mountains" also says "and July is not July." This in the course of a meditation on the Jew, son of a Jew, whose name is "unpronounceable" and who has nothing of his own, nothing that is not borrowed, so that, just like a date, what is proper to the Jew is to have no property or essence. Jewish is not Jewish. We will come back to this, as to this other fact: for the Ephraimites, in another way, *shibboleth* was also an "unpronounceable" name. One knows what this cost them.

We have spoken often of *constellations*: several heterogeneous singularities are consigned in the starry configuration of a single, dated mark. Let us recall here the "constellations of November."[q] They are associated with an ear, not of grain, as in *shibboleth*, but of corn:

BEIM HAGELKORN, im
brandigen Mais-
kolben, daheim,
den späten, den harten
Novembersternen gehorsam:

in den Herzfaden die
Gespräche der Würmer geknüpft —:

eine Sehne, von der
deine Pfeilschrift schwirrt,
Schütze.

WITH THE HAILSTONE, in
the rust-blighted ear
of maize, at home,
obedient to the late, the hard
November stars:

woven into your heart-thread, the
conversations of worms —:

a bowstring, from which
your arrow-script whirrs,
archer.*

The months come back as well, and especially March, and especially September. Among other places, in "Huhediblu." The return of the month is given to be read there, without mention of the year, and it signs the demarcation of the date, its partaking and its deportation. Chance for the ring, and fatality for all archiving. A date marks itself and becomes readable only in freeing itself from the singularity that it nonetheless recalls. It is readable in its ideality; its body becomes an ideal object: always the same, through the different experiences that point to or constitute it, objective, guaranteed by codes. This ideality carries forgetting into memory, but it is the memory of forgetting itself, the truth of forgetting. The reference to a singular event is annulled in the ring's annulation, when a month recalls and annually annuls a year. This is the moment when the year turns on itself. Poles and tropes; one recalls the "Meridian." A date: always a turning-about, a volte-face, *una volta*, a revolt, or a revolution. It replaces itself in its vicissitudes. Commemorating what can always be forgotten in the absence of any witness, the date is exposed in its destination or in its very essence. It is offered up to annihilation, but in truth it *offers* itself up. The threat is not external; it does not stem from an accident that would suddenly come along and destroy the archive's material support. The date lets itself be threatened in its coming due, in its conservation and its readability, by them, insofar as it remains, and gives itself to be read. Risking the annulment of what it saves from forgetting, it may always become no one's and nothing's date, essence without the essence of ash, about which one no longer even knows what was one day, only once, under some proper name, consumed there. The name shares this destiny of ash along with the date. This does not happen *empirically*, like a fact, which might come about once under certain conditions and which could be avoided at other times, for example, by multiplying precautions — or by chance. It belongs to the always eventful and damaged essence of the date to become readable and commemorative only in effacing what it will have designated, in becoming each time no one's date.

No one's — the possessive may be understood in two contradictory senses, which nonetheless form an alliance in the same tragedy. *Either . . . Or.*

Either the date remains encrypted — supposing, for example, that behind the allusion in "Huhediblu" to September ("unterm / Datum des Nimmermenschtags im September"), and beyond a certain number of identifiable things or persons, Celan has named and ciphered an event that he alone, or alone with but a few others, is able to commemorate. And those who commemorate are mortals; one must start with that. Then the date of this "Nevermansday in September" is destined, at least to this extent, *one day* to no longer signify at all for the survivors, that is to say, essentially, for the reader, the interpreter, the guardian of the poem. Finite surviving, this is their lot. In this case, a date becomes — from the moment it crosses the threshold of this surviving or revenance, from the moment, therefore, that it crosses the threshold of the poem — no one's date, nevermansday. The name *September* surfaces in a poem, a poem that "speaks!"; it lends itself to reading to the extent that it is caught up in, catches itself up in a net of signifying and, by convention, intelligible marks. It has its share in the "beauty" of the poem. But to this very extent, and here is the affect of bereavement that brings us back to "beauty," its readability is paid for by the terrible tribute of lost singularity. Mourning in the reading itself. What is encrypted, dated in the date, is effaced; the date is marked in marking itself off; and all the losses, all the beings whom we lament in this mourning, all the griefs are gathered in the poem of a date whose effacement does not await effacement.

Or, in an apparently inverse hypothesis, nothing is encrypted in the date. It makes itself available to all. And the result comes down to the same. The other's singularity is incinerated. The September rose, the no one's rose. "Die Nichts-, die / Niemandsrose" of "Psalm" belongs, so to speak, to the same generation as "die September- / rosen" of "Huhediblu"; "unterm / Datum des Nimmermenschtags im September" belongs to the same generation, too, as the untranslatable envoy, when the quasi-citation, metonymizing the flower of rhetoric, displacing the order of attribution, concludes the poem in *French*, without italics: "Oh quand refleuriront, oh roses, vos septembres?" ("Oh when will they reflower, oh roses, your Septembers?"). The to-come belongs to the date, months in the plural, the round of future Septembers. One awaits less the return of the flowers, their blossoming to come, than the re-flowering of returns. One does not place flowers on the stone of a date, one does not await a season, spring or autumn, one does not await the roses of this time, but the time of the roses, the dated time. What counts, what is born, flowers, opens, is not the flower, it is the date. It counts, and *September*, moreover, includes a cipher, a number, rather, in its name.

Either/Or. This does not constitute an alternative; the date's double demarcation does not make two. The two phenomena do not contradict each other; they are not even [*même*] juxtaposed in the poem. What is the same [*le même*] in all dating is here gathered and constituted. The possibility of reading and of recurrence, the ring, the anniversary and its keeping, the *truth* of the poem, its very reason, its essential raison d'être, its chance and its sense, this is also its madness.

A date is mad, that is the truth.

And we are mad for dates.

For the ashes that dates are. Celan knew one may praise or bless ashes. Religion is not necessary for that. Perhaps because a religion begins there, before religion, in the blessing of dates, of names, and of ashes.

A date is mad: it is never what it is, what it says it is, always more or less than what it is. What it is, is either what it is or what it is not.

It is not an effect of being, of some meaning of being; it is on this condition that its mad incantation becomes music. It *remains* without being, by force of music, remains for song; "Singbarer Rest"* is the incipit or title of a poem that *begins* by saying the remainder. It begins with the remainder—which is not and which is not being—leaving a song without words (*lautlos*) to be heard therein, a song perhaps inaudible or inarticulate, yet a song whose turn and whose line, whose outline, whose contour (*Umriß*) no doubt stems from the cutting, sharpened, concise, but also rounded, circumvenient form of a sickle, of yet another writing, of a sickle-script (*Sichelschrift*). This writing-sickle does not round what it slices, since it does not avoid it, not altogether, but rather cuts in coming around, all the way around. Another turning, another trope: to turn around and to go round are not the same thing for this sickle, which perhaps inscribes letters in cutting, all around. Shall one say that it circumcises words in silence, when speech is muted (*lautlos*), so that song may come: *singbarer Rest?* This will resonate later: *beschneide das Wort*, circumcise the word.

"Singbarer Rest" or "CELLO-EINSATZ / von hinter dem Schmerz" ("CELLO-ENTRY / from behind pain"), that other poem, sets into musical play something indecipherable or unsignifying (*Undeutbares*). It closes on these words, which say so little, yet more than all, unforgettable thenceforth and made to pass unperceived from memory, in their untranslatable simplicity, their nonetheless rhythmic simplicity:

alles ist weniger, als	everything is less, than
es ist,	it is,
alles ist mehr.	everything is more.*

What is most untranslatable stems at once from the scansion, or the caesura, and the absence of negation, whether grammatical or not. The ambiguous *als*, emphasized by its position at the end of the line, after the pause of a comma, disengages the *als es ist* (as it is, insofar as it is, as such, such as it is) from the apparent syntax of comparison with which it nonetheless plays.

If I say that the sense of a date opens up madness, a kind of *Wahnsinn*, this is not for emotional effect: only to say what *there is to read in a date*, in the injunction or chance of any reading.

Wahnsinn: the madness of the date, the madness of "when," the delirious sense of *wann*. The madness of the homophony (*Wahn/wann*) is not a play on words by Celan, any more than was the resemblance just before between *shibboleth* and *symbolon*, among Hebrew, Greek, and, here, Germanic. Madness slumbers in this aleatory encounter, this chance among heterogeneities that starts to give meaning and to date. Prior to the *Wahn/wann* of "Huhediblu," Scripture, the epistle, the epistolary, indeed epistolary espittle, cross their sendings with the name of the prophet, the trace and the posthumous, the postscript and the date:

Und — ja —
die Bälge der Feme-Poeten
lurchen und vespern und wispern und vipern,
episteln.
Geunktes, aus
Hand- und Fingergekröse, darüber
schriftfern eines
Propheten Name spurt, als
An- und Bei- und Afterschrift, unterm
Datum des Nimmermenschtags im September — :

And — yes —
the windbags of the poet-proscribers
toady and vesper and whisper and viper,
epistle.
Croaked things, out of
hand- and finger-tripe, on which
far from writing the
name of a prophet leaves its traces, as
at- and by- and behindscript, under the
date of Nevermansday in September — :

The question "When?," *Wann?*, which bears at first upon the roses (When do the roses of September flower?), comes to bear in the end upon the date itself ("Oh quand refleuriront, oh roses, vos septembres?") and becomes, in the meantime, mad itself:

Wann,	When
wann blühen, wann,	when bloom, when,
wann blühen die, hühendiblüh,	when bloom the, hoomendibloom,
huhediblu, ja sie, die September-	hoohedibloo, yes them, the
	September-
rosen?	roses?
Hüh — on tue . . . Ja wann?	Hoo — on tue . . . when then?
Wann, wannwann,	When, whenwhen,
Wahnwann, ja Wahn, —	manywhens, yes mania —
Bruder	brother*

The annulment[r] of the date, its becoming-anonymous in the nothing as well as in the ring, this given of the date leaves its trace in the poem. This trace is the poem. What it comes down to is not simply the trace of something, of a non-trace that happened, that took place in that it was lived, in one sense, and asks to be commemorated. It is also this, certainly, but it is first of all the trace *as* date, that which is bound to mark itself off if it is to mark, to bereave itself if it is to remain. It must expose its secret, risk losing it if it is to keep it. It must blur the border between readability and unreadability, crossing and recrossing it. The unreadable is readable as unreadable, unreadable insofar as readable; here is the madness that burns a date, consuming it from within. Here is what renders it ash, here is what renders ash from the first instant. And during the finite time of incineration, the password is transmitted, there is communication, the *shibboleth* circulates from hand to hand, from mouth to ear, from heart to heart—among a few, a finite number, always. For it can vanish with them, be left as an indecipherable sign, and yet a universal one (*de jure*, in principle): a token, a symbol, a tessera, a trope, a table, or a code.

Despite appearances, there is no dialectalizable contradiction here. To illustrate the paradoxes of this universalization of the "this, here, now" or of the "when," one could have cited the beginning of the *Phenomenology of Spirit*. But ellipsis, discontinuity, caesura, or discretion do not allow themselves here to be reduced or sublated (*aufheben*). No dialectic of sense-certainty can reassure us about an archive's safekeeping.

This is the gift of the poem, and of the date, their condition made up of distress and hope, the chance and the turn, the tone and the *Wechsel der Töne*.[s] This annulment of the return without return does not happen to experience via the only poem, *the* poem that there is not ("Ich spreche ja von dem Gedicht, das es nicht gibt!"), any more than there is the date, which, nonetheless, is there (*es gibt*) —to give. Annulment is at work everywhere a date inscribes its *here* and *now* within iterability, *when* it consigns itself to losing sense, in self-forgetfulness, thus succeeding only in effacing itself. Trace, or ash. These names stand for others. The destiny of a date is analogous to that of every name, of every proper name. Is there another desire than that of dating? of leaving a date? of fixing a date? of praising or blessing a commemoration without whose enunciation no event would ever take place?

Yet desire gets carried away. It gets carried away in praising or blessing the given letter, a date that, in order to be what it is, must give itself to be read in ash, in the nonbeing of its being, that remainder without remainder one calls ash. Of a date *itself* nothing remains, nothing of what it dates, nothing of what is dated by it. No one remains—*a priori*. This "nothing" or "no one" does not befall the date after the fact, like a loss—of something or someone—nor is it an abstract negativity that could be calculated here, avoided there.

We say "nothing" [*rien*] and "no one" [*personne*] according to French grammar, in which these words are neither positive nor negative. Despite the artifice or the randomness of this situation, the grammatical suspension is not unrelated to that in which Celan's *Nichts* and *Niemand* may resonate. Especially when he writes, in "Psalm":

Gelobt seist du, Niemand.   Praised be your name, no one.*

Or the following, in "Einmal" ("Once"), in which a certain *ichten* remains so difficult to translate; it repeats, in some sort, the annihilated without negation in that which also resonates like the production or constitution of an *I* (*ich*), one and infinite, once and infinitely, the step between nothing (*Nichts*) and light (*Licht*):

Eins und Unendlich,   One and Infinite,
vernichtet,   annihilated,
ichten.   ied.

Licht war. Rettung.   Light was. Salvation.*

If the date becomes readable, its *shibboleth* says to you: "I" (almost nothing, only one time, only once infinitely recommenced, but finite in precisely that, and de-fining repetition in advance), I am, I am only a cipher commemorating precisely what will have been doomed to oblivion, destined to become name, for a finite time, the time of a rose, name of nothing, "voices of no one," *name of no one*: ash.

Desire or gift of the poem, the date is borne, in a movement of blessing, toward ash.

I am not presupposing in this way some essence of blessing, realized here in a strange example. I am not saying: you know, we know, what a blessing is, well then, here is one addressed to ash. No, the essence of benediction enunciates itself perhaps from within poetic prayer, the song of a remainder without being, the experience of ashes in the incineration of the date, from within the experience of the date *as* incineration. The latter will no longer designate, in this place, the *operation* at times decided on or rejected by whoever asks himself whether or not to proceed with the cremation, with the destruction by fire, leaving no remains other than ashes, of this living being or of this archive. The incineration of which I speak takes place prior to any operation, it burns from within. There, the date is consumed by incineration in the very expiration that is its production, its genesis, or its inscription: its essence and its chance.

Like the September roses, the no one's rose calls for the blessing of what remains of what does not remain, what does not remain in this remainder (*singbarer Rest*), dust or ash. The mouth of the heart that comes to bless the dust of ash comes down to a blessing of the date. It sings, *yes, amen,* to this nothing that remains (a nothing does not remain), and even to the desert in which there would be no one left to bless the ashes. "Psalm," again:

Niemand knetet uns wieder aus Erde und Lehm, niemand bespricht unsern Staub. Niemand.	No one moulds us again out of earth and clay, no one conjures our dust. No one.
Gelobt seist du, Niemand. Dir zulieb wollen wir blühn. Dir entgegen.	Praised be your name, no one. For your sake we shall flower. Toward you.
Ein Nichts waren wir, sind wir, werden wir bleiben, blühend: Die Nichts-, die Niemandsrose.	A nothing we were, are, shall remain, flowering: the nothing-, the no one's rose.*

To address no one is not exactly not to address any one. To speak to no one, *risking*, each time, singularly, that there might be no one to bless, no one who can bless—is this not the only chance for blessing? for an act of faith? What would a blessing be that was sure of itself? A judgment, a certitude, a dogma.

I had suggested this: that the date, ash, and name was or will be the same, the same never holding in the present. And this same remains to be blessed. To be sung. It remains, the same, only in the call for blessing, it calls for the blessing that calls it. But the response is never assured, it is *given*, but by that very fact incalculable, nowhere a given, given in advance. "Chymisch":

Große, graue,	Great, gray,
wie alles Verlorene nahe	sisterly shape
Schwestergestalt:	near like all that is lost:
Alle die Namen, alle die mit-	All the names, all those
verbrannten	names
Namen. Soviel	burnt with the rest. So much
zu segnende Asche. Soviel	ash to be blessed. So much
gewonnenes Land	land won
über	above
den leichten, so leichten	the weightless, so weightless
Seelen-	rings
ringen.	of souls.*

There is ash, perhaps, but an ash is not. This remainder *seems* to remain of what was, and was presently; it seems to nourish itself or quench its thirst at the spring of being-present, but it emerges from being, it exhausts, in advance, the being from which it seems to draw. The remaining of the remainder—ash, almost nothing—is not being-that-remains, if, at least, one understands by that being-that-subsists. What is drawn, sucked up, drunk (*geschöpft*) with the scoop (*Kelle*; the spring or source, *Quelle*, is not far off), with the ash-scoop, with the ash-ladle (*mit der Aschenkelle*) comes out of the tub of being (*aus dem Seinstrog*). It comes from it, perhaps, but it comes out of it, and it comes out clean, soapy (*seifig*). This is why, in this scene of laundering and of ash (the spring or source is not far off), it is better to say tub of being than manger or trough (*Trog*):

MIT DER ASCHENKELLE GESCHÖPFT	DRAWN WITH THE ASH-LADLE
aus dem Seinstrog,	from the tub of being,
seifig	soapy*

All the rings, all the ashes—there are ever so many and each time unique—pass through the gift of a blessed date. Each tear. Innumerable gifts, ciphered beyond counting by ever so many poems, we will not cite them.

V

Until now, we have always been speaking of dates that are coded, not only ciphered, but coded according to the conventional grid of a calendar. A poem can mention these dates, while incorporating them in its phrasing: itself a daybook. The date thus marked does not necessarily correspond to that of the writing, to the event of the poem. It represents the poem's theme rather than its signature.

Though it has some necessity, this distinction appears nonetheless to be limited in pertinence. Where is this limit to be situated?

It has the form of a ring. By reason of the revolution of which we are speaking, the commemorating date and the commemorated date tend to rejoin and conjoin in a secret anniversary. The poem is this anniversary it sings or blesses, this given ring, the seal of an alliance and of a promise. It has, *it belongs to*, the same date as the one it blesses, it belongs *to it*, it gives and gives back again the date to which it *at one and the same time* belongs and is destined. At this point, in this place always passed, always to come, the border is effaced between the poem's "external" circumstance, its "empirical" date, and its internal genealogy. But this genealogy is dated; this is not an essential, universal, atemporal movement. A *shibboleth* also crosses this border: for a poetic date, for a blessed date, the difference between the empirical and the essential, between contingent exteriority and necessary intimacy, no longer has any place. This non-place, this utopia, is the taking place or the event of the poem as blessing, the (perhaps) absolute poem that Celan says there is not (*das es nicht gibt!*).

With this distinction between the empirical and the essential, a limit is blurred, that of the philosophical as such, philosophical distinction itself. Philosophy finds itself, *finds itself again* in the vicinity of poetics, indeed, of literature. It finds itself again there, for the indecision of this limit is perhaps what is most thought provoking. It finds itself again there, it does not necessarily lose itself there, as some believe, those who, in their tranquil credulity, believe they know where this limit runs and timorously keep within it, ingenuously, albeit without innocence, stripped of what one must call the *philosophical experience*: a certain questioning traversal of limits, uncertainty as to the border of the philosophical field—and above all the *experience of language*, always just as poetic, or literary, as it is philosophical.

Whence the privilege of what we are calling the code: the institution of the calendar, which permits one to call out, to class (*calare*), the years, the months, the days; or of the clock, which spaces and sounds the revolution of the hours. Like the calendar, the clock names the return of the other, of the wholly other in the same. But by *Uhr* and *Stunde*, named in so many poems, we must understand something else and something more than themes or objects. The hour writes, the hour speaks; it calls or assigns the poem; it provokes it, convokes it, apostrophizes it and addresses itself to it, as to the poet whom the hour claims. The hour summons the poem at its hour. "Nacht" speaks of a *Zuspruch der Stunde*:* an exhortation, perhaps a consolation, but above all a word addressed. And to this *Zuspruch* responds elsewhere a *Gespräch* of the hour, a dialogue, a conversation with the turning hour, a word shared with it:

Diese Stunde, deine Stunde,	This hour, your hour,
ihr Gespräch mit meinem Munde.	Its dialogue with my mouth.
Mit dem Mund, mit seinem	With the mouth, with its
Schweigen,	silence,
mit den Worten, die sich weigern.	with words refusing their
	compliance.*

Like a sundial or any other chart, the marking of the hour assigns the subject its place [*place*]; it opens a place for it [*lui donne lieu*]; its address seizes the signatory or the poet even before he has himself marked or given the hour. Mallarmé spoke of the initiative coming back to words: it also comes back to the hour, on the hour, on time. The poet is provoked, in other words, constituted by it. He appears to himself, as such, from within it. Discontinuous return and round of the hours, the here of the clock hand spaces the now. This discreteness, this "caesura of the hours" (*Stundenzäsur*),* cadence, chance, and sufferance, scans the poem from its origin. But this poetics of rhythm or of spacing not only concerns the form of the language, it also says something about the origin of meaning, and of the meaning of language. "Und mit dem Buch aus Tarussa" inscribes in its heart the "caesuras of the hours." The poem speaks in and of rhythm, rhyme, respiration ("mit / geatmeten Steppen- / halmen geschrieben ins Herz / der Stundenzäsur"; "with / breathed steppe- / grass written into the heart / of the caesura of the hours"), but also in and of language, the rhythm of language, the "language-scale, word-scale, home- / scale of exile" ("Sprachwaage, Wortwaage, Heimat- / waage Exile"). The Bremen address sees an affinity between this question of the meaning [*sens*] of language, of its sense and its place for an exile (German for a poet of the German language who was not German), and "the question as to which direction [*sens*] is clockwise" (*Uhrzeigersinn*):

In the midst of losses, only one thing remained attainable, near and not lost: language. . . .

In those years and in the years after, I have tried to write poems in this language: in order to speak, in order to orient myself, in order to find out where I was and where I happened to be going. . . .

It was, you see, event [*Ereignis*], movement, being underway [*Unterwegssein*], it was the attempt to find a direction. And whenever I ask about the sense of it, then I believe I must admit to myself that in this question is also implied *the question concerning which direction is clockwise.*

For the poem is not timeless. Certainly, it lays a claim to infinity, it seeks, through time, to reach through all the time, through time all the time, not above and beyond it.* (Emphasis mine)

The annulment, again, of the ring. The return upon itself of the hour. Consumption, becoming-ash, burning up or incineration of a date: on the hour, in the hour itself, at each hour. This is the threat of an absolute crypt: nonrecurrence, unreadability, amnesia without remainder, but nonrecurrence *as* recurrence, *in* recurrence itself. Such a risk appears no more inessential, no more an accident of the hour or of the day, than the possibility itself of recurrence, which carries with it both a chance and a threat, at once, each time.

Forgive me if I do not name, here, the *holocaust*, that is to say, literally, as I chose to call it elsewhere, the *all-burning*, except to say this: there is certainly today the date of that holocaust we know, the hell of our memory; but there is a holocaust for every date, and somewhere in the world at every hour. Every hour counts its holocaust. Every hour is unique, whether it recurs, and in the manner of a wheel that turns by itself, or whether, the last, it recurs no more, no more than the sister, its own, the same, its other revenant:

Geh, deine Stunde
hat keine Schwestern, du bist—
bist zuhause. Ein Rad, langsam,
rollt aus sich selber, die Speichen
klettern,

. . .

Jahre.
Jahre, Jahre, ein Finger
tastet hinab und hinan

. . .

Kam, kam.
Kam ein Wort, kam,
kam durch die Nacht,
wollt leuchten, wollt leuchten.

Go, your hour
has no sisters, you are—
are at home. A wheel, slow,
rolls on its own, the spokes
climb,

. . .

Years.
Years, years, a finger
gropes down and up,

. . .

Came, came.
Came a word, came,
came through the night,
wanted to shine, wanted to shine.*

And further on, in the same poem, which, therefore, I must cut into sections and on which these cuts inflict a measureless violence, since they wound not only the body of the song but, above all, the rhythm of its own caesuras, cutting into the cuts, the wounds and the scars, and the very sutures *this* poem speaks of, this poem that was the source of so many readings, further on, therefore, the ashes, the ashes repeated, ashes of ashes, night in night, night and night — but the two words (*Asche, Nacht*) call to one another, with their terrifying echo, only in this language:

Asche.	Ash.
Asche, Asche.	Ash, ash.
Nacht.	Night.
Nacht-und-Nacht.	Night-and-night.*

There is the commemorated date and the date of the commemoration, the commemorating. But how can one distinguish between them, at the very hour, today, of an anniversary? How can one differentiate between the date of which the poem speaks and that of the poem, when I write here, now, to recall that other here, now, which was another but *virtually* at the same date?

Virtually: not so much because this hour here, today, at this date, this *dated* here and now is not rigorously the same as, merely analogous to the other, but because the originary date, as coded mark of the other here-now, was *already* a sort of *fiction*, reciting singularity only in the fable of conventions and generalities, of what are, in any case, iterable marks.

Ashes in truth. If the date that is mentioned, commemorated, blessed, sung, tends to merge with its recurrence in the mentioning, commemorating, blessing, and singing of it, how then can one distinguish, in a poetic signature, between the *constative* value of a certain truth (here is when it took place) and that other order of truth which one would associate with poetic *performativity* (I sign this, here now, at this date)? Is a date true? What is the truth of this fiction, the untrue truth of this truth? Here, this, now, is a *shibboleth*. This is — *shibboleth*.

VI

Let us now go beyond what in language classifies the marks of dating according to the conventional fictions of the calendar or the clock.

Radicalizing and generalizing without artifice, we could say that poetic writing offers itself up, through and through, to dating. The Bremen address recalls this: a poem is underway from a place toward "something that stands open" ("an addressable you"), and it makes its way "through" time, it is never "timeless." In it there is merely the cipher of singularity, which opens onto, which recalls place, opening and recalling time,¹ at the risk of losing them in the holocaustic generality of return and in the readability of the concept, in the anniversary repetition of the unrepeatable. Wherever a signature has cut into an idiom, leaving in language the trace of an incision, the memory of an incision *at once* unique and iterable, cryptic and readable, there is date. Not *the* absolute date; there is none, no more than there is an "absolute poem"; but something of the date, the madness of "when," the *wann/Wahnsinn*, the unthinkable *Einmal*, the terrifying ambiguity of the *shibboleth*, sign of belonging and threat of discrimination, indiscernible discernment between alliance and war.

A date discerns and concerns a place, it is a *situation*. It can give place to calculations. But in the final account, it ceases to be calculable. The crypt ceases to be the result of a concealment, the work of a hermetic poet, one skilled at hiding or anxious to seduce with ciphers. A date fascinates, but it is not *made* to fascinate. The crypt takes place (it is a passion, not an action, of the poet) wherever a singular incision marks language. As one might engrave a date in a tree, burning the bark with ciphers of fire. But the voice of the poem carries beyond the singular cut. I mean by this that the cut becomes readable for certain of those who have no part in the event or the constellation of events consigned to it, for those excluded from partaking, yet who may thus partake and impart.

Within the bounds of this generality or this universality, insofar as its meaning is repeatable in this way, a poem acquires the value of a philosopheme. It may offer itself, and it must do so, to the work of a hermeneutics that does not require, for its "internal" reading, access to the singular secret once partaken of by a finite number of witnesses or participants. The poem itself is already such a hermeneutic event, its writing is a matter of *hermeneuein*, it proceeds from it. Looking at it from the side of the universal meaning that corresponds to the date, to that in it which might come again, in a publicly commemorated recurrence, one may always speak, as does one of the titles of the symposium, of "philosophical implications." But looking at it from the other side, from the side of an irreducibly singular date and of an untranslatable incision, if some such thing existed in all purity, there would be no "philosophical implication." The possibility of a philosophical reading would find here, as would any hermeneutics, its limit.

This limit would also be, symmetrically, that of a formal poetics, one concerned or sure about being able to keep meaning separate, at bay. Such a limit does not signify the failure of, even less the necessity of renouncing, philosophical hermeneutics or formal analysis. It turns us back, above all, toward the effaced but common provenance, toward the *possibility*, of philosophical hermeneutics, as well as of formal poetics. Both presuppose the date, the mark incised in language, of a proper name or an idiomatic event. What they thus suppose, they forget, it will be said. To be sure, but forgetting belongs to the structure of what they forget: one can only recall it to oneself in forgetting it. The date *succeeds only in effacing itself*; its mark effaces it *a priori*.

This is what I was suggesting, somewhat elliptically, when I began by saying: the question "What is?" dates. Philosophy, hermeneutics, and poetics can only come about in idioms, in languages, in the body of events and dates of which one could not say that any metalinguistic or metahistorical overview is possible—though such an overview is guaranteed from within, if one may say so, by the structure of marking off that pertains to the iterability of a date, that is to say, to its essential annulment. The effacement of the date or of the proper name inside the ring: here is the origin of philosophy, of hermeneutics, of poetics, their sendoff.

Annulling it in its repetition, the sending presupposes and disavows the date—in other words, the *shibboleth*. And we ought also to distinguish—but how?—between *shibboleth* and *the* or *a* shibboleth. How can one interpret this phrase or indication: "this = *shibboleth*"? This deictic, here, now? Who knows?

Formally, at least, the affirmation of Judaism has the same structure as that of the date. By affirmation, I also mean the claim, the engagement that does not limit itself to the acknowledgment of a fact but invokes a responsibility for it. "We are Jews" means, in this case, "We *take it on*, we take it upon ourselves," "We undertake to be it," and not merely "It turns out that in fact we are it." It means this even if the engagement cannot be reduced to the decisional act of an abstract will, but is rooted within the accepted memory of an unchosen destination. The "same structure as that of the date," we said. Is this only a formal analogy? When someone says "we Jews," does he intend the reappropriation of an essence? the acknowledgment of a belonging? the sense of a partaking?

Yes and no, once again. Celan recalls that there is no Jewish property. This is at least a common theme, as well as the title of a general question: "do you hear me, it is me, me, me and the one you hear, whom you think you hear, me and the other . . . for the Jew, you know, what does he have that really belongs to him, that isn't borrowed, lent, and not returned . . . ?"* The Jew is also the other, me and the other; I am Jewish in saying: the Jew is the other who has no essence, who has nothing of his own or whose own essence is to have none. Whence, *at the same time*, both the alleged universality of the Jewish witness ("All poets are Jews," says Marina Tsvetaeva, cited in the epigraph to "Und mit dem Buch aus Tarussa") *and* the incommunicable secret of the Judaic idiom, the singularity of "his name, his unpronounceable name,"* *sein Name, der unaussprechliche*.

The "name," what is for the Jew "unpronounceable," his proper name, is it a name? It says so many things:

—it says the *shibboleth*, a word that is unpronounceable in the sense that it *cannot* be pronounced by one who does not partake of the covenant or alliance. The Ephraimite *knows* how one *ought* to but *cannot* pronounce it. Here the fact serves the law;

—it says the name of God, which *must* not be pronounced by whoever partakes of the covenant or alliance. The Jew *can* pronounce it but *must not*; he may not pronounce it. The law commands the fact;

—it says the name of the Jew, which the non-Jew has trouble pronouncing, which he does not know how or does not want to pronounce correctly, and which he thereby scorns or destroys; he expels it as "foreign and outlandish";ᵘ he replaces it with a mocking name that is easier to pronounce or classify, as has happened at times on both sides of the Atlantic.

The unpronounceable keeps and destroys the name; it protects it, like the name of God, or dooms it to annihilation among the ashes.

Apparently different or contradictory, these two possibilities can always cross the border and exchange places.

The Jew, the name *Jew*, also exchanges places with the *shibboleth*, against it. Prior even to using the pledge or to being its victim, prior to all separation between communitarian separation or discriminating separation, whether safe or lost, master or exile, Jew is the *shibboleth*. Witness to the universal, but as absolute, dated, marked, incised, caesuraed singularity—as the other and in the name of the other.

(And I will also add that, in its fearsome political ambiguity, *shibboleth* could today name the State of Israel, the present state of the State of Israel. This deserves more than a parenthesis, it will be said. Yes. But what I say in parentheses is this: that it is a question here of nothing but this, everywhere and beyond the borders of this parenthesis.)

Witness to the universal as absolute singularity, as the other and in the name of the other, of the stranger, of you toward whom I must take a step that, without bringing me nearer to you, without exchanging me for you, without being assured a passage, lets the word pass and assigns us, if not to the one, at least to the same. We were already assigned to it, dwelling under the same tradewind. Let the word pass through the barbed-wire border, through, this time, the grid of language or thanks to it. The passage of the other, toward the other—respect *of* the same, of a same that respects the otherness of the other. Why did Celan choose the word *Passat*, the name of a wind, to say, in "Sprachgitter" (in parentheses) "We are strangers"?

(Wär ich wie du. Wärst du wie ich.	(Were I like you. Were you as I.
Standen wir nicht	Did we not stand
unter *einem* Passat?	under *one* tradewind?
Wir sind Fremde.)	We are strangers.)*

Strangers. Both strangers, the two of us. Strangers each to the other? Strangers the two of us to yet others, third parties? Both—the two of them, one *like* the other, *unter* einem *Passat*.

The impossible movement that designates the "Judaic," Jewishness—yours and not only mine, always something of the inappropriable other—we read it, for example, in the poem dated, as its title, "Zürich, zum Storchen." It is dedicated—every date is dedicated—to Nelly Sachs. The semantics of the *I* and the *you* figures here just as paradoxically (you, you are [a] me). This paradox exceeds any measure of being. Again the disproportion of too much or too little, of a more or less than being. You, the word *you*, may be addressed to the other as well as to me, to oneself as other. Each time it exceeds the *economy* of the discourse, its being alongside itself [*son être auprès de soi*]:

Vom Zuviel war die Rede, vom	Of too much was our talk, of
Zuwenig. Von Du	too little. Of the You
und Aber-Du, von	and You-Again, of
der Trübung durch Helles, von	how clarity troubles, of
Jüdischem, von	Jewishness, of
deinem Gott	your God.
. . .	. . .
Von deinem Gott war die Rede, ich	Of your God was our talk, I spoke
sprach	
gegen ihn.	against him.*

(Second parenthesis: several times I have abstained from mentioning the interpellation of Heidegger or to Heidegger. Its necessity can escape no one. For the same reason I will say nothing here of what could be said of other thinkers — Buber, Levinas, Blanchot, and still others.)

The "you," the "yours," may be addressed to the other as Jew but also to the self as other, as another Jew or as other than Jew. Is this a true alternative? "Die Schleuse," "The Lock Gate," addresses you, and your mourning, "all this mourning / of yours":* to tell you that what has been lost, and without remainder, is the word, a word that opens, like a *shibboleth*, onto what is most intimate. Now this lost word, the word that must be mourned, is not only the word "that had remained with me": "sister." It is also, and even more grievously, if this can be said, the word that opens the possibility of mourning what has been lost without remainder (the exterminated family, the incineration of the family name in the figure of the sister — for the word is "sister" — at the final hour that no longer has a sister: "your hour / has no sisters"). It is the very word that grants access to the Jewish mourning rite: *Kaddish.* This word addressed me, like the hour's interpellation, it came before me, it sought me out (*mich suchte*), it took the initiative. But then I lost it, like the word that had remained with me: *sister.* I lost the word that had remained with me, I lost the one that sought me out to mourn the one that had remained with me:

An einen Mund,	To a mouth
dem es ein Tausendwort war,	for which it was one of a thousand
verlor —	I lost —
verlor ich ein Wort,	I lost a word
das mir verblieben war:	that had remained with me:
Schwester.	sister.
An	To
die Vielgötterei	the worship of many gods
verlor ich ein Wort, das mich	I lost a word that was looking for
suchte:	me:
Kaddisch.	*Kaddish.**

Lost the word *sister* that had remained with me, lost the word *Kaddish* that sought me out in order to live the loss, lost too "my Jew's spot" ("wo / mein Judenfleck . . . ?"),* lost my "Jew's curl," which was also a "human curl" ("Judenlocke, wirst nicht grau / . . . / Menschenlocke, wirst nicht grau").*

When it goes as far as the death of the name, as far as the extinction of the proper name that a date, bereaved commemoration, still remains, loss cannot be worse. It crosses the boundary where mourning itself is denied us, the interiorization of the other in memory (*Erinnerung*), the preserving of the other in a sepulcher or epitaph. For in securing a sepulcher, the date would still make room for mourning, for what one calls its work. Whereas Celan also names the incinerated beyond of the date, words lost without sepulcher, "wie unbestattete Worte."* But once dead, and without sepulcher, these words of mourning, themselves incinerated, may still come back. They come back then as phantoms. One hears them roaming about the stelae,

wie unbestattete Worte,	like unsepulchered words,
streunend	roaming
im Bannkreis erreichter	in the orbit of attained
Ziele und Stelen und Wiegen.	goals and stelae and cradles.

Spectral errancy of words. This revenance does not befall words by accident, following a death that would come to some or spare others. *All* words, from their first emergence, partake of revenance. They will always have been phantoms, and this law governs the relationship in them between body and soul. One cannot say that we know this *because* we experience death and mourning. That experience comes to us from our relation to this revenance of the mark, then of language, then of the word, then of the name. What is called poetry or literature, art itself (let us make no distinction for the moment)—in other words, a certain experience of language, of the mark, or of the trait *as such*—is perhaps only an intense familiarity with the ineluctable originarity of the specter. One can, naturally, translate it into the ineluctable loss of the origin. Mourning, the experience of mourning, the *passage* through its limit, too, so that it would be hard to see here a law governing a theme or a genre. It is experience, and as such, for poetry, for literature, for art itself.

VII

An event seems to inaugurate the legitimate belonging of the Jew to his community, at the moment of the right of entrance or the rite of passage, and it takes place, we were saying at the outset, only once, at an absolutely set date: the circumcision. Such is, at least, the appearance.

Circumcision: can one say that it is precisely of this ciphered wound, this wound to be deciphered, that Celan speaks at the end of "Dein vom Wachen"? "Sie setzt / Wundgelesenes über" ("it carries across / the wound-read"),* these lines speak, in any case, of a passing beyond, over that which is *read* to the quick, to the point of bleeding, to the point of wounding, reaching the place where the cipher is painfully inscribed on the body itself. This body may be that of the "reader-collector," as Jean Launay's French translation, "lecteur ramasseur," rightly suggests,ᵛ but also the one on which there is a cipher to be read because it has remained there like the mark of a wound. The wound, or its scar, then becomes significant, it is held by some thread to reading. To say that it is readable would be literally abusive, for it is also very unreadable, and this is why it wears out reading to the very marrow. But it belongs to the experience of reading. I would even say to that of translation, for *setzt . . . über*— which would not under any circumstances be translatable by "translates"—also passes over this grammatical impossibility to beckon toward the translation of this reading-wound, passing over the border to the other side, the side of the other.

In the literality of its word (*Beschneidung*), circumcision appears rarely in Celan's text, at least to my knowledge. The example to which I will return in a moment concerns the circumcision of a word. But does one ever circumcise without circumcising a word? a name? And how can one circumcise a name without touching upon the body? First, upon the body of the name, which finds itself recalled by the wound to its condition as word, then as carnal mark, written, spaced, and inscribed in a network of other marks, carnal mark at once endowed with and deprived of singularity.

If the word *circumcision* appears rarely in its literality, other than in connection with the circumcision of the word, by contrast, the *tropic* of circumcision disposes cuts, caesuras, ciphered alliances, and wounded rings throughout the text. The wound, the very experience of reading, is universal. It is tied to both the differential marks and the destination of language: the inaccessibility of the other returns there in the same, dates and sets turning the ring. To say "all poets are Jews" is to state something that marks *and* annuls the marks of a circumcision. It is tropic. All those who deal with or inhabit language as poets are Jews—but in a tropic sense. And the one who says this, consequently, speaking as a poet and according to a trope, never presents himself literally as a Jew. He asks: What is literality in this case?

What the trope (again an intersection with the "Meridian") comes down to, then, is locating the Jew not only *as* a poet but also in every man circumcised by language or led to circumcise a language.

Every man, then, is circumcised. Let us translate, according to the same trope: therefore also every woman—even the sister. Consequently . . .

I am not in a position here to take up the question of the semantic charge of circumcision; I will not enumerate all the usages that the rich lexicon of circumcision may authorize in the language of the Scriptures, well beyond the consecrated operation that consists in excising the foreskin. The "spiritualization," as one often says, the interiorization that consists in extending the meaning of the word well beyond the sense of the cut into the flesh does not date from Saint Paul; it is not limited to the circumcision of the soul or the heart.

Keeping ourselves to a minimal semantic network, *circumcision* seems to involve *at least* three significations:

1. The cut, which incises the male sexual member, cuts into it, then turns around it to form a circumvenient ring;

2. A name given to the moment of covenant or alliance and of legitimate entry into the community: a *shibboleth* that cuts and partitions, then distinguishes, for example, by virtue of the language and the name given to each of them, one circumcision from another, the Jewish operation from the Egyptian operation from which it is said to derive, or, indeed, the Muslim operation that resembles it, or many others.

3. The experience of blessing and of purification.

Now, among all these meanings, a certain tropic may displace the literality of belonging to Judaism, if one can still speak of belonging to a community to which, as "Gespräch im Gebirg" reminds us, nothing properly belongs. Jews are then, in all senses of this word, the circumcised and the circumcisers, those who have the experience, a certain concise experience of circumcision. Anyone or no one may be a Jew. Jew, no one's name, the only one. No one's circumcision.

If all poets are Jews, they are all, the poets, circumcised or circumcisers. This opens up, in Celan's text, a tropic of circumcision that turns from ciphered sores toward reading-wounds, all cut words, notably in "Engführung," where a thread can be followed that passes through "points of suture," closed up tears or scars, words to be cut off that were not cut off, membranes stitched back together, and so on.

We said a moment ago *no one's circumcision*. The evocation of the exterminated race designates the race and root of no one: black erection in the sky, verge and testicle, race and root of no one. Uprooting of the race, but equally so of the sex (*Geschlecht*) in "Radix, Matrix":

Wer,	Who,
wer wars, jene	who was it, that
Geschlecht, jenes gemordete, jenes	lineage, the murdered, that looms
schwarz in den Himmel stehende:	black in the sky:
Rute und Hode—?	rod and bulb—?
(Wurzel.	(Root.
Wurzel Abrahams. Wurzel Jesse.	Abraham's root. Jesse's root. No
Niemandes	one's
	root—o
Wurzel—o	ours.)*
unser.)	

Circumcise: the word appears only once, in the imperative mode:
beschneide.

But the grammar of the verb, the modality of the imperative, does
not necessarily signify an imperious order. Injunction, appeal, desire,
supplication, prayer—these also may be conveyed through the same
grammar.

For this word, this word of command—injunction or appeal, desire, supplication, or prayer—bears this time *upon the word*. The verb
has the word as its object; it speaks about an operation to be performed on the word, in other words, on the verbum. The word says:
circumcise the word. Its complement is the word or, rather, the
Word: "beschneide das Wort."

Let us read this poem: "Einem, der vor der Tür stand."

It concerns the circumcision of the Word. The interpellation apostrophizes a rabbi, a circumciser, no doubt. Not any rabbi, but Rabbi
Löw:

Rabbi, knirschte ich, Rabbi	Rabbi, I gnashed, Rabbi
Löw:	Löw:
Diesem	For this one
beschneide das Wort.	circumcise the word.*

This word to be circumcised, this word to be circumcised for someone, this word of *someone's* to be circumcised, this word which must
thus be given, and given *once* circumcised, we may understand it as
an opened word.

Like a wound, you will say. Yes and no. Opened, first of all, like a
door: opened to the stranger, to the other, to the neighbor, to the
guest, to whomever. To whomever no doubt in the figure of the absolute to-come (the one who will come, more precisely who *would come*,
for this to-come, *this* to-come, its coming must be neither assured nor

calculable), thus in the figure of the monstrous creature. The absolute to-come can only announce itself in the form of monstrosity, beyond all forms and norms that could be anticipated, beyond all genres or kinds. And I am passing over here what the sudden appearance of Rabbi Löw may recall for us of the Golem, the inventor of the monster: the narrative is given over in the poem to a transmutation, a transfigurative translation [*traduction*], meticulous in its letter and detail — yet another stone in the Prague cemetery — but totally emancipated. The transfer [*translation*] is beholden to the narrative, but absolved from and having no relationship to its literality.

A word opened to whomever in the figure as well, perhaps, of some prophet Elijah, of his phantom or double. He is unrecognizable, through this monstration of monstrosity, but one must know how to recognize him. Elijah is the one to whom hospitality is due, promised, prescribed. He may come, one must know this, at any moment. He may cause the event of his coming to happen at each instant. I will situate in this place that which speaks of or summons the coming of the event (*kommen, geschehen*) in so many of Celan's poems.

The prophet Elijah is not named by Celan, and perhaps he was not thinking of him. I take the risk of recalling as well that Elijah is not only the guest, the one to whom, as *relationship* [rapport] itself, the door [*porte*] of the word [*parole*] must be opened. Elijah is not simply a messianic and eschatological prophet. By God's command, says one tradition, he must be present at every circumcision, each time, every time. He watches over them. The one who holds the circumcised infant must be seated on what is called Elijah's chair (*Kise Eliyahu*). How could he be absent from this poem, which says "Diesem / beschneide das Wort"?

Right here, the monster, or Elijah, the guest or the other, is standing before the door, at the poem's first step, on the threshold of the text. "Einem, der vor der Tür stand" is its title. He stands before the door as before the law. We may think of Kafka's "Vor dem Gesetz," "Before the Law," but also of everything that, in Judaism, associates the door and the law.

And the one who says *I*, the poet, if you like, one of those poets "all" of whom "are Jews," no doubt opens the door to him, but the door turns into the word. He opens to him not the door but the word:

EINEM, DER VOR DER TÜR STAND,   TO ONE, WHO STOOD BEFORE THE
       eines   DOOR, one
Abends: evening:

| ihm | to him |
| tat ich mein Wort auf—: | I opened my word—: |

Let us call this—by way of allegory—an *allegory*, the bearing [*portée*] of a word for the other, to the other or from the other. The allegory follows the revolution or *vicissitude* of the hours, from evening to morning, the *times in their turns, in vicem, vice versa*. The vicissitude begins one evening, *eines Abends*, in the Occident of the poem. The poet, the one who says "I," opens the word and addresses the Rabbi, the *Mohel*, the one whom he appoints as circumciser, since he says to him, "Circumcise." What does he ask of him? To close the door of the evening and to open the door of the morning (*die Morgentür*). If what the door [*porte*] says is the word [*parole*], then he asks him for the morning word, the Oriental word, the poem of the origin—once the word [*mot*] has been circumcised.

Wirf auch die Abendtür zu, Rabbi.	Slam shut the evening door too, Rabbi.
. . .	. . .
Reiß die Morgentür auf, Ra—	Fling the morning door open, Ra—*

A violent opening and closing. *Aufreißen* is to open brusquely, rapidly, and wide, to break or sometimes to *tear* in one stroke, like a veil. *Zuwerfen* similarly marks some brutality; the door is slammed, as though flung in someone's direction, signifying its closing to someone. As for *Ra-*, the name interrupted at the final caesura, the first syllable of an appellation that is not completed and finally remains in the mouth, the Rabbi cut in two, this is perhaps the Egyptian God as well, the sun or light, at the opening of the "morning door."

I will not claim I can read or decipher this poem. A poem about the poem, it also names the becoming-poetic of the word, its becoming-Jewish, in short, if "all poets are Jews." It describes the becoming-circumcised of the word of origin, its circumcision. It is a narrative of circumcision.

I use this word, *circumcision*, to designate an operation, the surgical act of cutting, but also and equally the state, the quality, the condition of being circumcised. In this second sense, one may speak of the circumcision of a word or utterance, as one also speaks of the concision of a discourse. Circumcision will designate being circumcised or circumscribed. Blake's *Jerusalem*, that great poem of circumcision, regularly associates these three turns or turns of speech, these three revolutions: *circumcision, circumscription,* and *circumference* — for example, that of the four senses, which are like four faces turned toward the four cardinal points, from the west ("the Tongue") to the east ("the Nostrils"), from the north ("the Ear") to the south ("the Eye," "Eyed as the Peacock"): "Circumscribing & Circumcising the excrementitious / Husk & Covering into Vacuum evaporating revealing the lineaments of Man . . . rejoicing in Unity / In the Four Senses in the Outline the Circumference & Form, for ever / In the Forgiveness of Sins which is Self Annihilation; it is the Covenant of Jehovah" (98:18–23).

I have cited this "covenant" of Blake's to emphasize that, in all of what we are calling its tropic dimensions, circumcision remains a matter of the senses and of the body. It offers itself to be written and read on the body. Rather: the sense of the senses, the body, thus offers itself to be thought, signified, and interpreted, as revealed in *this* response to the question "What is the body proper, said to be proper?": a place of circumcision.

Before Saint Paul, the Bible tells of the circumcision or uncircumcision of the lips, that is to say, in this tongue, of the tongue (Exod. 6:12, 30), of the ears (Jer. 6:10), and of the heart (Lev. 26:41).

The opposition of the clean and the unclean, the proper and the improper, the pure and the impure, coincides often with that of the circumcised and the uncircumcised, extending without limit the semantic field of circumcision and thus defining it only at the limits of definition, of limitation, of circumscription itself, which is to say, conferring on it a singular indefiniteness.

The circumcision of a word must thus be understood as an event of the body. There is an essential analogy between this event, on the one hand, and the diacritical difference between *shibboleth* and *sibboleth*, on the other. It is in the body, by reason of a certain impotence coming over their vocal organs, but an impotence of the body *proper*, of the already cultivated body, limited by a barrier neither organic nor natural, that the Ephraimites experienced their inaptitude to pronounce what they nonetheless knew ought to be pronounced *shibboleth* — and not *sibboleth*.

An "unpronounceable name" for some, *shibboleth* is a circumcised word. For this one, Rabbi, circumcise the word, *beschneide das Wort.* Give him the word of partition, give it to him to partake of, also, to this one also.

One must pretend to close a lecture, and to have gone full circle around the topic. I will limit myself in concluding to some remarks or questions.

The word to be circumcised is, above all, opened, like a door, offered, given, or at least promised to the other.

The other remains indeterminate—unnamed in the poem. He has no identifiable face; he simply has a face since he must see the door and receive the word, even if this face remains invisible. Nothing lets it be seen in the poem. It is *no one*, anyone, the neighbor *or* the stranger, because for the other it all comes down to the same.

The one who is not yet named, the one who perhaps awaits his name, which is bestowed by circumcision, is the one-and-only, the unique, *this one*. He draws the whole poem toward him, destines it to himself, the destinatory, inspires it toward his own pole in absolute dissymmetry.

The other, *this one*, is always placed *at the head*, as it were, *alone*, very much alone on a line—a poetic line. It is to him, *to this one* (*Diesem*) that the word must be opened, given, circumcised, *for him* that the living Nothing must be inscribed in the heart ("diesem / schreib das lebendige / Nichts ins Gemüt"), to him, for him, this one: *ihm*, then *Diesem, diesem, diesem, Diesem*, four times the same demonstrative pronoun, the same word framing a strophe, four times alone on a line, twice, to begin and to end, in the grammar of the capital letter.

ihm	to him
tat ich mein Wort auf	I opened my word
. . .	. . .
Diesem	For this one—
beschneide das Wort,	circumcise the word,
diesem	for this one
schreib das lebendige	write the living
Nichts ins Gemüt,	Nothing in the heart,
diesem	for this one
spreize die zwei	spread the two
Krüppelfinger zum heil-	cripplefingers in the hal-
bringenden Spruch.	lowing sentence.
Diesem.	For this one.*

The offering of this word for circumcision is indeed the giving of a word, indeed, of one's word, since it is said that "I open my word," *mein Wort*. Given word, promise, engagement, signature, date, and "saving word" also, in the form of a poem or a decision (*Spruch*: sentence or aphorism, strophe or poem, judgment or verdict, decision of justice: circumcision would be *just* this, this decision of the word, its sentence, inscribed right on the body, right at the heart, *precisely*).

This word of opening permits one to pass through the doorway. It is yet another *shibboleth*, the *shibboleth* at the origin of all the others, yet still one among others, *in a given language*.

The *shibboleth* is given or promised by *me* (*mein Wort*) to the singular other, "this one," that he may partake of it and enter, or leave, that he may pass through the doorway, across the line, the border, the threshold.

But this word, given or promised, in any case, opened, offered to the other, also asks. It asks intercession, or, rather, it intercedes with the Rabbi—still an other—that he might bestow, him, a third party, the value of circumcision upon this word, the *shibboleth* of the community before the law, the sign of the covenant. The Rabbi is a wise man invested with this right; he has the knowledge and the power to circumcise the word. He is the guardian and the guarantor; through him the transmission of the *shibboleth* passes at the moment of passing through the doorway. And this doorway is nothing other than circumcision as *shibboleth*, the place of decision for the right of access to the legitimate community, the covenant or alliance, the given name of a singular individual, but the *dated* name, singular but inscribed right on the body, on a given day in a genealogical classification, one could say in a calendar. The name counts *at the same time one time and several times*. There is a turning and a vicissitude of names.

The intercessor seems to hold all the powers and all the rights, whether one thinks of the poem's intercession, of mine, or of the Rabbi's. This—a *shibboleth*—intercedes. But here knowledge and power are in themselves annulled. The knowledge and the ability of Rabbi Löw are annulled, his knowing-to-be-able-to-circumcise, which amount in truth to the same thing, which are but one—are immediately annihilated in the *objectless*. They know and can infinitely, but must also infinitely annihilate themselves. For the writing of circumcision which *I* ask of him, for which I intercede with the intercessor, is a *writing of Nothing*. It performs its operation on Nothing, an incisive surgery that, to the point of bleeding, to the point of wounding (*Wundgeschriebene*, one might say this time), embeds the inscription of Nothing in the flesh, in the living word, in the flesh of the pronounceable and circumcised word: "Diesem / beschneide das Wort, / diesem schreib das lebendige / Nichts ins Gemüt." Write, slice, inscribe, cut, separate, *schreiben, schneiden, scheiden*. But Nothing. One gives the word, *one's* word, in inscribing this Nothing in the heart; thus one should not cut in, but on the contrary allow the word passage. In "Engführung," it is said of a stone, that of the threshold, perhaps, or of the path, or of the first circumcisers, that "it / was hospitable, it / did not cut in": "er / war gastlich, er / fiel nicht ins Wort."* As often, the break in the line comes after the pronoun.

How can one write nothing?

(Let us place here, not to close it, but on the contrary so as to leave it open, like a wound, the necessity of an immense parenthesis: for the question of Nothing and the meaning of being in Celan, of a truth of being that *passes* through the *experience* of Nothing, for the question, here, of circumcision left unanswered at the time or date of Todtnauberg, when it was, in effect, put to another kind of wise man, one summer's day in 1967.)*

No one's circumcision, the word's circumcision by the incision of Nothing in the circumcised heart of the other, of this one, you.

Circumcise the word [*parole*] for him, circumcise his word [*mot*] — what is meant by this demand? More than one can *mean-to-say*, more and less than this or that meaning, more or less than this *determination*. Circumcision is also a determination: it defines and it decides. But to ask for circumcision is not to ask for something determinate, a meaning or an object.

The circumcised word [*parole*] is *above all* written, at once incised and excised in a body, which may be the body of a language and which in any case always binds the body to language: word that is entered into, wounded in order to be what it is, word that is cut into, written because cut into, caesuraed in its origin, with the poem.

The circumcised word is, *next*, readable, starting from *nothing*, but readable, *to be read* to the point of wounding and to the point of bleeding (*Wundgelesene*).

By the same stroke, as it were, the circumcised word grants access to the community, to the covenant or alliance, to the partaking of a language, in a language. And in the Jewish language as poetic language, if all poetic language is, like all poets according to the epigraph, Jewish in essence; but this essence promises itself only through dis-identification, that expropriation in the nothing of the non-essence of which we have spoken. The Germanic language, like any other, but here with what privilege, must be circumcised by a rabbi, and the rabbi becomes then a poet, reveals the poet in him. How can the German language receive circumcision at this poem's date, that is to say, following the holocaust, the solution, the final cremation, the ash of everything? How is one to bless ashes in German?

Finally, *fourth* and in consequence, at once both readable and secret, mark of belonging and of exclusion, the wound of partaking, the circumcised word reminds us also of the *double edge*ʷ of a *shibboleth*. The mark of a covenant or alliance, it also *intervenes*, it interdicts, it signifies the sentence of exclusion, of discrimination, indeed, of extermination. One may, thanks to the *shibboleth*, recognize and be recognized by one's own, for better and for worse, in the partition of partaking, according to these *two senses* of the word *partage*: *on the one hand* [d'une part], for the sake of the partaking and for the ring of the covenant, but also, *on the other hand* [d'autre part], on the other side of partaking, that of exclusion, for the purpose of denying the other, of denying him passage or life. One partition [*partage*] always refuses the other, the meaning of the one — such is the lot [*partage*] — proscribes the other. Because of the *shibboleth* and exactly to the extent that one may make use of it, one may see it turned against oneself. Then it is the circumcised who are proscribed or held at the border, excluded from the community, put to death, or reduced to ashes: at the mere sight, in the mere name, at the first reading of a wound.

How is one to guard oneself against this double edge? With what? With nothing. Perhaps Nothing, the annulment of all literal circumcision, the effacement of this *determinate* mark, perhaps the inscription as circumcision of Nothing or nothing in circumcision. Perhaps Rabbi Löw understood himself to be asked or ordered to do this, *precisely* this, nothing, the inscription of "the living Nothing in the heart." Perhaps, but precisely: this would not reduce the demand to nothing.

There must be circumcision, circumcision of the word, writing, and it must take place once, precisely, each time one time, the unique time.

This time awaits its coming, as its vicissitude. It awaits a date, and this date can only be poetic, an incision in the body of language. It remains to come, always. How are we to transcribe ourselves into a date? Celan asks.

When we speak here of a date to come for circumcision, we are not yet speaking, not necessarily, of history. We are not speaking of the date *in* the history of an individual (we know, for example, that this date was variable until it was fixed, for Jews, at the eighth day after birth) or *in* the history of Judaism (we know that other peoples practiced it already and still do; a *shibboleth* passes the blade of a slight difference between several circumcisions; we also know that circumcision only beçomes law at a certain date; the first codes of Israel did not make a ritual injunction of it).

No, the circumcision of the word is not dated in history. In this sense, it has no age, but it opens the place of and for the date. It opens the word to the other, and the door, it opens history and the poem and philosophy and hermeneutics and religion. Of all that calls itself—of the name and the blessing of the name, of yes and of no, it sets turning the ring, to affirm or to annul.

I have kept you too long and ask your pardon.

Permit me to let fall, by way of envoy or *shibboleth*, that is to say, in the economy of an ellipsis that circulates only in the partaking and partition of a given language, here my own, by way of signature here, today, this: circumcision—dates.

Seattle, October 14, 1984

Poetics and Politics of Witnessing

> The world becomes its language and its language becomes
> the world. But it is a world out of control, in flight from
> ideology, seeking verbal security and finding none beyond
> that promised by a poetic text, but always a self-unsealing
> poetic text.
>
> —Murray Krieger, *A Reopening of Closure: Organicism Against Itself*

> [I]t is the role of art to play the unmasking role—the role
> of revealing the mask as mask. Within discourse it is liter-
> ary art that is our lighthouse. . . . It would seem extrava-
> gant to suggest that the poem, in the very act of becoming
> successfully poetic—that is, in constituting itself poetry—
> implicitly constitutes its own poetic. But I would like here
> to entertain such an extravagant proposal.
>
> —Murray Krieger, *Ekphrasis: The Illusion of the Natural Sign*

Signing, sealing, revealing, unsealing. This will be about bearing witness. And about poetics as bearing witness—but testamentary witness: attestation, testimony [in English in the original], testament.

A poem can "bear witness" to a poetics. It can promise it, it can
be a response to it, as to a testamentary promise. Indeed it must, it
cannot not, do so. But not with the idea of applying a previously existing art of writing, or of referring to one as to a charter written

somewhere else, or of obeying its laws like a transcendent authority, but rather by itself promising, in the act of its event, the foundation of a poetics. It would be a matter, then, of the poem "constituting its own poetics," as Krieger puts it, a poetics that must also, *through* its generality, become, invent, institute, offer for reading, in an exemplary way, signing it, at the same time sealing and unsealing it, the possibility of *this* poem. This would come about in the event itself, in the verbal body of its singularity: at a particular date, at the both unique and repeatable moment of a signature that, in the reference that carries it beyond itself, toward the other or toward the world, opens the verbal body to things other than itself.

As testimony of warm gratitude, I would like to take, in my turn, a certain risk, in order to share it with Murray Krieger—the risk of "entertain[ing] such an extravagant proposal." And to try it out, I would like to put to the test this experience of bearing witness. Wanting to recall places where, for over ten years, I have enjoyed living near Murray Krieger, I chose to return to a particular text of Celan that I happened to read with my students at the University of California, Irvine, in the course of a three-year seminar about witnessing. And especially about responsibility, when it engages a poetic signature, at a singular date. Hypothesis to be verified: all responsible witnessing engages a poetic experience of language.

I

Without renouncing, far from it, thinking about the secret within the horizon of responsibility, how must one come up against the question of testimony (*testimonium*)? And why is the question of *testimonium* no different from that of the *testamentum*, of all the testaments, in other words, of surviving in dying, of *sur-viving* before and beyond the opposition between living and dying?

ASCHENGLORIE hinter . . .

. . .
Niemand
zeugt für den Zeugen.

CENDRES-LA GLOIRE revers . . .

. . .
Nul
ne témoigne
pour le témoin.
    (du Bouchet)

GLOIRE DE CENDRES derrière . . .

. . .

Personne
ne témoigne pour le
témoin.
   (Lefebvre)

ASH-GLORY behind . . .

. . .

No one
bears witness for the
witness.
   (Neugroschel)[1]

If we want to keep the poetic resonance to which, already, on the page, these words intend to respond, we must remember that they come to us in German. As always, the idiom remains irreducible. This invincible singularity of the verbal body already introduces us into the enigma of testimony, next to the irreplaceability of the singular witness, which is exactly, perhaps, what this poem is speaking to us about. Which thus speaks *of itself*, signifying itself in speaking to the other about the other, signing and de-signing itself in a single gesture —*sealing and unsealing itself*— or again, to quote and displace a little the words of Murray Krieger: *sealing while (by, through) unsealing itself as a poetic text.*

This idiom is untranslatable, at bottom, even if we translate it. These three lines resist even the best translation. They come to us, moreover, at the end of a poem that, however little certainty there may be about its meaning, about all its meanings and all its possible intended meanings, it is difficult not to think of as also referring, according to an essential *reference*, to dates and events, to the existence or the experience of Celan. These "things" that are not only "words": the poet is *the only one who can bear witness to them*, but he does not name them in the poem. The possibility of a secret always remains open, and this reserve inexhaustible. That is more than ever so in the poetry of Celan, who never ceased encrypting (*sealing, unsealing*) these references. Some have been able to bear witness to this, in fact, such as Celan's friend and reader-interpreter Peter Szondi, who shared at least some of his experiences, not that such testimony exhausts or, above all, proves what he speaks of, far from it.

This poem also remains untranslatable to the extent that it may refer to events to which the German language will have been a privileged witness, namely, the Shoah, which some call by the proper name (and metonymic name—an immense problem that I leave hanging here) of "Auschwitz." The German language of this poem will have been present at everything that was capable of destroying by fire and reducing to "ash" (*Aschenglorie* is the first word of the poem, a double and divided word) existences of innumerable number—innumerably. Innumerably but also unnameably, unspeakably, revoltingly, incinerating thus, together with the name and the memory, even the *guaranteed* possibility of testimony. And since I have just said "even the *guaranteed* possibility of testimony," we will have to ask whether the concept of testimony or bearing witness is compatible with a value of certitude, of warrant, and even of knowing as such.

Ash, this is also the name of what annihilates or threatens to destroy even the possibility of bearing witness to annihilation. Ash is the figure of annihilation without remainder, without memory, or without a readable or decipherable archive. Perhaps that would lead us to think of this fearful thing: the *possibility* of annihilation, the *virtual* disappearance of the witness, but also of the capacity to bear witness. Such would be the only condition for bearing witness, its only condition of possibility as condition of its impossibility—paradoxical and aporetic. When testimony appears guaranteed and then becomes a demonstrable theoretical truth, part of a legal proceedings or report, a substantiation of evidence or even a piece of evidence, it risks losing its value, its sense or its status as testimony. That comes down to saying—always the same paradox, the same paradoxopoetic matrix—that *as soon as* it is guaranteed, certain as a *theoretical proof*, a testimony *can no longer* be guaranteed *as* testimony. For it to be guaranteed as testimony, it cannot, it must not, be absolutely certain, absolutely sure and certain in the order of knowing as such. This paradox of *as such* is the paradox we can experience—and there is nothing fortuitous about this—apropos of the secret and responsibility, of the secret of responsibility and the responsibility of the secret. How can one manifest a secret *as* secret? To take up Murray Krieger's words again, how can one reveal a mask *as* a mask? And in what way is a poetic *opus* called upon to put this strange operation to work?

So it is necessary first to hear these lines in their own tongue, and to see them in their space. Necessary out of respect for their spacing, but above all because the spaced writing of this language does not admit of translation into a simple *speech*, French or English. We see already announcing itself the poignant question of untranslatable testimony. Because it must be linked to a singularity and to the experience of an idiomatic mark—for example, that of a language—testimony resists the test of translation. It thus risks not being able to cross the frontier of singularity, if only to deliver its meaning. But what would an untranslatable testimony be worth? Would it be a non-testimony? And what would a testimony that was absolutely transparent to translation be? Would it still be a testimony?

Ash, we were saying, annihilates or threatens to annihilate even the *possibility* of bearing witness to annihilation.

It so happens that Celan's poem has as its title its own *incipit*. Its first line speaks of ashes, and it appears quite translatable. Du Bouchet translates *Aschenglorie*, a single word, with *three* words, as *Cendres-la gloire*; Lefebvre does the same, in *Gloires de cendres*; Neugroschel uses *two* hyphenated words, *Ash-glory*. *Word-for-word* translation is already impossible. Infidelity has begun, and betrayal and perjury, from the very threshold of this arithmetic, with this accountability of the incalculable. The poetic force of a word remains incalculable, all the more so, surely, when the unity of a word (*Aschenglorie*) is that of an *invented* composition, the inauguration of a new body. All the more so, surely, when the birth of this verbal body gives the poem its first word, when this first word becomes the word that comes at the beginning. *En arkhē ēn ho logos*. And if for John this logos is a light, here it is a light of ashes. In the beginning was (the word) *Aschenglorie*.

This glory of ashes, this glory of ash, this glory which is that of ashes but is also of ash, in ashes—and glory, at the very least, the light or shining brightness of fire—here sheds light on a poem that I shall not even attempt to interpret with you. Light is also knowing, truth, meaning. Now this light is no more than ashes here, it becomes ash, it falls into ashes, as a fire goes out. *But* (and the mobile and unstable articulation of this "but" will be important for us) ashes are also of glory, they can still be renowned and renamed, sung, blessed, loved, if the glory of the renowned and renamed is not reducible either to fire or to the light of knowing. The brightness of glory is not only the light of knowing [*connaissance*], and not necessarily the clarity of knowledge [*savoir*].

Why not even attempt to *interpret* this poem? I'd like to try to explain this limit here. What matters is not what this poem means, or that it mean, or that it bear witness to this or that, or even *that* it names and *what* it names—*elliptically*, as always. Ellipsis and caesura and the cut-off breath no doubt designate here, as always in Celan, that which, in the body and in the rhythm of the poem, seems most *decisive. A decision,* as its name indicates, always appears *as* interruption, it decides *inasmuch* as it is a cut that tears. What counts, then, is not that the poem *names* some motifs we know in advance must be at the heart of a reflection on responsibility, bearing witness, or poetics. What matters most is the strange limit between what can and cannot be determined or decided in *this poem's bearing witness to bearing witness.* For this poem says something about bearing witness. It bears witness to it. Now in this bearing witness to bearing witness, in this apparent meta-witnessing, a certain limit makes meta-witnessing — that is, absolute witnessing — at the same time possible and impossible.

Let us try to go into the region of this limit, to the passage of this line. We will be guided by a hypothesis: this line is perhaps also the line of necessary "extravagance" of which Murray Krieger speaks.

We have just alluded to some motifs that are in some way signaled by this poem and that we know in advance intersect at the heart of the questions of responsibility, of the secret, of bearing witness.

What, then, are these motifs? Well, for example, the *three,* the figure of everything that carries beyond the two, the duo, the dual, the couple. *Three* is named *two times,* in the first stanza and close to the final stanza, which names, precisely, the *Aschen (Aschenglorie,* to repeat, in *one single word* in the first line, but *Aschen-glorie,* cut or gathered by a hyphen across two lines, near the end). Two times there is a tripleness, which affects the road (*Weg*) and the hands (*Händen*), the *knotted* hands (let us also keep hold of the knot, the knotting of the link and the hands).

ASCHENGLORIE hinter
deinen erschüttert-verknoteten
Händen am Dreiweg.

Let us quote French and English translations; they are not wholly satisfactory, but no one should pose as an authority here, by definition:

CENDRES-LA GLOIRE revers
de tes mains heurtées-nouées pour jamais
sur la triple fourche des routes.
   (du Bouchet)

GLOIRE DE CENDRES derrière
tes mains nouées-bouleversées
au Trois-chemins.
   (Lefebvre)

ASH-GLORY behind
your shaken-knotted
hands on the three-forked road.
   (Neugroschel)

It would also be possible to translate as follows:

GLOIRE POUR LES CENDRES, derrière
tes mains défaites effondrées — toutes nouées
à la fourche des trois voies.

GLORY FOR ASHES, behind
thy demolished collapsed hands — all knotted
at the fork of the three ways.

I am not satisfied with this "pour les cendres," "for ashes," because the phrase concerns the glory *of* ashes as much as the glory
promised *to* ashes. If, as I also considered doing, we translated this
as "*gloire* aux *cendres* [glory *to* ashes]," it would be necessary to hear
in it not only the glorification of ashes, but, as one might say of a still
life, the figure of glory surrounded by ashes, having a background or
an ornament of ashes. So many ways of noting the poetic stroke of
genius in this untranslatable *Aschenglorie*. The composite word remains untranslatable, untranslatable word for word, one word for
the other, there where it does not decompose. For in the original version it is not divided, as it will be lower down, near the end, disarticu-
lating and unifying itself with itself, this time, at the end of the line,
via a strange hyphen. Such a hyphen is also an act of poetical memory. It re-marks, *in return*, the incipit; it gives a reminder of the initial
undividedness of *Aschenglorie*:

Aschen-
glorie hinter
euch Dreiweg
Händen.

Cendres-
la gloire, revers
de vous — fourche triple,
mains.
   (du Bouchet)

Gloire de
cendres
derrière vous, mains
au Trois-chemins
   (Lefebvre)

Ash-
glory behind
your three-forked
hands.
    (Neugroschel)

One could also translate another way:

Gloire
de cendres derrière
vous les mains
du triple chemin.

Glory
of ashes behind
you the hands
of the triple road.

Euch (plural you) has just replaced the *deinen* of the second line ("deinen erschüttert-verknoteten / Händen am Dreiweg"; thine, thy hands, the hands that are thine). The addressee of the apostrophe is pluralized. At any rate, it is no longer simply the same, no longer reducible to the being in the singular, masculine or feminine, to whom the first stanza is addressed. The two stanzas turn, they *turn round*, as a stanza [*strophe*] and an apostrophe always do. The latter, in a line [*vers*], *turns toward* [vers]. The two stanzas apostrophize more than one addressee. They turn from one toward the other; they turn away from one toward others; they return, they turn round, they turn around, from one to the other.

Why even point out this allusion to the *three*, whether in connection with the road (*Dreiweg*) or hands (*Dreiweg/Händen*)? Because in fact we will soon be butting up against this motif of the third in the scene of possible/impossible testimony, of possible testimony *as* impossible. In its Latin etymology, witness, *témoin* (*testis*), the one testifying, is the one who is present as a third (*terstis*).[2] We would have to look very closely to understand what this might imply. *Testis* has a homonym in Latin. It usually occurs in the plural, to mean "testicles." Plautus plays on the word in *Curculio*, and exploits this homonym. *Testitrahus* means at once complete and male, masculine. Some feminists, men or women, could, if they wanted, playfully or not, derive from this an argument about the relations between a certain thinking of the third and testimony, on the one hand, and the chief, the head and phallocentric capital, on the other. It is true that, in English, *testis, testes* has kept the sense of testicle—which could be an incitement to militancy.

In the chapter "Religion and Superstition" in his *Vocabulaire des institutions européennes (Indo-European Language and Society)*,[3] Benveniste analyzes a word, *superstes*, which can mean *témoin*, "the one testifying," in the sense of surviving: someone who, having been present then having survived, plays the role of the one who testifies. He both associates *superstes* and *testis* and distinguishes between them: "We can now see the difference between *superstes* and *testis*. Etymologically *testis* means the one who is present as the 'third' person (*terstis*) at a transaction where two persons are concerned; and this conception goes back to the common Indo-European period." As always, Benveniste analyzes the etymology by following the line of a genealogical recollection that goes back to institutions, customs, *practices*, *pragmatics*. In this invaluable but profoundly problematic work, which wants to be a "vocabulary of Indo-European *institutions*," words are selected and then placed in a network according to *institutional* figures, to which they are also supposed to testify.[4] The words *testify* to institutions; the vocabulary *attests* to an institutional meaning. But even assuming that the meaning exists before and outside of these words (an improbable hypothesis, or one with little sense), it is at any rate sure that the meaning does not exist without these words, which is to say, without that which testifies to it, in a sense of testifying that remains highly enigmatic but inescapable. If the words *testify* to a usage and an institutional practice,[5] the paradox here is concentrated in the analysis of the word *testis, terstis*, which attests, with regard to knowledge, thus giving rise to this putative knowledge, to the existence of an institution or a practice, a social organization, a "conception"—Benveniste's word—which, he says, "goes back to the common Indo-European period." In order to illustrate—in reality, to *establish*—this filiation, to prove this fact, Benveniste adds:

> A Sanskrit text has it: "every time two persons are together, Mitra is there as the third person," thus Mitra is by nature "the one who testifies." But *superstes* describes the one who testifies as the one "who survives," as the one who testifies in virtue of his surviving, or as "the one who keeps to the thing," who is present at it.
>
> We can now see what *superstitio* can and must theoretically signify, namely the quality of being a *superstes*. This would be the "property of being present" as "the one who testifies."[6]

Here Benveniste's statements open onto a larger context that we should reconstruct, in particular around *superstes*, the one who survives determined *as* one who testifies, and around *testis, terstis*, determined *as* third. The one who testifies is the one who will have been present. He or she will have *been present at*, in the present, the thing to which he testifies. The motif of presence, of being-present or of being-in-presence, always turns out to be at the center of these determinations. In *The Différend*, a book in which the question of the witness plays a large role, Jean-François Lyotard addresses this question of the witness as third person a number of times, without reference to Benveniste or to Celan. But by privileging the example of Auschwitz and the debate about "revisionism" (which is, naturally, a debate about the status of testimony and of survival), he problematizes the idea of God as absolute witness.[7]

Obviously, we must take into account an undeniable fact: like the institutions to which it is thought to refer, which it ought to reflect, represent, or incarnate, Latin semantics (*testis, terstis, superstes*) denotes only one etymologico-institutional configuration among others—even one among others for "us," assuming that we can say "we" Westerners. It cannot, for example, be found in German.

The family *Zeugen, bezeugen, Bezeugung, Zeugnis*, translated as "witness," "to bear witness," "testimony," "attestation," belongs to a completely different semantic network. One would be hard put, in particular, to find in it explicit reference to the situation of the third, not to mention presence. All these words, in a family that we would not dare simply to call homonymy, recur in a fundamental way in Celan's poem (*Zeug, Zeugen, Zeugung*). Elsewhere, they also mean "tool, procreation, engendering," and, precisely, "generation"—at the same time biological and familial. Following what the word *témoin* (*terstis, testis*) *testifies to* by its supposed genealogy, we have also what the word *Zeugen bears witness* to in its supposed genealogy or generation. If we consider the *témoin*, the one who testifies, to be *terstis superstes*, the surviving third, even the testamentary heir, guardian, guarantee, and legatee, in principle, of what was and is now gone, then the crossover between, *on the one hand*, a genealogical or generational semantics of *Zeugen* and, *on the other hand*, the semantics of *terstis superstes* becomes vertiginous.

Crossover of a *vertiginous* filiation, yes, perhaps. But it is a vertigo that turns our heads, a vertigo in which we will turn and let ourselves be turned round, even sink down, and not only in between the tropes, stanzas or strophes, and apostrophes of Celan.

In English, with *testimony* and *to testify, attestation, protest, testament* [in English in the original], the Latin root does, of course, remain. It thus articulates for us the two themes of survival and testimony. But the family of *witness* and *bearing witness* [in English in the original] is something else altogether. It opens, no doubt, onto the aspect of seeing (a privileging of ocular witnessing), and thus toward another semantic and poetic space in the final words of Celan's poem in [English] translation: "No one / bears witness for the / witness." Finally—but this is where we should have begun—Greek makes no explicit reference to the third, to surviving, to presence, or to generation: *martus, marturos*, the witness, who becomes the martyr, the witness of faith, does not literally entail any of these values (third, surviving, presence, generation). *Marturion* means, following the institutional usage, "bearing witness," but also "proof."

Here we touch on a sensitive and deeply problematic distinction: between bearing witness, the act or experience of bearing witness as "we"[8] understand it, on the one hand, *and*, on the other hand, proof—in other words, between bearing witness *and*, on the other hand, theoretical-constative certitude. This conceptual distinction is as essential as it is unsurpassable in principle, *de jure*. But the confusion always remains *de facto* possible, so fragile and easily crossed can the limit sometimes appear, whatever the language and word may be. For this is not limited to the Greek *marturion* alone: the Latin *testimonium*—testimony, deposition, attestation—can come to be understood as proof. Therefore, language cannot of itself alone, as a lexicon or dictionary would do, be guardian and guarantor of a usage. A pragmatic slippage from one sense to another, sometimes in the passage from one sentence to another, can always occur. We should ask for what necessary—not accidental—reasons the sense of "proof" regularly comes to contaminate or divert the sense of "bearing witness." For the axiom we ought to respect, it seems to me, even though it may be problematized later, is that *bearing witness* is not *proving*. Bearing witness is heterogeneous to producing proof or exhibiting a piece of evidence. In the case of a statement under oath, bearing witness appeals to the act of faith [*acte de foi*], and thus takes place in the space of pledged or sworn word [*foi jurée*] ("I swear to tell the truth"), or of a promise engaging a responsibility before the law, a promise always open to betrayal, always hanging on the possibility of perjury, infidelity, or abjuration.

What does "I bear witness" mean? What do I mean when I say "I bear witness" (for one only bears witness in the first person)? I do not mean "I prove," but "I swear that I saw, I heard, I touched, I felt, I was *present.*" That is the irreducible *sense-perceptual* dimension of presence and past presence, of what can be meant by "being present" and especially by "having been present," and of what that means in bearing witness. "I bear witness"—that means: "I affirm (rightly or wrongly, but in all good faith, sincerely) that that was or is present to me, in space and time (thus, sense-perceptible), and although you do not have access to it, not the same access, you, my addressees, *you have to believe me*, because I engage myself to tell you the truth, I am already engaged in it, I tell you that I am telling you the truth. Believe me. You have to believe me."

The addressee of the testimony, the witness of the witness, does not see what the first witness says she or he saw; the addressee did not see it and never will see it. This direct or immediate non-access of the addressee to the object of the testimony is what marks the absence of this "witness of the witness" to the thing itself. This ab-sence is essential. It is connected to the speech or the mark of testimony to the extent that speech can be dissociated from what it is witness to: for the witness is not *present* either, of course, presently present, to what he recalls, he is not present to it in the mode of perception, to the extent that he bears witness, at the moment when he bears witness; he is no longer present, now, to what he says he was present to, to what he says he perceived; he is no longer present, even if he says he is present, presently present, here and now, through what is called memory, memory articulated in a language, to his having-been-present.

II

This "you have to believe me" must be rightly understood. "You have to believe me" does not have the sense of the theoretico-epistemic necessity of knowledge. It is not presented as a *probative* demonstration, where we cannot but subscribe to the conclusion of a syllogism, to the chain of an argumentation, or, indeed, to the display of a thing present. Here, "you have to believe me" means "believe me because I tell you to, because I ask it of you," or, equally well, "I promise you to tell the truth and to be faithful to my promise, and I engage myself to be faithful." In this "you have to believe me," the "you have to," which is not theoretical but performative-pragmatic, is as determining as the "believe." At bottom, it is perhaps the only rigorous introduction to the thought of what "to believe" might mean. When I subscribe to the conclusion of a syllogism or to the production of proof, it is no longer an act of belief, even if the one who conducts the demonstration asks me to "believe" in the truth of the demonstration. A mathematician, a physicist, or a historian does not seriously, as a scholar, ask me to *believe* him or her. He does not appeal, in the final analysis, to my belief at the moment when he presents his conclusions.

"What is believing?"—what are we doing when we *believe* (which is to say all the time, and as soon as we enter into relationship with the other): this is one of the questions that cannot be avoided when one tries to think about bearing witness.

In spite of the examples invoked to begin to make things a little clearer, bearing witness is not through and through and necessarily discursive. It is sometimes silent. It has to engage something of the body, which has no right to speak. We should thus not say, or believe, that bearing witness is entirely discursive, through and through a matter of language. But we will not, in general, call "bearing witness" something that is not open to the order of the *comme tel*, of the present or having-been-present *comme tel, en tant que tel*, of the *as such* or of this *as* that Murray Krieger rightly stresses—as truth itself, the truth of the lie or the simulacrum, the truth of the mask—in the sentence quoted in the epigraph ("the role of revealing the mask *as* mask").

This "as such" is presupposed by language, unless on its side it presupposes at least the possibility of a mark, or a pre-linguistic experience of the mark or the trace "as such." This is where the whole formidable problem of the apophantic opens up—of the *as such*, of presence and of language. We will not enter into it directly here in its own right.[9]

Whoever bears witness [in English in the original] does not provide proof; he is someone whose experience, in principle singular and irreplaceable (even if it can be cross-checked with others in order to become proof, in order to become probative in a verification process) attests, precisely, that some "thing" has been present to him. This "thing" is no longer present to him, of course, in the mode of perception at the moment when the attestation takes place; but it is present to him, if he alleges this presence, as presently *re-presented* in memory. At any rate, even if—something unusual and improbable—it were still contemporary at the moment of attestation, it would be inaccessible, as *perceived* presence, to the addressees receiving the testimony, who are placed in the order of believing or are asked to place themselves there. The witness marks or declares that something is or was present to him that is not so to the addressees to whom he is joined by a contract, an oath, a promise, by a sworn word [*foi jurée*], whose performativity is constitutive of the testimony and makes it a pledge [*gage*], an engagement. Perjury even presupposes this sworn word, which it betrays. Perjury does indeed threaten all bearing witness, but this threat is irreducible in the scene of the sworn word and attestation. This structural threat is at once distinct and inseparable from the finitude that any testimony also presupposes, for any witness can make a mistake in good faith; he can have a limited, false perception, one that in any number of ways is misleading about what he is speaking about; this finitude, which is just as irreducible and without which there would be no place for bearing witness, is nonetheless other, in its effects, than the kind that obliges us to believe and makes lying or perjury always possible. There are thus two heterogeneous effects of the same finitude here, or two essentially different approaches to finitude: one that goes by way of error or hallucination in good faith, and one that goes by way of deceit, perjury, bad faith. Both must always be *possible* at the moment of bearing witness.

But the very possibility of lying and perjury (lying being a kind of perjury) attests that for us bearing witness, if there is such a thing, gains a sense only before law, before the promise, the pledge. It has a sense only in regard to a cause: justice, truth as justice. Here we will merely situate this difficulty at the moment where we encounter in the same word, *marturion*, and in a way that is not fortuitous, two heterogeneous meanings: (1) *on the one hand*, bearing witness (which belongs to the space of believing, of the act of faith, of pledge and signature, and we will constantly have to ask and re-ask ourselves: What does *believe* mean?); and (2) *on the other hand*, proof, guaranteed determination, the order of knowledge. It is always the alternation between *Glauben und Wissen*, the title of a work of Hegel, but also of an interminable debate between Kant and Hegel.

Whether it is phenomenological or semantic, we will not go so far as to say that this distinction between *bearing witness* and *proof de facto exists*, in the strong and strict sense of the word. We will not go so far as to say that it *holds in reality, solidly, actually or presently*. We are dealing here with a border that is at once rigorous and inconsistent, unstable, hermetic, and permeable, uncrossable *de jure* but *de facto* crossed. The entire problem stems from the fact that the crossing of such a conceptual limit is at once forbidden and constantly practiced.

But if there is bearing witness and if it answers properly, *incontest-ably*, to the name and the sense intended by this name in our "culture," in the world that we think we can, precisely, inherit and to which we can bear witness, then this bearing witness must not essentially consist in proving, in confirming a knowledge, in ensuring a theoretical certitude, a determinant judgment. It can only appeal to an act of faith.

To complete this inspection of the Greek vocabulary, next to *marturion* there is *marturia*, which means the action of deposing or giving a deposition: it is the attestation, the deposition of a witness. *Marturomai* is to call to witness, to invoke witnesses, to take as witness. A good example of this "take as witness," a sentence from the *Civil Wars* of the historian Appian of Alexandria, says: *marturamenos emauton tēs philotimias*, "I take myself as witness to my zeal, to my ambition, to my taste for honors." Another common translation: "I take my conscience as witness to my ambition." Someone bears witness in front of others, because he is speaking, because he is addressing others; but he takes the others as witnesses to what he first of all takes *himself* as witness to, the fact that he is sufficiently conscious, self-present, to bear witness in front of others, of what he bears witness to, of *the fact that* he bears witness, and *of that to which* he bears witness, in front of others.

Why this translation? Why this example? Because in it we encounter one of the irreducible folds of bearing witness and presence, of being present as witness [*de l'assistance*], of being present as witness, in existence, as presence: it is the fold of presence *as self-*presence. A witness can claim his having been present at this or that, having been witness to this or that, having had the experience of or having experienced this or that, only on the condition of being and having been sufficiently *self*-present *as such*, only on the condition of claiming, at any rate, to have been sufficiently conscious of himself, sufficiently self-present to know what he is talking about. There are no masks here any longer. If there still were, the masks would be exhibited *as* masks, in their truth of being masks. I can claim to offer reliable testimony only if I claim to be able to witness about it in front of myself, sincerely, without mask and without veil, only if I claim to know what I saw, heard, or touched, only if I claim to be the same as yesterday, if I claim to know what I know and mean what I mean. And thus to reveal or unveil—beyond the mask or the veil. In bearing witness, self-presence, the classic condition of responsibility, must be coextensive with presence to other things, with having-been-present to other things and to the presence of the other, for instance, to the addressee of the testimony. It is on this condition that the witness can respond, can answer for himself, be *responsible* for his testimony, as well as for the oath by which he commits himself to it and guarantees it. In their very concepts, perjury or lying *as such* presuppose that the liar or the perjurer is sufficiently self-present; he has to keep, self-present, the meaning or the true meaning, in its truth, of what he is concealing, falsifying, or betraying—and of which he can then keep the secret. Keep it *as such*—and the *keeping* of this safekeeping is the movement of *truth* (*veritas, verum, wahr, wahren,* which means to keep; *Wahrheit*: truth).

Here is one of the joints linking the problematics of the secret, of responsibility, and of testimony. There is no lie or perjury without responsibility, no responsibility without self-presence. This self-presence is, of course, often interpreted as self-consciousness. Under this heading, bearing witness before the other would imply bearing witness before one's own consciousness; this can lead to a transcendental phenomenology of consciousness. But this self-presence is not necessarily the ultimate form of consciousness or of self-consciousness. It can take other forms of existence: that of a certain *Dasein*, for instance. Think of the role (phenomenological in another sense) that the value of testimony or attestation can play in Heidegger's *Sein und Zeit* (*Being and Time*), especially around the passages concerning, precisely, *Dasein's* attestation (*Bezeugung*) to its originary possibility and its authenticity (*Eigentlichkeit*).[10] *Dasein* must be able to testify about itself: that is, in *Being and Time*, the axiom or testimony of the existential analytic of *Dasein*. From the beginning, Heidegger announces the bringing to light, the manifestation, the phenomenological presentation (*Aufweis*) of such an attestation (*der phänomenologische Aufweis einer solcher Bezeugung*), namely, the phenomenology of an experience that is itself phenomenological, in other words, that consists in a *presentation*. It is the presentation of a presentation, the testimony of or about a testimony: here there is witness for the witness, testimony for the testimony.

To return now to the Celan poem, let us again stress this double reference to attestation (*Bezeugung*) in "Niemand / zeugt für den / Zeugen," as a reference to the enigmatic and recurrent figure of the three. While taking note of this crossover between the semantics of the witness and that of the "three" or the third, let us beware of being overhasty. Let us not pre-interpret this co-occurrence of the two motifs in the Celan poem. Although this crossover is irreducible *a priori* wherever there may be a question of the witness and of the three, nothing allows us to go beyond this *a priori* in the reading of this poem.

The same is true for the reference to the *oath*. The poem names the oath and the *petrified* oath, that which sounds so deeply at the bottom of the petrified oath, of the oath of stone, of the oath become stone:

> Pontisches Einstmals: hier
> ein Tropfen,
> auf
> dem ertrunkenen Ruderblatt
> tief
> im versteinerten Schwur
> rauscht es auf.

Published translations:

> Pontique une fois: ici
> telle une goutte,
> sur
> le plat de la rame submergée,
> au profond
> du serment mué en pierre,
> sa rumeur.
>   (du Bouchet)

> L'Autrefois pontique: ici,
> une goutte,
> sur
> la pale d'aviron noyée,
> tout au fond
> du serment pétrifié,
> son bruit revient.
>   (Lefebvre)

> Pontic once-upon: here
> a drop
> on
> the drowned oar-blade,
> deep
> in the petrified vow,
> it roars up.
>   (Neugroschel)

Another possible translation:

Autrefois Pontique: ici
une goutte
sur
la palme d'une rame noyée
au fond
du serment pétrifié
bruit.

Once Pontic: here
a drop
on
the palm of a drowned oar
at the bottom
of the petrified oath
sounds.

Suppose that we refrain, as I would wish to do here, from "commentary" on this poem. Even before doing so, in any case, and whatever the poem or its signatory *means*, whatever he intends to be bearing witness to, one cannot not link *a priori* this figure of the oath to that of bearing witness, which comes up at the end. There is no bearing witness without some involvement of an oath (*Schwur*) and without some sworn word [*foi jurée*]. What distinguishes an act of bearing witness from the simple transmission of knowledge, from simple information, from the simple statement or mere demonstration of a proven theoretical truth, is that in it someone *engages* himself with regard to someone else, by an oath that is at least implicit. The witness *promises* to say or to manifest something to another, his addressee: a truth, a sense that was or is in some way present to him as a unique and irreplaceable witness. This irreplaceable singularity links the question of bearing witness to that of the secret but also, indissociably, to that of a death that no one can anticipate or see coming, neither give nor receive in the place of the other. With this attestation, there is no other choice but to *believe* it or *not believe* it. Verification or transformation into proof, contestation in the name of "knowledge," belong to a foreign space. They are heterogeneous to the moment proper to bearing witness. The experience of bearing witness as such thus presupposes the oath. It takes place in the space of this *sacramentum*.[11] The same oath links the witness and his addressees, for example—but this is only an example—in the judicial scene: "I swear to tell the truth, the whole truth, and nothing but the truth." This oath (*sacramentum*) is sacred: it marks acceptance of the sacred, acquiescence to entering into a holy or sacred space in the relationship to the other. Perjury itself implies this sacralization in sacrilege. The perjurer commits perjury *as such* only insofar as he keeps in mind the sacredness of the oath. Perjury, the lie, the mask, only appear as such ("the role of revealing the mask as mask") where they confirm their belonging to this zone of sacral experience. To this extent, at least, the perjurer remains faithful to what he betrays; he pays the homage of sacrilege and perjury to the sworn word; in betrayal, he sacrifices to the very thing he is betraying; he does it on the altar of the very thing he is thereby profaning. Whence at the same time the wiliness and the desperate innocence of he who would say: "in betraying, in betraying you, I renew the oath, I bring it back to life, and I am more faithful to it than ever, I am even more faithful than if I were behaving in an objectively faithful and irreproachable way, but was all the while forgetting the inaugural *sacramentum*." For the unshareable secret of the oath or perjury, for this secret that cannot even be shared with the partner in the oath, with the ally of the alliance, there is consequently only bearing witness and belief. An act of faith without possible proof. The hypothesis of proof does not even make sense any more. But because it remains alone and without proof, this bearing witness cannot be authorized through a third party or through another bearing witness. For this witness there is no *other* witness: there is no witness for the witness. There is never a witness for the witness. This is also, *perhaps*, what the Celan poem might mean. It is also this that all the world's "revisionisms" might always allege, inversely, when they reject all testimonies on the pretext that testimonies will never, by definition, be proofs. What is one to answer to an allegation that might be translated like this: I can bear witness to this before my conscience, I am betraying you, I am lying to you, but in doing so I remain faithful to you, I am even more faithful than ever to our *sacramentum*? No objection can be made, nothing can be proved either for or against such a testimony. To this act of language, to this "performative" of testimony and declaration, the only possible response, in the night of faith, is another "performative" that consists in saying or testing out, sometimes without even saying it, "I believe you."

How can this belief be thought? Where should we situate this faith, which does not necessarily have to take on the grand appearances of so-called religious faith? This act of faith is implied everywhere one participates in what are called scenes of bearing witness.

And in truth, as soon as you open your mouth. As soon as you open your mouth, as soon as you exchange a look, even silently, a "believe me" is already involved, which echoes in the other. No lie and no perjury can vanquish this appeal to belief; they can only confirm it; in profaning it, they can only confirm its invincibility. I can lie, perjure, or betray only by promising, under oath (be it implicit or explicit) to say what I believe to be the truth, only by pretending to be faithful to my promise.

Can this "believe" be thought? Is it accessible to the order of thought? The reason we referred to *Being and Time* and to what it demands of *Bezeugung*, of the phenomenology of attestation, and precisely on the subject of *Dasein*'s authentic *potentiality-of-being-one's-self*, is that Heidegger in several other places excludes or at any rate dissociates the order of faith or belief from that of thinking or philosophy. He does this very often, but in particular in an abrupt, late statement, from "Der Spruch des Anaximander" ("The Anaximander Fragment").[12] This statement radically excludes the order of belief from that of thinking in general. Heidegger then touches on a problem of translation. (I point it out because we too are caught up, right here, in the scene of translation and bearing witness, and of the translation of the poem by Celan on bearing witness, of a poem that is virtually untranslatable and that bears witness about bearing witness.) It is for Heidegger precisely a question of the translation of a *Spruch*. *Spruch*: saying, maxim, decree, decision, poem, in any case, a saying that is not a theoretical or scientific statement and that is tied in a singular and "performative" way to language. Now what does Heidegger say in a passage that also concerns, precisely, presence (*Anwesen, Präsenz*), the presence that founds the classical value of bearing witness, this time presence as representation, in the "representation of representing" ("die Präsenz in der Repräsentation des Vorstellens")? After proposing a translation of Anaximander's saying, Heidegger declares: "Belief has no place in the act of thinking [*Der Glaube hat im Denken keinen Platz*]." This phrase is taken from an argument that must be reconstructed, at least in part:

> We cannot prove [*beweisen*] the translation scientifically, nor should we, in virtue of some authority, have faith in it [give it credit, believe it, *glauben*]. The reach of proof [understood: "scientific" proof] is too short [*Beweis trägt zu kurz*]. Belief has no place in the act of thinking. Translation can be rethought [reflected, *nachdenken*] only in the thinking [*im Denken*] of the saying [saying, *Spruch*: it is necessary to think the *Spruch*, the

engaged saying, as poem, maxim, decision, pledge, in order to think, to rethink, on the basis of this, the possibility of translation, and not the other way around]. But thinking [*das Denken*] is the *Dichten* [the poem, poetizing, the poetical act or operation, the poetic that Krieger is perhaps speaking of in the passage quoted as epigraph—but the words *act* and *operation* are not quite right: there's something there other than the activity of a subject, perhaps we should say "the event," the "coming" of the poetic] of the truth of Being [*der Wahrheit des Seins*] in the historic conversation [dialogue, dual language] of thinkers [*geschichtlichen Zweisprache der Denkenden*].[13]

Heidegger thus dismisses both scientific proof and belief, which might suggest that to this degree he gives credit to a non-scientific testimony. In this context, the believing of belief is the credulity that accredits authority, the credulity that shuts its eyes and acquiesces dogmatically to authority (*Autorität* is Heidegger's word). Heidegger extends with no less force and radicality the assertion according to which believing has no place in thinking. Is this believing foreign to that which in thinking itself (in particular, the thinking that thinks in the *Zweisprache* and holds itself in relation to the *Spruch* of a thinker, in the experience of thinking translation) concerns the *Bezeugung*, the attestation of which *Being and Time* speaks? Is there not a belief in the recourse to attestation (*Bezeugung*) in the discourse that brings it into play? And in the experience of thinking in general, thinking as Heidegger refers to it, is there not an experience of *believing* that is not reducible to the credulity or passivity before authority that Heidegger here too easily excludes from thinking? And doesn't the authority of some "believing," "making believe," "asking to believe" always necessarily insinuate itself in the invocation of a thinking of the truth of Being? What, in that which is not proof, holds the place of this *Glauben* in the thinking that Heidegger intends to think at the very moment when he excludes belief or faith?

III

"Raise your right hand and say, 'I swear.'" To these words a witness must respond, when he appears before a French court. Whatever the meaning of the raised hand, it engages the visible body in the act of the oath. The same is true for the wedding ring worn on the finger. Now *Schwurfinger* means the three fingers that are raised in taking an oath. That is perhaps not unrelated to "Händen am Dreiweg," or "Dreiweg- / Händen," which recurs on two occasions in Celan's poem. They are, first, tied to the *tie*, the knot (*knoten, verknoteten*). One might imagine that these "knots" are not unrelated to the ties of the oath, for instance, the oath of stone the poem mentions: "im verstein-erten Schwur." Second, they are tied to the knots of the hands ("er-schüttert-verknoteten Händen") and of pain ("Schmerzknoten").

Stricto sensu, the *inherited* concept of bearing witness, determined culturally, implies, we were saying, some kind of oath, law, or sworn word. That's the reference to *sacramentum*, namely, to what is at issue between the parties involved in a trial, or in a dispute. The issue was entrusted, during the hearing, during the procedure known as *per sac-ramentum*, to the pontiff. "Pontiff" is not far from *Pontisches, Pontisches Einstmals*, about which we will have occasion to speak later.

But that does not necessarily mean that in every testimony we have to raise our hands and swear to tell the truth, the whole truth, and nothing but the truth. It does not necessarily mean that every time we do what is called *témoigner* or *déposer sous la foi du serment*: *unter Eid bezeugen, unter Eid aussagen*, or *to testify* or *to bear witness*—which almost always has the value of "attesting under oath," before the law—we do it ritually. No, but even when the scene is not formal-ized in this way by an institutional code of positive law that would oblige us to observe this or that rite, there is in all testimony an impli-cation of oath and of law.

This extension of the oath's implication may appear extraordinary and abusive, even extravagant, but I believe it to be legitimate, I will even say incontestable. Logically, it obliges one to take any address to another to be a testimony. Each time I speak or manifest some-thing to another, I bear witness to the extent that, even if I neither say nor show the truth, even if, behind the "mask," I am lying, hid-ing, or betraying, every utterance implies "I am telling you the truth; I am telling you what I think; I bear witness in front of you to that to which I bear witness in front of me, what is present to me (singularly, irreplaceably). And I can always be lying to you. So I am in front of you as in front of a judge, before the law or the representative of the law. As soon as I bear witness, I am in front of you as before the law, but, as a result, you who are my witness, you who witness my bear-ing witness, you are also judge and arbiter, judge and party as much as judge and arbiter." We will come back to this essential possibility of the judge's becoming-witness or the witness's becoming-judge and becoming-arbiter.

I have already admitted: I will not attempt to interpret this poem. Not even its last lines:

Niemand
zeugt für den
Zeugen.

What then are we doing with this poem? And why are we quoting it? Why are we invoking its poetic force? Why are we borrowing its force even when and no doubt because, beyond all we might decipher of this poem, we don't finally know *to what* it is bearing witness? What we are calling here the force, the energy, the virtue of the poem, and above all in its language, is what makes us have to cite it, again and again, with an irresistible compulsion. For it is cited and re-cited, we tend to learn it by heart while knowing that we do not know what, in the end, it means, when we do not even know *to what* or *for whom* and *for what* it is bearing witness. For we do not know it, even if we can know a lot and learn a lot from it. We can "read" this poem, we can desire to read, cite, and re-cite it, while giving up on interpreting it, or at least on going over the limit beyond which interpretation encounters, at the same time, its possibility and its impossibility. What we have here is a compulsion to cite and re-cite, to repeat what we understand without completely understanding it, feeling at work in the economy of the ellipsis a power more powerful than that of meaning and perhaps even than that of truth, of the mask which would manifest itself *as* mask. The reciting compulsion, the "by heart" desire, stems from this limit to intelligibility or transparency of meaning.

Is not this limit that of a crypt, and thus of a certain secret? In bearing witness for bearing witness and for the witness, the poem says that there is no witness for the witness. No one bears witness for the witness. It is no doubt an indicative, a constative description, but also, implicitly, perhaps, a prohibiting prescription: no one in fact bears witness for the witness, no one can, of course, but first of all because no one should. No one can, for it must not be done. The possibility of the secret must remain sealed at the very moment when bearing witness unveils it—or claims to reveal anything at all.

The poem bears witness. We don't know about what and for what, about whom and for whom, in bearing witness *for* bearing witness, it bears witness. But it bears witness. As a result, what it says of the witness it also says *of itself* as witness or as bearing witness. As poetic bearing witness. Can we not, then, here transfer to bearing witness, to *this* poetic bearing witness, as to that which in *all* bearing witness must always appear as "poetic" (a singular act, concerning a singular event and engaging a unique, and thus inventive, relationship to language), that "extravagant proposal" of Murray Krieger: "the poem, in the very act of becoming successfully poetic—that is, in constituting itself poetry—implicitly constitutes its own poetic"?

Moreover, *taken by itself alone*, the last stanza

Niemand
zeugt für den
Zeugen.

may vacillate or pivot; it seems to turn-re-turn around the axis of its own syntax. To the point of vertigo. The "for" (*für*)—what does it mean? We can offer at least *three* hypotheses.

1. Is it about bearing witness *on behalf* of someone (I bear witness for you, I bear witness on your behalf, I am a witness for the defense, etc.)? *Zeugen für jenen* does in fact generally mean to bear witness *on behalf of* someone, as opposed to *zeugen gegen jenen*, to bear witness against someone.

2. Is it rather about "bearing witness for" the other in the sense of "in the place of" the other? And here refuting this possibility, this ability, this right, by recalling that no one can bear witness *in the place of* another, no more than anyone can die *in the place of* another? In this impossibility of substitution, we are put to the test of an alliance between death and the secret. The secret always remains the very experience of bearing witness, the privilege of a witness for whom no one can be substituted, because he is, in essence, the only one to know what he has seen, lived, felt; he must thus be *believed*, taken at his word, at the very moment when he is making public a secret that nonetheless remains secret. A secret *as* secret. Now even if we cannot say anything definite about it, *Aschenglorie* clearly remains a poem of death and the secret. The poem survives by bearing witness, through this alliance, to the surviving of the *testis* as *superstes*.

If no one can replace anyone as witness, if no one can bear witness *for* the other as witness, if one cannot bear witness for a bearing witness without taking from it its worth as bearing witness (which must always be done in the first person), isn't it difficult to identify the witness with a third? We readily represent the third as anyone, as a replaceable first person: the third is a singular "I" in general. Now, nothing is both more and less substitutable than an "I." The question being announced on the horizon is indeed that of what one calls a first person, a discourse in the first person (singular or plural, *I* or *we*). Who is the "I" of the poem? This question displaces itself; it gets divided or multiplied, like the question of the signature, between the "I" of which the poem speaks, or to which the poem refers, reflexively (which can also sometimes be *a mentioned* or even *a cited* "I," if we want), the "I" who writes it or "signs" it in all the possible ways, and the "I" who reads it. How then is this self-referentiality determined, this autodeictic quality that is always posited or alleged by whoever says "I," thereby demonstrating, even if he is masked, that the speaker is showing himself and referring to himself? The form of this self-referential self-presentation is not only grammatical; it can be simply *implied* by discourses that are not conjugated in the first person present tense. As soon as I say "you," "your," and so on, I say or imply "I."

3. But there is still a third possibility: to bear witness "for" someone not in the sense of "on behalf of" or "in the place of" but "for" someone in the sense of "in front of" someone. One would then witness *for* someone who becomes the *addressee* of the testimony, someone to whose ears or eyes one is bearing witness. Then the phrase "no one bears witness for a witness" would mean that no one, no witness, delivers his or her testimony in front of someone who is also a(nother) witness. A witness, as such, is never in a position to receive the testimony of another; he is never entitled to do so. The judge or the tribunal, the representatives of the law, presupposed to be neutral and objective, can certainly receive a testimony, but another witness cannot, since he is as singular and as involved as the first witness. The judge or the tribunal, the arbiters, those who judge and decide, those who conclude, are not mere witnesses; they must not, should not, be only witnesses, in other words, subjects who find themselves in a singular fashion in the situation of being present at or participating in that for which testimony is given. They would be suspected, as any witness is suspect, of being interested parties, partial subjectivities, themselves involved, situated in the space described by the testimony. The judge, the arbiter, or the addressee of the testimony is thus not a witness: he cannot and must not be. And yet, in the final analysis, the judge, the arbiter, and the addressee *also* have to be witnesses; they have to be able to bear witness, in their turn, before their consciences or before others, to what they have attended, to what they have been present at, to what they have been in the presence of: the testimony of the witness at the witness stand. Only on the basis of this testimony will they be able to justify, in just

this way, their judgment. The judge, the arbiter, the historian also remains a witness, a witness of a witness, when he receives, evaluates, criticizes, interprets the testimony of a survivor, for instance, a survivor of Auschwitz. Whether he accepts or contests this testimony, he remains a witness of the witness. He remains a witness even if he contests the first testimony by alleging that, since he has survived, the survivor cannot be a certain and reliable witness to what happened, namely, a witness to the existence of gas chambers or crematoria being put to this purpose, to put people to death—and that therefore he cannot bear witness *for* the only true witnesses, those who have died, and who by definition can no longer bear witness, confirm or refute the testimony of another. In this context, *Aschenglorie* also lets one hear, between the words, rising from the light of the ashes, something like a desperate sigh: no witness for the witness in this perverse situation, which will permit all judges, arbiters, all historians to hold the revisionist thesis to be fundamentally indestructible or incontestable.

Although he cannot be a witness "at the stand," the judge-arbiter-historian must also and still bear witness, if only to what he has heard attested. He must bear witness to the experience in the course of which, having been present, put in the presence of the testimony, he has been able to hear it, understand it, and can still reproduce the essence of it, etc. There would be here a third and testimony to testimony, witness for the witness.[14]

"Niemand / zeugt für den / Zeugen": *für* is thus at the same time the most decisive and the most undecidable word in the poem.[15] Nothing prohibits any of these three readings. They are different, but not necessarily incompatible. On the contrary, they accumulate their potential energy deep in the crypt of the poem, thereby giving it its force of appeal and inducing our compulsion to cite-recite it without knowledge, beyond knowledge. In these *three* readings of *für*, which intensify the *three* with which we have not finished, even the verb of the stanza vacillates. Its tense vacillates; it makes its mood and the negation that affects it (*Niemand zeugt*) vacillate with it. The present indicative can signify a fact to be noted: no one bears witness. But, as is often the case (in French, too, especially when it is a question of law), "no one bears witness" implies: "no one *can* bear witness," "no one can, has been able, and will ever be able to bear witness for the witness" (with the three possible senses of "for" that we have just recalled). And as a result, this *being able*, this "not being able," is displaced and translates easily into a "must not" or an "ought not to":

no one *can*, which is to say, no one *must*, no one *ought* to bear witness for the witness, replace the witness, defend the witness, bear witness in front of the witness, and so forth. One *cannot* and (in addition or moreover or above all) one *must* not bear witness *for* the witness, in all the senses of "for." One cannot and must not (claim to) replace the witness of his own death, for instance, someone who perished in the hell of Auschwitz (but that does not mean that this poem is a poem *on* Auschwitz—and for the very reason that I am in the process of pointing out again, namely, that no one bears witness for the witness). One cannot and must not replace (thus bear witness *for*) the witness of his or her own death, or the witness of others' deaths, the one who was present and survived, for instance, at the hell of Auschwitz.

And yet, in its own way, the poem bears witness to this impossibility. It attests to this prohibition imposed on bearing witness, in the very place where one has to go on appealing to it. This impossibility and this prohibition manifest themselves *as such*. Non-manifestation manifests itself (*perhaps*) *as* non-manifestation. Is this possible? How? How is one to understand this "perhaps"? Its possibility or its necessity?

It is a matter of death, if death is what one cannot witness *for* the other, and above all because one cannot witness it *for oneself*. The surviving of surviving, as place of testimony and as testament, would here find at once its possibility and its impossibility, its chance and its threat. It would find them in this structure and in this event.

That this is a poem on *the subject of death*, a poem *of* death, a poem that speaks death *as such*, can be affirmed at no great risk. It can be affirmed where one cannot separate questions of the secret, the crypt, and testimony from questions of surviving and death. It can also be affirmed by taking as testimony the naming of ashes, of course. There are ashes there, *but* they are of glory. Or again, there is glory, light, fire, *but* already in ashes. Double possibility of the "but"—ash, certainly, and death, *but* glorious; glory, certainly, *but* of ash and death without memory. The double possibility of this implied "but" is, indeed, implied in the hyphen, which *is now stressed* at the end of the line to articulate and disarticulate the relationship between ashes and glory

Aschen-
glorie

(double word: we don't know which is the subject and which the predicate), and *is now effaced*, in a single, simple word, as in the incipit

(*Aschenglorie*). There, too, one does not know whether the glory is of ashes or the ashes are glorious, ashes of glory. This explains du Bouchet's French translation, which reads "Cendres-la gloire [Ashes-glory]" rather than "Gloire de cendres [Glory of ashes]." "Ashes" is always in the plural here, of course: ashes never gather together their dissemination, and that is exactly what they consist in. They consist in not consisting, in losing all consistence. They have no more existence; they are deprived of any substance that gathers together and is identical to itself, deprived of any self-relation, any power, any ipseity.

That is confirmed (perhaps) via the association of the *Dreiweg* with the *Pontisches*, with the petrifaction of the oath in its crypt, especially with the Tartar moon (*Tatarenmond*). There are at least two proper names (*Pontisches* and *Tatarenmond*) whose referent seems unavoidable. Namely, perhaps, the goddess Hecate. Here is the stanza we have not yet read:

(Auf dem senkrechten
Atemseil, damals,
höher als oben.
zwischen zwei Schmerzknoten, während
der blanke
Tatarenmond zu uns heraufklomm,
grub ich mich in dich und in dich.)

The published translations say:

(Perpendiculaire, alors,
sur cette corde le souffle,
plus haut que le faîte,
entre deux nœuds de douleur, cependant
que la blanche
lune tatare jusqu'à nous se hisse,
je m'enfouis en toi et toi.)
    (du Bouchet)

(Sur la corde de souffle
verticale, autrefois,
plus haute qu'en haut,
entre deux nœuds de souffrance, tandis que,
blanche,
la Lune des Tatares grimpait vers nous,
je me suis creusé en toi et en toi.)
    (Lefebvre)

(On the perpendicular
breath-rope, at that time,
higher than above,
between two pain-knots, while
the shiny
Tartar moon climbed up to us,
I burrowed into you and into you.)
    (Neugroschel)

It could also be translated:

(Sur la corde verticale
du souffle [corde vocale?] autrefois [*damals*, responding to *Einstmals*; il
                                        était une fois],
plus haut qu'en haut,
entre deux nœuds de douleur, pendant que
La nue [luisante, lisse, blanche] lune tatare se haussait [s'élevait] vers
                                        nous
je m'enfouissais [je m'enterrais, je m'encryptais, je m'inhumais] en toi et
                                        en toi.)

(On the vertical cord
of breath [vocal chord?], long ago [*damals*, which responds to *Einstmals*,
                                        from above; once upon a time],
higher than on high,
between two knots of pain, while
the bare [shiny, smooth, white] Tartar moon was raising itself [rising]
                                        toward us
I buried myself [I interred myself, I encrypted myself, I inhumed myself]
                                        into you and into you)

The name of the goddess Hecate is not pronounced. It remains, it
will perhaps remain ineffaceable, beneath the surface of this poem,
because of the association of the moon, the Pontic, and the three of
the *Dreiweg*. However little one knows about the goddess Hecate, the
first thing one remembers is that her most important trait is the
three — and the tripleness of the way or road. She is *trimorphic*; she has
three forms and three faces (*triprosōpos*). She is also the goddess of
the crossroads, in other words, as the name at once indicates and
does not indicate (*quadrifurcum*), of a road branching off in four
rather than three directions. Of course, but apart from all the Oedi-
pal associations that multiply with every crossroads, we know that a
crossroads can be made by the crossing of two, three, or four roads,
hence in three ways. Now Hecate, goddess of crossroads, is called
trioditis (a word that comes from *triodos*, three ways: it is an epithet

meaning "honored at the crossroads"). Hecate protects roads and is polyonymous, endowed with many names. We are selecting only the features that matter most to us here. An account of Hecate could be prolonged *ad infinitum*. For this goddess of the *Dreiweg* also has a privileged relationship with fire, with brightness, with burning—and so with consuming by fire, with ashes, as much as with glory. Her mouth exhales fire, she is *pyripnoa* ("breath of fire") (*Atem*, that word dear to the author of *Atemwende*, the title of the collection that includes *Aschenglorie*, *Atem*, which we come across here again in *Atem-seil*). Her hands brandish torches. The Chaldaean Oracles associate her with implacable thunderbolts and call her "flower of fire." Transporting fire from on high (think of the verticality and *höher als oben* in Celan), she is life-giving and fertile. But another chain of associations inverts these meanings and turns Hecate toward the moon and death. Her signs and her triadic nature then couple her with Mene or Selene, the moon, the goddess of the moon—which we see appearing in Celan's poem. Some prayers to the moon invoke Hecate and Selene as one and the same goddess (three heads, crossroads, etc.): "This is why you are called Hecate of many names, *Mene*, you who split the air like Artemis the arrow-darter. . . . [I]t is from you that all proceeds and in you, who are eternal, that all comes to an end." Elsewhere, she becomes Aphrodite, universal procreator and mother of Eros, at the same time low and high "in the Underworld, the abyss and the *aiōn* (the forever, being in all times, the eternal)." Goddess of light but also of night, she keeps her festival in the crypts and the tombs. Hence she is also a goddess of death and the subterranean underworld, a goddess of Hades. This is the guise in which Hecate appears in *Macbeth*. Apart from the general knowledge that one might have of this, we know that Celan also translated Shakespeare. In the apparition of Hecate (Act 3, Scene 5), the three surfaces again in the form of the three witches who meet Hecate and speak with her ("Why, how now, Hecate! you look angerly!"). Hecate's reply is about nothing other than death ("How did you dare, / To trade and traffic with Macbeth / In riddles and affairs of death"), glory ("or show the glory of our art"), the "pit of Acheron," the moon ("Upon the corner of the moon"), and so on.

With Acheron, or the Styx, we could return to Celan's poem, to *Pontisches Einstmals*, the only time we cross the waves of the Black Sea. Because we cross them only once, the "Pontic once-upon" perhaps designating the passage of death. That is also where Odysseus is allowed to pass through only *one single time* to go and see the dead, when he goes to consult Tiresias. At the moment of death—and to reassure themselves about their fate after death, even if they were cremated—the Greeks needed a witness. They had to go by way of a *trivium*, where the path and the place of their destination would be decided.

There would be much to say here as well about Odysseus, or Elpenor, about his drunkenness and his oar, to which there is *perhaps* a reference, could we ever know, in the words *ertrunkenen Ruderblatt*, the blade of a drowned or drunken oar. There would be much to say as well on the subject of the vertical cord, the breath-rope (*Atemseil*), which perhaps, *perhaps*, alludes to the death of Tsvetaeva. We know what she represented for Celan. Tsvetaeva hanged herself in 1941 *unwitnessed*. She lived in the Tartar republic. Thus the Tartar moon (*Tatarenmond*) may condense at least two encrypted allusions, thereby—as is most often the case—foiling the unity of reference, and thus of reading, and thus of bearing witness, without, however, effacing the singularity of each event, of each date thereby re-lated, re-marked.

Whatever their probability or improbability, the "perhaps" of these singular references, which all appeal to dated testimony (e.g., we have to know who Tsvetaeva was and who she was for Celan, and how, where, and when she killed herself, she too, like him, etc.), we can say *a priori* that this poem speaks of death (for which there is no witnessing), perhaps of suicide, and that the "grub ich mich in dich und in dich" may mean not only "I burrow, I bury" but also "I inter, I encrypt myself into you inside you": *graben, grub*. *Grab* is the tomb: you are my tomb, my own tomb, you to whom I address myself, whom I take as witness, if only to say (to you) "no one bears witness for the witness."

Beyond or before everything that could be thought, read, or said of this poem, according to the "perhaps," the probability and the act of faith that a poetic experience is, beyond or before all the possible translations, a mark remains and is here re-marked: it is a certain limit to interpretation. In the end, it is in all certainty impossible to put a stop to the meaning or the reference of this poem, the meaning or the reference to which it bears witness or responds. Whatever one might say about it, and this can be drawn out *ad infinitum, there is a line*. It is not only marked by the poem. It is the poem, poetics, and the poetics of the poem—which conceals itself by exhibiting its concealment *as such*. But it is this "as such" that turns out to be doomed to the "perhaps." Probable and improbable (possible but removed

Poetics and Politics of Witnessing ■ *95*

from proof), this "as such" takes place as poem, as *this* poem, irreplaceably, in it, *where* nothing or no one can reply in its place, *where* it is silent, *where* it keeps its secret, all the while telling us that there is a secret, revealing the secret it is keeping *as* a secret, not revealing it, as it continues to bear witness that one cannot bear witness for the witness, who in the end remains alone and without witness. In *The Step Not Beyond* Blanchot speaks of a "word still to be spoken beyond the living and the dead, *attesting for the absence of attestation.*"[16]

I would have liked to speak of this essential solitude of the witness. It is not just any solitude—or just any secret. It is solitude itself and the secret itself. They speak. As Celan says elsewhere, it speaks, the poem does, secretly, of the secret, through the secret, and thus, in a certain way, in it beyond it: "Aber das Gedicht spricht ja! Es bleibt seiner Daten eingedenk, aber—es spricht [But the poem does speak! It remains mindful of its dates, but—it speaks]."[17] It speaks to the other by keeping quiet, keeping something quiet from him. In keeping quiet, in keeping silent, it still addresses. This internal limit to all witnessing is also what the poem says. It bears witness to it even in saying "no one bears witness for the witness." Revealing its mask *as* a mask, but without showing itself, without presenting itself, perhaps presenting its non-presentation as such, representing it, it thus speaks about bearing witness in general, but above all about the poem that it is, about itself in its singularity, and about the bearing witness to which every poem bears witness.

Left here to itself, in its essential solitude, in its performance or in its event, the poetic act of the work perhaps no longer derives from self-presentation *as such*.

Language Is Never Owned
An Interview

Évelyne Grossman: In "Shibboleth," the book dedicated to Paul Celan, you mention at some point, very briefly, the friendship that bound you to him, not long before his death. You then enter into a long reflection upon dates in Celan's poems and, pointing to the "spectral revenance" of the date, you say: "I will not give myself over here to my own commemorations; I will not hand over my dates." Could you, however, speak a little about your encounter with Celan in Paris, in 1968, I believe it was?

Jacques Derrida: I will try to speak about it. I must say that the sentence you quote about "my dates" perhaps referred to the dates of my encounters with Celan or dates shared with Celan. As you know, I repeatedly allude, on the subject of this or that poem, to witnesses, such as Peter Szondi, who have interpreted certain poems on the basis of the knowledge they had of dated events in Celan's life — his stay in Berlin in December 1967, for instance. At issue there were dates, dated events. I do not know whether, in that sentence, I was alluding to more secret dates or dates shared with Celan. I cannot even say. What I can try to do, nevertheless, is to recount, if only briefly, these encounters with Celan. It so happens that Celan had been my colleague at the École Normale Supérieure for years without my meeting him, without our ever really meeting each other. He was a language instructor in German. He was a very discreet man, self-effacing and withdrawn. So much so that one day, during a meeting about some administrative matters in the director's office at the École, the director said something that implied he did not even know who Celan was. My colleague in German replied: "But, sir, do you not know that the language instructor we have here is the greatest living poet in the German language?" That says something about this director's ignorance, but also about the fact that Celan's presence was, like his whole being and all his gestures, extremely discreet, elliptical, and self-effacing. This explains, at least in part, why there was no exchange between us, although for some years I was his colleague. It was only after a trip that I made to Berlin in 1968, at Peter Szondi's invitation, that I finally met Celan. Szondi, who became my friend, was a great friend of Celan, and when he came to Paris later he introduced me to Celan. It's a rather curious situation, but there you have it, he introduced me to my own colleague, and we spoke a little. From then on, a series of meetings can be dated, always brief, silent, on his part as on mine. The silence was his as much as mine. We exchanged books that we had signed, a few words, then we would then lose sight of one another. Apart from these bare hints of conversation, which ended almost as soon as they had begun, I also remember a lunch at Edmond Jabès's place. Jabès, who knew Celan, invited the two of us to his home — he lived close to the École. Once again, it was the same: Celan remained silent during the meal and the time that followed. I do not know how to interpret this. I believe there was in him a kind of secrecy, silence, and exactingness that made him find words not indispensable, no doubt especially the words you exchange during a meal. At the same time, there was perhaps something more negative. I learned through other sources that he was often depressed, angry, or not very happy because of what surrounded him in Paris. His experience with many French people, academics, and even fellow poets and translators was, I believe, rather hopeless. I believe he was, as one says, very difficult, in the sense of both very demanding and trying one's patience. Nevertheless, through this silence, there was a great bond of affection between us, which I could detect through the inscriptions in the books he gave me. I believe it was two years later that he committed suicide. I met him in 1968 or 1969, and thus I am talking about a period of three years at the most . . . No, a lot less . . . In fact, this is an extremely brief sequence, on which I later meditated, more or less constantly. That's all I can say about these encounters. It is, rather, the memory of them that, later, after his death, kept on working, reinterpreting itself, and weaving itself into what I heard about him, about his life in Paris, his friends, so-called friends, alleged friends, about all the conflicts of translation and interpretation, of which you are aware. With regard to Celan, the image that comes to my mind is a meteor, an interrupted blaze of light, a sort of caesura, a very brief moment leaving behind a trail of sparks that I try to recover through his texts.

ÉG: You analyze in "Shibboleth" what you call "the experience of language" in Celan's works, a certain way of "inhabiting the idiom" ("signed: Celan from a certain place in the German language, which was his property alone"). And at the same time, you say that Celan suggests there is a "Multiplicity and migration of languages, certainly, and within language itself." "Your country," Celan says, "migrates all over, like language. The country itself migrates and transports its borders." Should we see in this, in your opinion, a phantasm of belonging, the opposite of a phantasm of belonging, or both? How can we attempt to understand that: *inhabiting the place of a multiple and migrating language*?

JD: Before trying to answer this difficult question in a theoretical manner, we must recall obvious facts. Celan was not German; German was not the only language of his childhood; and he did not write only in German. Nonetheless, he did everything he could in order, I will not say to appropriate the German language, since what I suggest is precisely that one never appropriates a language, but rather to carry on a hand-to-hand, bodily struggle with it. What I try to think is an idiom (and the idiom, precisely, means *the proper*, what is proper to) and a signature in the linguistic idiom that at the same time causes one to experience the fact that language can never be appropriated. I believe Celan tried to leave a mark, a singular signature that would be a counter-signature to the German language and, at the same time, something that *happens* to the German language — that *comes to pass* in both senses of the term: something that approaches the language, that reaches it, without appropriating it, without surrendering to it, without delivering itself to it; but also something that enables poetic writing to *occur*, that is to say, to be an event that marks language. In any case, that is how I read Celan, when I can read him, because I have my troubles with German and with his German language. I am far from being sure I can read him in a precise or fair way, but it seems to me he *touches* [touche] the German language both by respecting the idiomatic spirit of that language and in the sense that he displaces it, in the sense that he leaves upon it a sort of scar, a mark, a wound. He modifies the German language, he tampers with [*touche à*] language, but, in order to do so, he has to acknowledge it—not as his language, since I believe that language is never owned, but as the language he made up his mind to struggle with, to have it out with, precisely in the sense of debate, of *Auseinandersetzung*, to work out his differences with the German language. As you also know, he was a great translator. Like many poets who are also translators, he knew what the risks and the stakes of his translations were. He not only translated from English, Russian, and so forth, but within the German language itself he performed an operation that it might not be an exaggeration to construe as a translating interpretation. In other words, there is, in his poetic German, a source language and a target language, and each poem is a kind of new idiom in which he passes on the inheritance of the German language. The paradox is that a poet who was German neither by nationality nor by mother tongue should not only have insisted on doing that, but even imposed his signature in a language that could be for him, apparently, none other than German. How can we explain that, although he was a translator of so many European languages, German was the privileged site for his writing and signing his poetry—even if, within the German language, he welcomed a different kind of German, or other languages, or other cultures, since there is in his writing quite an extraordinary crossing—almost in the genetic sense of the term—of cultures, references, literary memories, always in the mode of extreme condensation, caesura, ellipsis, and interruption? That is the genius of this writing.

Now, concerning the question of "dwelling poetically," Hölderlin is of course one of his great references. What is "inhabiting a language" where one knows both that there is no home and that one cannot appropriate a language . . .

ÉG: . . . not to mention a "migrant" language.

JD: Exactly! He was a migrant himself, and he marked in the thematics of his poetry the movement of crossing borders, as in the poem "Shibboleth." I do not wish to emphasize too readily, too easily, as is sometimes done, the great migrations under Hitlerism, but one cannot let that go unspoken. Those migrations, those exiles, those deportations are the paradigm of the painful migration of our time and, obviously, the work of Celan, as well as his life, bears many of its marks.

ÉG: Since you have just evoked the question of national and linguistic borders, I would like to broach what you call, in *The Monolingualism of the Other*, your monolingualism. You develop at length the following paradox, which is not only yours but also of a general order: "Yes, I have only one language; it is not mine." In particular, you say there: "the jealous guard that one mounts in proximity to one's language, even as one is denouncing the nationalist politics of language (I do the one and the other), demands the multiplication of shibboleths as so many challenges to translators, so many taxes levied at the frontier of languages." And you conclude: "Compatriots of every country, translator-poets, rebel against patriotism!"[1] How do you conceive of the political role of translator-poets or translator-philosophers who play with the "non-identity to itself of any language"?

JD: As a preamble, I shall say that one cannot, for a thousand all too obvious reasons, compare my experience, my history, or my relation with the French language to Celan's experience and history and to his experience of the German language. For a thousand reasons. That being said, what I wrote there I also wrote in memory of Celan. I knew that what I was saying in *The Monolingualism of the Other* was valid to a certain extent for my individual case, to wit, a generation of Algerian Jews before the Independence. But it also had the value of a universal exemplarity, even for those who are not in such historically strange and dramatic situations as Celan's or mine. I would venture to claim that the analysis is valid even for someone whose experience of his own mother tongue is sedentary, peaceful, and without any historical drama: to wit, language is never owned. Even when one has only a single mother tongue, when one is rooted in the place of one's birth and in one's language, even then language is not owned. It is of the essence of language that language does not let itself be appropriated. Language is precisely what does not let itself be possessed but, for this very reason, provokes all kinds of movements of appropriation. Because language can be desired but not appropriated, it sets into motion all sorts of gestures of ownership and appropriation. What is at stake here politically is that linguistic nationalism is precisely one of these gestures of appropriation, a naïve gesture of appropriation. What I am trying to suggest is that, paradoxically, what is most idiomatic, that is to say, what is most proper to a language, cannot be appropriated. What one must try to think is that, when you look for what is most idiomatic in a language—as Celan does—you approach that which, throbbing within the language, does not let itself be grasped. Therefore I would like to try to dissociate, paradoxical as it may seem, idiom from property. The idiom is what resists translation, and hence is what seems attached to the singularity of the signifying body of language—or of the body, period—but which, because of such singularity, eludes all possession, any claim of belonging to. Here lies the political difficulty: how can one be in favor of the greatest idiomaticity—which one must be, I think—while resisting nationalist ideology? How can linguistic difference be defended without yielding to patriotism, in any case, to a certain type of patriotism, and to nationalism? That is what is at stake, politically, in our time. Some think that, in order to fight for the just cause of antinationalism, we must rush headlong into universal language, transparency, and the erasure of differences. I would like to think the contrary. I think there should be a treatment of and a respect for the idiom, which dissociates itself not only from the nationalist temptation but also from what binds the nation to a State, to the power of a State. I believe that today one should be able to cultivate linguistic differences without yielding to ideology or to state-nationalist or nationalist politics. The key element in the politics I would advocate is this: it is *because* the idiom is not owned—and cannot therefore become a thing or a possession of a national, ethnic community or nation-state—that every kind of nationalist appetite and zeal for appropriation pounces on it. It is very difficult to get some people to understand that one can love what resists translation without yielding to nationalism, without yielding to any nationalist policies. Because—and this is another motive—the moment I start to respect and cultivate the singularity of the idiom, I cultivate it as "my home" and as "the other's home." In other words, the other's idiom (the idiom being first of all other, even for me my idiom is other) is to be respected and, as a result, I must resist any nationalist temptation, which is always the imperialist or colonialist temptation to overstep borders. Here, beyond the bodies of work we are talking about, arises a whole political form of reflection that seems to me to have a general significance both in and outside of Europe. It's obvious that there is at present a problem with European languages, with the language of Europe, and that a certain Anglo-American is becoming hegemonic, irresistibly. We all experience this. I have just returned from Germany, and I spoke English for three days, only English. When Habermas and I spoke of these problems, we spoke of them in English. What can be done so that a new kind of inter-nation, such as Europe, can find the means to resist linguistic hegemonies, and in particular the Anglo-American? It is very difficult, all the more so because this Anglo-American does violence not only to other languages but also to a certain English or American genius. These are very difficult debates, and I believe that translator-poets, when they experience what we are at this moment describing, are politically exemplary. It is their task to explain, to teach, that one can cultivate and invent an idiom, because it is not a matter of cultivating a given idiom but of producing the idiom. Celan produced an idiom; he produced it from a matrix, from a heritage, without, for obvious reasons, yielding in the least to nationalism. In my opinion, today such poets have a political lesson to teach to those who need it about the question of language and nation.

ÉG: What you have just said about how Celan reactivates the heritage of the idiom allows me to raise a question I wanted to ask you about the life and death of languages. Everyone is familiar with George Steiner's statement that the enigma of Auschwitz can be penetrated only in German, that is to say, in writing "from within the language of death itself." The phrase is controversial, of course, but it can perhaps shed light on one aspect of Celan's writing. Might we say that his experience of language is that of a language that lives eternally insofar as it is haunted by death and negativity? For instance, in "Shibboleth" you quote this line by Celan: "Speak — / But keep yes and no unsplit." You yourself claim the right not to renounce a form of discourse that can at times seem contradictory: "I live in this contradiction," you write somewhere, "it is even what is most alive within me, so I assert it."

JD: Yes, on the condition you yourself clearly stated, that "to keep alive" is also to welcome mortality, the dead, the specters (you spoke of "negativity").[2] If exposing oneself to death and keeping the memory of the mortal and of the dead is a manifestation of life, then yes. I would not want to yield—and I am sure it is not the direction you are inviting me to take—to a sort of linguistic vitalism. It is a matter of life in the sense that life is not separable from an experience of death. So, yes, that is the first type of contradiction: the life of language is also the life of specters; it is also the work of mourning; it is also impossible mourning. It is not only a matter of the specters of Auschwitz or of all the dead one may lament, but of a spectrality proper to the body of language. Language, the word—in a way, the life of the word—is in essence spectral. It is a little like the date: it repeats itself, as itself, and is every time other. There is a sort of spectral virtualization in the being of the word, in the very being of grammar. And it is therefore within language already, right on the tongue, that the experience of life-death makes itself felt.

ÉG: And is this what one should not flee?

JD: Indeed. Even if the statements one signs on this subject are or seem contradictory: going in this or that direction. One must cultivate the idiom and translation. One must inhabit without inhabiting. One must cultivate linguistic difference without nationalism. One must cultivate one's own difference and the other's difference. Besides, when I say "I only have one language; it is not mine," such a statement defies common sense and is self-contradictory. Such a contradiction is not someone's personal heartrending contradiction, but a contradiction inscribed within the possibility of language. Without this contradiction, there would be no language. I believe, therefore, that one must endure it . . . One must . . . I do not know if one must . . . One endures it and this stems from the fact that language is, at bottom, an inheritance. One does not choose an inheritance: one is born into a language, even if it is a second language. For Celan, it is German. Was he born into German? Yes and no. When one is born into a language, one inherits it because it is there before us, it is older than us, its law precedes us. One starts by recognizing its law, that is to say, a lexicon, a grammar, all this being almost ageless. But to inherit is not simply to receive passively something that is already there, like a possession. To inherit is to reaffirm through transformation, change, and displacement. For a finite being, there is no inheritance that does not imply a kind of selection, or filtering. Moreover, there is inheritance only for a finite being. An inheritance must be signed; it must be countersigned—that is to say, at bottom, one must leave one's signature on inheritance itself, on the language that one receives. That is a contradiction: one receives and, at the same time, one gives. One receives a gift, but, in order to receive it as a responsible heir, one must respond to the gift by giving something else, that is to say, by leaving a mark on the body of what one receives. These are contradictory gestures, an intimate, bodily struggle. One receives a body and one leaves one's signature on it. This bodily struggle, when translated into formal logic, gives rise to contradictory statements.

So, should one flee from, avoid, the contradiction, or should one try to account for what takes place, to justify what is—that is to say, this experience of language? As for myself, I choose contradiction, I choose to expose myself to contradiction.

ÉG: I want, in conclusion, to ask you to comment on this very beautiful passage from "Shibboleth," in which you speak about the "spectral errancy of words":

> This revenance does not befall words by accident, following a death that would come to some or spare others. *All* words, from their first emergence, partake of revenance. They will always have been phantoms, and this law governs the relationship in them between body and soul. One cannot say that we know this *because* we experience death and mourning. That experience comes to us from our relation to this revenance of the mark, then of language, then of the word, then of the name. What is called poetry or literature, art itself (let us make no distinction for the moment) — in other words, a certain experience of language, of the mark, or of the trait *as such* — is perhaps only an intense familiarity with the ineluctable originarity of the specter.

Is this "spectral errancy" of words a definition of the poetic and philosophical experience of language (by both Celan and you)? Are words eternally suspended between life and death, becoming thereby, as Artaud would say, "sempiternal"?

JD: What I am trying to say there, it seems to me, would be valid for the experience of language in general. I am attempting there a sort of analysis of the structure of language in general. I do not much like the term "essence" of language. I would prefer to give a more living and dynamic meaning to this way of being, to this manifestation of linguistic spectrality, which is valid for all languages. The common, universal experience of language in general becomes here an experience *as such* and appears *as such* in poetry, literature, and art. There would be much to say about this "as such". . .

I would give the name of poet to the one who experiences this most intimately, *in the quick, the living flesh* [à vif]. Whoever has an intimate, bodily experience of this spectral errancy, whoever surrenders to this truth of language, is a poet, whether he writes poetry or not. One might be a poet in the statutory sense of the term, inside the literary institution, that is to say, writing poems inside the space that is called "literature." I call "poet" the one who gives way to events of writing that give this essence of language a new body and make it manifest in a work. I do not want to take the word *work* in any easy sense. What is a work? To create a work is to give a new body to language, to give language a body so that this truth of language may appear *as such*, may appear and disappear, may appear as an elliptic withdrawal. I believe that Celan, from this point of view, is an exemplary poet. Others, in other languages, create works that are equally exemplary, but Celan, in this century and in German, put his name to an exemplary work. This, once again, has a general value, and this general value is exemplified in singular and irreplaceable ways in Celan's work. This is valid for everyone and for Celan in particular.

ÉG: Would you say that one must have been able, like Celan, perhaps, to live the death of language in order to be able to try to tell about this experiencing "in the flesh"?

JD: It seems to me that he must have, at every instant, lived this death. In several ways. He must have lived it everywhere he felt the German language had been killed in a certain way, for instance, by subjects of the German language who put it to a certain use; it is murdered, it is killed, it is put to death by what one makes it say in this or that way.[3] The experience of Nazism is a crime against the German language. What was said in German under Nazism is a death. There is another death in the mere banalization, the trivialization of language, for instance, the German language, no matter where, no matter when. And then there is another death, the death that comes over language because of what language is: repetition, lethargy, mechanization, and so forth. The poetic act therefore constitutes a sort of resurrection: the poet is someone permanently engaged with a dying language that he resuscitates, not by giving back to it a triumphant line, but by sometimes bringing it back, like a revenant or phantom. He wakes up language, and in order to experience the awakening, the return to life of language, truly *in the quick, the living flesh*, he must be very close to its corpse. He needs to be as close as possible to its remnants, its remains. I do not want to yield too much to *pathos* here, but I imagine that Celan was constantly working with a language that was in danger of becoming a dead language. The poet is someone who perceives that language, his language, the language he inherits in the sense I was just emphasizing, is in danger of becoming a dead language again, and he therefore has the responsibility, a very grave responsibility, of waking it up, of resuscitating it (not in the sense of Christian glory but in the sense of a resurrection of language), not like an immortal body or a glorious body, but like a mortal body, frail, sometimes indecipherable, as is each poem by Celan. Each poem is a resurrection, but one that engages us to a vulnerable body, one that may be forgotten again. I believe that all Celan's poems remain in a certain way indecipherable, retain some indecipherability, and the indecipherable can either call endlessly for a sort of reinterpretation, resurrection, or new interpretative breath, or, on the contrary, it can perish or waste away once more. Nothing insures a poem against its own death, either because the archive can always be burnt in crematoria or in flames, or because, without being burnt, it can simply be forgotten, or not interpreted, or left to lethargy. Oblivion is always possible.

June 29, 2000

4

Majesties

I

In the "Meridian" of Celan, which we will be approaching, the word *majesty* (*Majestät*) appears at least once. The word *Majestät* appears at least once *in the German text*, and, as we will later see, it is taken up or repeated *a second time in the translation of the text* by Jean Launay, the exemplary translator and editor of an admirable volume, *Le Meridien et autres proses* (Seuil, 2002).

In the "Meridian," then, the word *majesty* appears in the vicinity of the word *monarchy* and its lexicon—which is in question throughout this speech, the monarchy decapitated during the French Revolution. This proximity is there for contrast, as we will see, to mark a difference between the majesty that Celan is talking about and that of the monarchy. But it is too early to be specific; we will have to wait a little. And to proceed by approaching slowly and prudently, for things are here, more than ever, complex, subtle, slippery, unstable, even undecidable.

Let us come back to the marionette. There's more than one, we were saying. We will look closely at Celan's marionette ("Die Kunst, das ist, Sie erinnern sich, ein marionettenhaftes . . . kinderloses Wesen"; "art, you will remember, has the qualities of the marionette . . . it is incapable of producing offspring"), where, as I suggested last time, the marionette in the "Meridian" comes to us, gives itself to be read and thought, through an experience of the strange (*das Fremde*) and of the *Unheimliche* (*das Unheimliche*),[1] which all the marionettes and the marionettes of marionettes of "Monsieur Teste" *seemed most often* (I want to be careful)—to try to reduce or to suppress, to repress or to purify of its ambiguity.

Marionettes. There is more than one kind of marionette, that's the hypothesis, the bet that I ventured last time. There would be two experiences, rather, let us say, two arts of the marionette. But also, perhaps, two fables of the marionette. Two marionettes whose fables cross, two marionettes.

If I insist so much on the fable and the fabulous, it is no doubt and too evidently because of fables, like those of La Fontaine, that politically or anthropomorphically stage animals who play a role in civil society or in the State, often the statutory roles of the subject or the sovereign. But there is another reason for my insistence on the fabulous. It is because, as the fables themselves show, political force or power, in laying down the law, in laying down its own law, in appropriating legitimate violence and legitimating its own arbitrary violence, is in essence such that this unleashing and restraining of power passes by way of the fable, in other words, by way of a language that is both fictional and performative, a language that consists in saying: well, I am right because, yes, I am right because I am called the lion and you will listen to me, I am talking to you, stand in fear, I am the strongest, and I will finish you off if you object. In the fable, within a narrative that is itself fabulous, power is shown to be an effect of the fable, of fiction and fictive language, of the simulacrum. Just like the law, like the force of law, which Montaigne and Pascal said is, in essence, fictional.

Of the two fables of marionettes, one would perhaps be a poem, the other not; one would perhaps be an invitation to thinking, the other not. I continue to say "perhaps." Perhaps two, we can never be sure.

The difference between the two would be, perhaps, almost nothing, barely the time or the turning of a breath, the difference of a breath, a turning of a breath that is barely perceptible. (*Atemwende*, as Celan would say. *Atemwende* is not only the title of one of his collections of poetry, it is the word that he uses in the "Meridian" to try to define poetry: "Dichtung: das kann eine Atemwende bedeuten": "Poetry: that might mean a turn of the breath.") But we are never sure of this. Both the poem, if there is one, and thinking, if there is any, are there because of this im-probability of breath. But breath remains, in some living things, at least, not only the first but also the last sign of life, of living life. The first and last sign of living life. Without breath there would be neither speech nor speaking, but before speech and in speech, at the beginning of speech, there is breath.

Not only is the certainty of this distinction between these two (marionettes and arts of the marionette) never established in any living present, but this point is *necessarily* not certain. This "necessarily" (or "not necessarily" or "necessarily not") perhaps disqualifies or discredits the presence, the self-presence of every living present. If I use, with emphasis, the expression *the living present* (*lebendige Gegenwart*: the living now), an expression to which Husserl gave, as you know, phenomenological status and philosophical privilege, it is, of course, in order to make a strategically essential and necessary reference to Husserlian phenomenology and to the transcendental phenomenology of time; I also use it for other reasons, which will appear in the course of an attempt to read Celan and what he says about the present or the now, precisely about its "majesty." But it is above all in order to interrogate once more this manner of naming life, more precisely, living [*le vivant*]: not Life [*LA vie*], the Being or Essence or Substance of something like LIFE [*LA VIE*], but living, the presently living, not the substance called Life that remains alive, but an attribute called "living" that qualifies or determines the present, the now, a now [*maintenant*] that would be essentially living, presently living, maintaining [*maintenant*] qua living (*die lebendige Gegenwart*). As those who have been attending this seminar for the last few years know well, what we have been trying to think together under the headings of forgiveness, pardon, death penalty, and sovereignty, what we have always kept in sight, has always been nothing other than that which, I would not say presents itself as the living of life, the enigma of living (in the sense of *zoē* just as much as *bios*, life, *Leben*, *Lebendigkeit*, as Husserl says, *vivance*, that is, that which now maintains [*maintenant maintient*] life as living), but rather that which remains at a certain remove precisely where the question "What is the living of life?" holds its breath before the problematic legitimacy of submitting the question of life to the question of Being, of life to Being.

To think of a difference between the marionettes, to think *the* marionette, is to attempt to think the living of life, and a living "being" [*un "être" vivant*] that perhaps is not, a *living without Being* [*un vivant sans l'être*: a living being without being (one)]. As I put it long ago, "God without Being," an expression to which {Jean-Luc}[2] Marion has given majestic form and force as the title to one of his books. A living being without being (one) [*un vivant sans l'être*] — or that "is" only a simulacrum of a being [*∂'étant*]. Or is only a prosthesis. Or is only a substitute for the being or for the thing itself, a fetish. A marionette is all that: a simulacrum, a prosthesis (remember Kleist's allusion to the art of the English artist who made a wooden leg with which to dance gracefully), a fetish. People can and must make marionettes, even a theater of marionettes. Will we jump to the conclusion that those called animals cannot do so? No. To be sure, most do not, but then most human beings never make puppets or Kleist's marionette theater. But are some non-human animals capable of producing simulacra or of attaching themselves to them, to masks and to signifying prosthetic substitutes? The answer would be "yes"; it would be easy to build up an argument starting either from our common experience or from ethological or primatological knowledge.

It is along this a-venue that I was proposing, last time, an attempt at a timid or intimidated, partial, very selective reading, following the marionettes of "Monsieur Teste," of the marionettes of Celan in the "Meridian." I have already cited twice, the last two times [the last two seminar sessions], the first words of this speech, which you know was given in October 1960 in Darmstadt, on the occasion of receiving the Georg Büchner prize, a fact that explains and justifies, to a great extent, context obliging, the central and organizing character of references to Büchner's work, to *Danton's Death*, *Woyzeck*, and so forth. I have already cited twice, the last two times, the first words of this speech ("Die Kunst, das ist, Sie erinnern sich, ein marionettenhaftes, / kinderloses Wesen"). But before proceeding to encounter what is said in this speech of the encounter (*Begegnung*, the secret of the encounter, *im Geheimnis ∂er Begegnung*),[3] and of what is there named "majesty" — and it is not just any majesty, but the majesty of the present, of the *Gegenwart* of which we just spoke in reference to the *∂ie leben∂ige Gegenwart*, and of the present of man or the human ("They are a tribute to the majesty of the present, which bears witness to human presence, the majesty of the absurd"; "Gehuldigt wird hier der für die Gegenwart des menschlichen zeugenden Majestät des Absurden," 175/64[4]), before going further to encounter what is said about the encounter in this speech, and of what is there named "majesty," I want now to tell you what I had in mind when I insisted not only on the magnitude of grandeur in the lexicon and semantics of sovereign majesty but, since last time, on the fact that there are two marionettes, two arts and two senses of the marionette, and thus a difference in the body, and at the heart, of the marionette. And this difference between two marionettes within the marionette is still one of sexual difference, which we have been talking about since the beginning of the seminar.

*　　*　　*

Instead of encountering this immense question head-on, it is time to come back to the "Meridian," which we have kept obliquely in sight since the beginning of this session. What is said there of the marionette, of the Medusa's head, of heads in general and of majesty, allows us to make the transition. But I would also like to stress the strange (*Fremde*), the other (*Andere*), and the strangely familiar or disquieting (*unheimliche*). I had to choose between a continuous reading of Celan's speech, an interpretation that would follow the apparent order and linear time of the text, its very consecutiveness, and another reading, less diachronic and more systematic, which would insist on making appear, for purposes of demonstration, a configuration of motifs, of words and themes, of figures that do not usually appear in this order. I have made this second choice, first, because we would not have the time to read together, linearly, the whole text from *A* to *Z* (but I recommend that you do so on your own), and second, because the actively interpretive, selective, oriented reading that I am about to propose to you requires it. You understand, of course, that I do not hold this interpretive reading to be the only or even the best one possible, but it does not seem impossible to me, and it is important to me from the perspective of this seminar.

Even before starting to consider—too fast, certainly—the motifs that I propose to articulate together (even if Celan does not do so explicitly), namely, art, the marionette, the automaton, the Medusa's head, heads in general, and majesty, the strange and the *Unheimliche*: two preliminary remarks.

First preliminary remark. Dates are important in this text, a text that is also a sort of poetics of the date. When, some fifteen years ago, I devoted a little book, "Shibboleth," to it, I made this a privileged theme of reflection and analysis, or of interpretation, notably around a certain *20th of January*, which returns regularly, at least three times, in the text (Büchner's Lenz who "walked through the mountains on the 20th of January" [179/71], then "perhaps one can say that every poem has its '20th of January'?" [180/73], and then "I started to write from a '20th of January,' from my own '20th of January'" [184/81]). In "Shibboleth," I insistently expounded upon dates, upon the question of anniversaries and of the calendar, and upon this example of the 20th of January. But thanks to Jean Launay's (invaluable and exemplary, as I have said) edition, I have been able to discover one more bearing for this "January 20." Referring to Celan's manuscript, Launay recalls in a note (p. 107, n. 50) that "the 20th of January is also the day when, in Berlin, the so-called Wannsee Conference took place, in the course of which Hitler and his collaborators finalized plans for the 'final solution.'" Cf. *Der Meridian*,[5] p. 68 (and here is the translation of this manuscript passage of Celan: "We still write, even today, January 20, *this* January 20 [*this* underlined: diesen *20 Jänner*], to which is added ever since then the writing of so many days of ice [*zu dem sich (seitdem) soviel Eisiges hinzugeschrieben hat*].") "January 20": anniversary of death, then, of the crime against humanity, of the sovereignly, arbitrarily genocidal decision. "January 20": the eve of the anniversary of the beheading of the monarch, King Louis XVI, of which it is also a question, between so many "Long live the Kings!" of Lucile and of Lenz, of which we will talk later.

Second preliminary remark. The apparently surprising contiguity of our readings of "Monsieur Teste" and "The Meridian"—texts nonetheless so different, so distant from each other in so many ways, including the dates, precisely—this contiguity or proximity of two texts apparently so anachronistic, is justified not only, beyond mere juxtaposition, by the fact that both treat, each in its manner, the marionette and everything tied to it. It turns out that Valéry is not absent from the "Meridian." Celan wonders at a particular moment, concerning the radical calling-into-question of art, whether we should not "follow Mallarmé to his logical conclusion [*Mallarmé konsequent zu Ende denken*]." There again a long note by Launay (p. 105, n. 43) indicates a manuscript by Celan that refers to a passage by Valéry in "Variété" (*Oeuvres*, 1:784). Valéry there cites a remark of Mallarmé in response to poor Degas, who complained of not being able to finish his little poem, although he was "full of ideas." Mallarmé, reports Valéry, then responded: "But Degas, it is not with ideas that one makes verses, but with words." And Valéry concludes: "That is a great lesson."

Let us now attempt, around or through this announced configuration (art, the marionette, the Medusa's head or the automaton, heads in general and majesty, the strange and the *Unheimliche*), to decipher a certain poetic signature. I do not say a poetics, a poetic art, or even a poetry; I will, rather, say a certain poetic signature, the unique signature of a unique poem, always unique, which attempts to express not the essence, the presence or what *is* there of the poem, but where the poem comes and goes, that attempts, then, to set itself free, through art, from art.

What line is there to follow to the the unique encounter of a unique poem? You know that the concept of encounter, the "secret of the encounter" (*Geheimnis der Begegnung*) of which we spoke a moment ago, is the secret of the poem, of the presence, or presencing [*mise en présence*], or presentation of the poem, the secret of the encounter as the secret of the poem, in the double sense of this expression "secret of": in the sense of that which, *on the one hand*, in the first place, makes a poem, in the sense of its construction, of its making, of its possibility of taking form, if not of its art and its *savoir faire*, I prefer to say of its signature (that's the secret as the genesis of the poem, its condition of possibility, as when one says "this one, he has the secret," implying "the art of" and so forth, but here it is not essentially art that holds the secret of this act or, rather, of this event, it is the encounter) and then, double sense of the secret, thus, *on the other hand*, second, as what in the present itself, in the very presentation of the poem, in this present now upon which Celan insists so much, in the experience of the encounter, continues to remain secret, at bottom a present that does not present itself, a phenomenon that does not phenomenalize itself. Nothing shows itself, the nothing, the absurd shows itself in manifesting nothing. We will come to this, to this manifestation as non-manifestation.

But I believe I know, having read it so many times, that the trajectory of this poem follows a line that defies any reconstitution in the form of a logical or narrative exposition. The few initial figures or feints [*esquisses ou esquives*] that I propose to you today are therefore only an invitation to go and see for yourselves, to go and seize with your own eyes and hands, to go precisely to the encounter of the poem. The line (I keep the word *line*, but in a moment we will have to say link, for the line is a link, *Verbinden*), the line as link that links to the other, to the Thou in the encounter, the line as link that I am seeking to sketch or reconstitute, is exactly that which is sought, that which Celan acknowledges having sought throughout this journey and on this path, and which he describes in the end, and I will, in short, start out from there, namely, from the end, via the end, as "the impossible path" or "the path of the impossible." Yet "the impossible path" and "the path *of* the impossible" are not exactly the same thing. One can imagine that the path *of* the impossible remains, as path, as the path-making of the path [*cheminement du chemin*], possible, which immediately would make the impossible path possible in its turn; and

it is doubtless deliberately, and in view of the inextricable knot holding them together but distinct, that Celan says, juxtaposing and
crossing the two, "the impossible path" *and* "the path *of* the impossible": "Ladies and gentlemen, I find something that offers me some
consolation for having . . . in your presence . . . [*in ihrer Gegenwart*:
this *in ihrer Gegenwart*, which looks like a conventional banality, a polite phrase suitable for addressing the audience on the day of a prize,
is of remarkable gravity, given that the whole text will have turned
around the enigma of the "now," *Gegenwart*, and of presence; in a moment I will take up, among other possible ones, just *three examples* of
this *by making three returns*, after having cited this phrase to the end]
Ladies and gentlemen, I find something which offers me some consolation for having traveled the impossible path, the path of the impossible, in your presence [*in ihrer Gegenwart diesen unmöglichen Weg, diesen
Weg des Unmöglichen gegangen zu sein*]" (185/84).

This impossible path of the impossible constitutes, as link, the line
Celan *believes* he has found, even *touched* ("habe ich ihn soeben wieder
zu berühren geglaubt," these are the very last words), and that he
will call, precisely, the meridian. This line is a link that leads to the
encounter (*Begegnung*), to your encounter, to the encounter of you, to
the nomination of Thou, by which he will more than once have
named the poem and the present of the poem. But before pursuing
this citation to the end, I would like, in circling back, in *three returns*,
as I said, to show you why this "in your presence [*in ihrer Gegenwart*]"
was not a concession to convention (there are none in this extraordinary text). This "in your presence [*in ihrer Gegenwart*]" was invested
in advance, charged, aggravated by the question of the poem, the
poem in its difficult and tumultuous explication with art. The question that is about art and about poetry ("Frage nach der Kunst und
nach der Dichtung," Celan says above, adding: "I had to encounter
this question on the path that is my own (own does not mean I have
decided upon it), so that I could seek that of Büchner" [177/67].)[6]
Now, this question becomes that of the poem, defined by Celan as
present and as presence, as now and presence.

First return, toward what is implied by the word *majesty*, precisely
in the essence, or rather the event, the chance, of poetry. After several appearances of art, to which we will be coming back (art as marionette, art as monkey, etc.), here is Lucile from *Danton's Death*, the
one who is "blind to art [*die Kunstblinde*]," surprising us by shouting,
"Long live the King!" As you can see, with this scene of the French
Revolution and of the putting to death of the King, on the scaffold,

but also with the evocation of marionettes and of the monkey, we are close to our principal question concerning "the beast and the sovereign."

Lucile cries, "Long live the King!" and Celan stresses with an exclamation point to what extent this cry surprises, so close to the bloodstained scaffold and after having just recalled the "artful words *kunstreiche Worte*]" of Danton, Camille, and so on. Lucile, who is blind to art, shouts, "Long live the King!" Celan calls this a counterword (*Gegenwort*):

> After all the words spoken on the platform (the scaffold [*es ist das Blutgerüst*: literally, Blood-Scaffold])—what a word [*welch ein Wort*]!
>
> It is a counter-word [*Es ist das Gegenwort*], a statement that severs the "wire," that refuses to bow before the "loiterers and parade horses of history." It is an act of freedom. It is a step [*Es ist ein Akt der Freiheit. Es ist ein Schritt*]. (175/63)

In order to support the view [*propos*] that the "Long live the King" of the one who is blind to art is a "step" and an "act of freedom," a manifestation without manifestation, a counter-manifestation, Celan must detach this cry, this "counter-word," from its political code, that is, from its counter-revolutionary meaning, indeed from everything that a counter-manifestation may still owe to this politicizing code. Instead, Celan believes he recognizes in it, as an act of freedom, a poetic act, or rather—if not a poetic act, if not a poetic making, still less a poetic art by someone who "is blind to art"—poetry itself (*die Dichtung*). In order to hear poetry in this "act of freedom," in this "step" (and the reference to the step, to walking, to coming or going, is always decisive in the "Meridian"), Celan states that this homage "Long live the King!" this stand, this profession of faith, this tribute (*gehuldigt*) is not pronounced, politically, in favor of the Monarchy, thus of his majesty King Louis XVI, but in favor of the majesty of the present, of the *Gegenwart*. This *Gegenwort* speaks in favor of the majesty of the *Gegenwart*. In the passage that I will now read in {Launay's} translation, I will stress *four words*, for reasons that will be all too obvious and on which I will hardly need to comment; they are words that fall within the lexicon of "bearing witness," of "majesty," of "the present," and of "the human": "To be sure, it sounds like an expression of allegiance to the ancien régime. . . . But . . . these words are not a celebration of the monarchy and a past which should be preserved. They are a tribute to the majesty of the present, which bears witness to human presence, the majesty of the absurd. [*Gehul-digt wird hier der für die Gegenwart des Menschlichen zeugenden Majestät des Absurden*]. That, ladies and gentlemen, has no universally recognized name, but it is, I believe . . . poetry [*aber ich glaube, es ist . . . die Dich-tung*]" (175/63).

(This "I believe," so close to the majesty of the absurd [the word *absurd* recurs more than once in the text, no doubt to signal what remains beyond meaning, beyond idea, beyond theme and even rhetorical tropes, beyond all the logic and all the rhetoric to which one believes a poetics should submit] seems to suggest "I believe where I believe, because it is absurd, *credo quia absurdum*." Faith in poetry as faith in God, here in the majesty of the present.)

This move on Celan's part, his recourse to the word *majesty* —and this is what is most important to me here, at least in the context of this seminar—consists in placing one majesty above another, thus in bidding up on sovereignty. A bidding up that attempts to change the sense of *majesty* or of *sovereignty*, to displace its sense, while keeping the old word or claiming to restore its most dignified meaning. There is the sovereign majesty of the sovereign, of the King, and there is, more majestic or otherwise majestic, more sovereign and otherwise sovereign, the majesty of poetry, or the majesty of the absurd insofar as it bears witness to human presence. This hyperbolic bidding up is inscribed in what I will call the dynamic of majesty or of sovereignty, a *dynamic* because it is a matter of a movement whose acceleration is inescapable, a *dynamic* (I choose this word deliberately) because it is a matter of the sovereign, precisely, of might, of power (*dynamis*), of the deployment of the potentiality of the dynast and of the dynasty. In other words, there is something "more majestic" than the majesty of the King, just as it was said, you remember, that Monsieur Teste is superior to superior men, or as the Nietzschean superman is above the superior man. As in Bataille, sovereignty, in the sense Bataille understands it and wants to give it, exceeds classic sovereignty, namely, mastery, supremacy, absolute power, and so forth. (We will come back to this.)

Why keep the word, then?

What counts most here, with Celan, is that this hyper-majesty of poetry, beyond or outside the majesty of the king, the sovereign, or the monarch, this supreme majesty of the absurd, as the majesty of *Dichtung*, turns out to be determined by four equally serious values, among which, I believe, one must still be privileged or, rather, recognized in its singular privilege, and that is the present (*Gegenwart*).

These four weighty values or significations are: *bearing witness*, of course; *majesty*, insofar as it bears witness (*zeugenden Majestät*); the *human*, for which it bears witness; but above all, I will say, because it never stops confirming and repeating itself, the present ("Gehuldigt wird hier der für die Gegenwart des Menschlichen zeugenden Majestät des Absurden"). Majesty is here majestic, and it is poetry, insofar as it bears witness to the present, to the now, to the "presence," as Launay translates, of the human. And because to bear witness is always to manifest presence, through speech, through speech that addresses the other and thereby attests to a presence, well, then, what counts here, and what signs, is a presence attesting to a presence, or rather to a present, a human present.

I would not privilege to such an extent the present, the presence of this present, if, apart from all the reasons that you can easily imagine, Celan had not himself kept coming back to it with an evident and, I believe, undeniable insistence. I will be briefer, for lack of time today, about my two other promised examples or returns.

Second return. Some six pages later (181/76), after an itinerary that I cannot reconstitute, though we will pursue a few of its essential stages next time, Celan speaks of what he calls a "language become reality" (*aktualisierte Sprache*), under the sign of "an individuation which is radical." Adding presence to the now, reinforcing *Gegenwart* with *Präsenz*, he says: "Then a poem would be—even more clearly than before—the language of an individual which has taken form; and, in keeping with its innermost nature, it would be present and presence [*Dann wäre das Gedicht—deutlicher noch als bisher—gestaltgewordene Sprache eines Einzelnen, —und seinem innersten Wesen nach Gegenwart und Präsenz*]."

Third return. On the next page (182/77), Celan specifies something essential regarding, let's call it the structure of this present now, and it is from this specification, which risks complicating everything, that I will start off again next time. He specifies that this present-now of the poem, *my* present-now, the punctual present-now of the punctual *I*, my here-now, has to *let* [laisser] *speak* the present-now of the other, the of the other. My here-now has to *leave* [laisser] time, it has to *give* to the other its time.

It has to leave or give to the other *its* time. *Its own time.*

It has to leave or give *its* time. It has to leave or give *its* proper time. This formulation is not literally Celan's, but I attach to it this ambiguous, even *unheimlich* grammar, where one no longer knows to whom the possessive adjective refers: to oneself or to the other. To leave or give to the other *its* time: I give or leave to this formulation a grammatical ambiguity in order to translate what I believe to be the truth of Celan's intention [*propos*]: *to leave or give* to the other *its* own time.

That is, of course, what introduces into the present-now a divisibility or an alterity that changes everything. It calls forth a complete rereading of the predominant authority, indeed, of the majesty of the present, which becomes that of the other or that of an asymmetrical partaking with the other, turned toward the other or coming from the other. I will now read the passage in question, and its wording sometimes, when necessary, in two languages.

> The poem becomes—and under what conditions!—a poem of one who—as before—perceives, who is turned [*zugewandten*, I stress this turn, the turn of this "turned"] toward that which appears [*dem Erscheinenden Zugewandten*]. Who questions this appearing and addresses it [*dieses Erscheinende Befragenden und Ansprechenden* . . . this *Ansprechen*—this turning toward the other in order to address speech to the other, to address the other, to speak to the other, indeed to apostrophize the other—this *Ansprechen* is doubtless the *turning* and the *turn* that responds to everything in this passage, as in the "Meridian"; and I say this "turn" less to suggest a figure, a turn of phrase, indeed, one of these rhetorical tropes of which Celan is so wary, than to signal toward *Atemwende*, the turn, the turning of breath, which is so often, in its letter, the very inspiration, the spirit of the "Meridian"]. It becomes dialogue—it is often despairing dialogue [*es wird Gespräch—oft ist es verzweifeltes Gespräch*]. (182/77)

The poem is thus a speaking of two (*Gespräch*, a speaking together), a speech of more than one, a speech whose now maintains more than one in it, a speaking that *gathers* more than one in it (I say "gathers" because, in what is maintained in this now, there is, as you will hear, a movement of gathering [*rassemblement*], a being-together [*être-ensemble*], a chance of gathering, *Versammlung*—once again, a very Heideggerian motif—a movement, a momentum [*un élan*], a step that gathers more than one in it), and the address of one to the other—even if it fails, even if the address is not received or does not arrive at its destination, even if the despair of the other, or about the other, is always waiting, and even if it must always be waiting, as its very possibility, the possibility of the poem. Celan continues:

Only in the realm of this dialogue does that which is addressed [*das Angesprochene*] take form and gather around [*versammelt es sich*] the I who is addressing and naming it. But the one who has been addressed [*das Angesprochene*] and who, by virtue of having been named, has, as it were, become a Thou [*zum Du Gewordene*] also brings its otherness [*bringt . . . auch sein Anders-sein mit*] along into the present, into this present [*in diese Gegenwart*]. In the here and now of the poem [*Noch im Hier und Jetzt des Gedichts*] it is still possible — the poem itself, after all, has only this one, unique, punctual present [*diese eine, einmalige, punktuelle Gegenwart*] — only in this immediacy and proximity does it let what the Other has as its most proper, its time, speak also [*noch in dieser Unmittelbarkeit und Nähe lässt es das ihm, dem Anderen, Eigenste mitsprechen: dessen Zeit*]. (182/77–78)

What the poem lets speak at the same time (*mitsprechen*: lets speak *also*, says Launay's translation, and the *mit* of *mitsprechen* deserves stress; this speaking is originally, *a priori*, a speaking *with* the other or *to* the other, even before speaking alone; and this *mit* does not necessarily break solitude; we might even say it is its condition, as it is sometimes of despair), what the poem lets speak with it, lets partake in its speech, what it lets con-verse, con-voke (so many ways to translate *mit-sprechen*, which means more than a dialogue), what it lets speak, indeed sign with it (co-sign, consign, countersign), is the time of the other, *its* time in what it has as its most proper: the most proper, and thus most untranslatably other, of the time of the other.

One could comment infinitely on the wording of these sentences. As you see, it is not only a matter of a gathering in dialogue. What is not even a poetics here is even less a politics of dialogue — of a dialogue in the course of which, helped by communication experts and advisers, one would learn with great effort to let the other speak. It is not a matter of a democratic debate in the course of which the other is given "equal time" to speak, under the watchful eye of one of those clocks that, along with the calendar, is in question in the "Meridian." It is not a matter of allotting a certain amount of time but of leaving to the other, thus of giving to the other, without acting out of generosity, thereby effacing oneself absolutely, of *giving* to the other its time (and giving here is leaving, as one gives to the other only what is proper to it, irreducibly proper), it is not only a matter of letting the other speak, but of letting time speak, its time, what its time, the time of the other, has as its most proper. It is time that one must let speak, the time of the other, rather than leaving to the other its time of speech. It is a matter of letting time speak, the time of the other in what it has that is most proper to the other, thus, in what it has as its most other—which arrives [*arrive*], which I let arrive, as the time of the other, in the present time of "my" poem. In *letting* arrive what arrives (of the other), this "letting" neutralizes nothing, it is not a *simple* passivity, even if some passivity is required here. It is, on the contrary, the condition of an event occurring [*advienne*] and of something happening [*arrive*]. What I *would make* happen instead of *letting* happen, well, that would no longer happen. What I *make* happen does not happen, of course, and one must draw consequences from this apparently paradoxical necessity (but of course the *lassen* in Celan's German means both *letting* and *making*: "noch in dieser Unmittelbarkeit und Nähe lässt es das ihm, dem Anderen, Eigenste mitsprechen: dessen Zeit").

Starting from there, so to speak, though I will have to stop here, the "Meridian" sets off again, and we make a half-turn. After having said that the poem seeks this place (*Ort*), Celan approaches the question of place (*Ort*, place of rhetoric, *Bilder und Tropen*), the question of *topoi* and of u-topia, while recalling that he speaks of a poem that is not there, of an absolute poem that cannot be there ("das gibt es gewiss nicht, das kann es nicht geben!").

I had announced that, after these three returns and three examples, I would finish reading this conclusion, which I had started to cite. I will do so, and next time I will come back again to the "Meridian" (which I ask you to read in the meantime). I will thus come back, hoping that the necessity of this will become clearer, to the themes of the Other and of the strange, of the *Unheimliche*, of the head (the "Meridian" moves between heads and beheadings; it often speaks of falling in the *Grund* and *Abgrund*); and then we find again, among other heads, the Medusa's head (in relation to erection and castration); and, finally, we will return toward the monkey, toward the marionette as a question of art ("Die Kunst, das ist, Sie erinnern sich, ein marionettenhaftes . . . kinderloses Wesen").

I am also seeking the place of my own origin, since I have once again arrived at my point of departure.

I am seeking all of that on the map with a finger which is uncertain, because it is restless—on a child's map, as I readily confess.

None of these places is to be found, they are not there, but I know where they would have to be—above all at the present time—and . . . I find something!

Ladies and gentlemen, I find something which offers me some consolation for having traveled the impossible path, this path of the impossible, in your presence.

I find something which links and which, like the poem, leads to an encounter.

I find something, like language, abstract, yet earthly, terrestrial, something circular, which traverses both poles and returns to itself, thereby—I am happy to report—even crossing the tropics and tropes. I find . . . a *meridian*.

With you and Georg Büchner and the state of Hesse I believe that I have just now touched it again.

II

The question of the sovereign, of standing upright, of the magnitude or highness of the Most High, led us last time not only from the Roman *majestas*, as the sovereignty of the State or of the Roman people, to the majesty in La Fontaine's fable "The Wolf and the Lamb," to His Majesty the wolf, but also to a double division, if I can put it this way, a division of division itself, in what I will venture to call, through this poem on poetry that is "The Meridian," on this side of or through this poem, the Celanian discourse, the logic or discursive axiomatics that underlies or gives its rhythm to his poem; a double division, then, namely:

1. *on the one hand*, a first difference, dissociation, or division between the majesty of the Monarch (here of the monarch Louis XVI, of the one who will lose his head in a Revolution) and the majesty, let us say, of the present or of poetry (*Dichtung*, for as you recall, Celan, after having spoken of the "für die Gegenwart des Menschlichen zeugenden Majestät des Absurden," adds, "but I believe it is . . . poetry [*aber ich glaube, es ist . . . die Dichtung*]"); this second majesty, this second sovereignty, poetic sovereignty, is not, Celan says, the political sovereignty of the monarch.

2. *and on the other hand*, the division in the point [*point*], in the very point [*pointe*], in the very punctuality of the now, as the very presence of the present, in the majesty itself of the poetic present, in the poem

as encounter, the dissociation, then, the partition that is also a partaking, of my present, the present itself, the very presence of the present, of the same present, in the present of the same, and, on the other hand—and this is the other part of partition and of partaking—the other present, the present of the other to whom the poem makes present its time, letting thus speak, in a *Mitsprechen*, the time of the other, its proper time. ("Das Gedicht selbst hat ja immer nur diese, einmalige, punktuelle Gegenwart—noch in dieser Unmittelbarkeit und Nähe lässt es das ihm, dem Anderen, Eigenste mitsprechen: dessen Zeit": "In the here and now of the poem, it is still possible—the poem itself, after all, has only this one, unique, punctual present—only in this immediacy and proximity does it let what the Other has as its most proper, its time, also speak" [182/77–78].)

We have specified at great length the time of this speech left to the other in the encounter of the poem, beyond its politico-democratic interpretation, beyond the calculable time of speech or the counting of voices in an election of the sovereign.

Having reached this point, and so as not to lose sight of our question of the proper of man, of the phallic majesty and revolutionary decapitation of the sovereign, I would like, while privileging these motifs, as well as those of the animal, the monkey, the marionette and especially the Medusa's head, to reconstruct as quickly and schematically as possible an itinerary that will take us back to what Celan evokes as a stepping outside the human ("ein Hinaustreten aus dem Menschlichen").

This stepping outside the human, the human to which the poetic majesty of the Absurd bears witness, *would be* (here the conditional must be kept, you will see why one must always say "perhaps") what is proper to art according to Büchner, but proper to an art that would be *"unheimlich"* (the word, as you will hear, appears twice, translated {by Launay} once as *étrange*, ["uncanny"], once as *étrange, dépaysant* ["uncanny, disorienting"][7]) —an art that would be *unheimlich* because in this art these apparently inhuman things would find themselves at home (*zuhause*), these three apparently inhuman or unhuman things in the figures of which art has, from the beginning of the speech, made its appearances, three appearances that would be (1) a Medusa's head (which is evoked through the mouth of Büchner's Lenz, in whom Celan claims to hear the voice of Büchner himself); (2) "the form of a monkey" (*die Affengestalt*, which also made its appearance above); and (3) the automata or the marionettes.

Here, as always, one must be very attentive to ellipses and furtive shifts of meaning, to cursory allusions. This stepping outside the human, which Celan describes as one describes the gesture or movement of the other, the Lenz of Büchner or Büchner himself, has the character, according to Celan, of the *unheimlich*. That is, the character that Celan acknowledges, attributes to, or confers on this movement is *unheimlich*. You know that this word has two apparently contradictory and undecidable meanings; we have talked a lot about that here (cf. Freud and Heidegger): the familiar, but as the unfamiliar; the terribly disquieting of the strange [*étranger*],[8] but as the intimacy of one's proper home. The word appears two times in the following passage, and even more often elsewhere:

> Here we have stepped outside the human, gone outward and entered an *unheimlich* realm, yet one turned toward that which is human, the same realm in which the monkey, the automaton, and, accordingly . . . alas, art, too, seem to be at home.
>   This is not the historical Lenz speaking, it is Büchner's Lenz. We hear Büchner's voice: even here art preserves something *unheimlich* for him. (177/66–67)

Here the word *unheimlich* carries all the charge, precisely where it remains equivocal and so difficult to translate; it expresses the essential bearing of the "Meridian," it seems to me. It shows up elsewhere in the text, appearing together with a word just as recurrent: the strange [*étranger, fremd*].

> And poetry? Poetry, which, after all, must travel the path of art? In that case we would in fact be shown here the path to the Medusa's head and the automaton!
>   At this point I am not searching for a way out, I am just asking, along the same line, and also, I believe, in the line suggested in the Lenz fragment.
>   Perhaps—I'm just asking—perhaps poetry, in the company of the I which has forgotten itself, travels the same path as art, toward that which is *unheimlich* and strange. And once again— but where? but in what place? but how? but as what?—it sets itself free. (178/69)

Although the uncanniness of the *Unheimliche*, which is a familiar uncanniness, which stems from the fact that the figures of the automaton, the monkey, and the Medusa's head are at home (*zuhause*), is often associated with the strange in this way, it is not at all by chance that this uncanniness should also be so close to what creates the secret of poetry, that is, the secret of the encounter. In German "secret" is *Geheimnis* (the intimate, the withheld, the withdrawn into retreat, the concealed interior of one's home, of the house), and this secret of the encounter is at the innermost heart of that which is present and presence (*Gegenwart und Präsenz*) in the poem.

> Then the poem would be—even more clearly than before—the language of an individual which has taken on form; and in keeping with its innermost nature, it would also be present and presence.
>
> The poem is alone. It is alone and underway. Whoever writes it must remain in its company.
>
> But doesn't the poem, for precisely this reason, at this point participate in an encounter—*in the secret of an encounter*?
>
> The poem wants to reach the Other, it needs this Other, it needs a vis à vis. It searches it out and addresses it.
>
> Each thing, each person is a form of the Other for the poem, as it makes for this Other. (181/76)

Before returning to the concept of the strange thus appearing together with the uncanny, with the uncanniness of what is *unheimlich*, I would just like to indicate to you the way [*voie*] of a long detour through the texts of Heidegger. It was right here that I stressed, some years back, the decisive importance, until recently noticed little if at all, of the lexicon of the *Unheimliche* or of *Unheimlichkeit* in Heidegger (where it has an importance just as great, however different, in appearance at least, as it does in Freud). Now, without wanting or being able to reopen fully here the question of the *unheimliche* in Heidegger, from *Being and Time* to the end, I will merely signal to you, precisely because it concerns the human and the unhuman within the human, a particular passage in the *Introduction to Metaphysics* (1935) that resonates uncannily (*unheimlich*) with what Celan says of the *Unheimliche*, as that which, at home in art, seems to exceed the human in the human, seems to step outside the human in human art.

I reopen, with some violence, and guided by what is important to us here at this moment, the *Introduction to Metaphysics* at the point where Heidegger relaunches the question "What is man?" (p. 142 sq. of English tr. and 108 sq. of the original, Niemeyer).[9] Let me recall two essential markers before coming to what interests us here in this section, namely, the *Unheimliche*.

1. *First marker*: Heidegger starts by stating the secondary, derived, in short, late and at bottom very unsatisfying character, from
an ontological point of view, of a definition of man as "rational animal" or as *zōon logon ekhōn*. This definition, which he calls, in an interesting and unchallengeable manner, "zoological," not exclusively but
also in the sense in which it allies *logos* to *zōon*, and in which it claims
to account for and explain (*logon didonai*) the essence of man by saying that man is above all a "living thing," an "animal": "Die genannte
Definition des Menschen ist im Grunde eine zoologische." But the
zōon of this zoology remains in many respects *fragwürdig*. In other
words, as long we have not interrogated, ontologically, the essence
of Being in life, the essence of life, to define man as *zōon logon ekhōn*
remains problematic and obscure. Now, it is on this uninterrogated
ground, on this problematic ground of a non-elucidated ontological
question of life, that the entire West, declares Heidegger, has con-
structed its psychology, its ethics, its theory of knowledge, and its
anthropology. Heidegger then describes with irony and hauteur the
state of culture in which we live, where one can receive books bearing on their cover the title *What Is Man?* without the slightest question being posed beyond the cover of such a book, a book that, he
then notes (in 1935), the *Frankfurter Zeitung* praises as "an extraordinary, magnificent, and courageous work."

2. *Second marker*: From then on the answer to the question "What
is man?" cannot be an answer but a question, a questioning, an act
or an experience of *Fragen*, for in this question it is man himself who
determines himself in interrogating himself about himself, about his
Being, discovering himself thus as a questioning essence in the *Fragen*. From this Heidegger draws *two conclusions in one*, namely—I will
cite the {French} translation, which does not seem very illuminating
to me and which I will attempt to clarify later: "Only as a questioning
being does man come to himself; only as such is he a self [*der Mensch
kommt erst als fragend-geschichtlicher zu ihm selbst und ist ein Selbst*]."[10]
And so this *Selbst*, this himself, this *ipseity* (as *Selbst* is sometimes
translated), which is as yet neither an "I" nor an individual, neither
a we nor a community, is a "who," before every "I," every individual,
every somebody, every we, and every community (*a fortiori*, I will
add, for what interests us, neither a subject nor a political animal, for
Heidegger's suspicion regarding man as *zōon logon ekhōn*, as rational
animal, equals his suspicion regarding man as political animal, Aris-
totle's phrase, to which we will return at length later). So that, second conclusion wrapped in the first, the question of man concerning

his proper Being (*nach seinem eigenen Sein*) transforms itself; it is no longer "What is man?," "What is it that is man?," "*Was* ist der Mensch?," but "Who is man?," "*Wer* ist der Mensch?"

Having recalled these two markers, you'll then find, if you reread the text, as I ask you to, that Heidegger temporarily abandons Parmenides, whom he is reading, and turns toward Sophocles' *Antigone*, seeking there a poetic outline of what could be the Greek ear for the essence of man. In the interpretation of this poetic outline, he proposes a retrieval of what he takes to be a more originary sense of the Greek *polis*, for which, he says, the translation as "city" or "city-state," *Stadt und Stadtstaat*, does not render the "full meaning" ("dies trifft nicht den vollen Sinne"). Before the city-state, thus before what we call politics, the *polis* is the Da, the *there* in which and as which the *Da-sein* is *geschichtlich*, happens [*advient*] as history, as the historical origin of history. To this place and scene of history belong not only the sovereigns (*Herrscher*), the men who hold power, the army, the navy, the council of elders, the assembly of the people, but also the gods, the temples, the priests, the poets, the thinkers. But what is most important to us here, in the course of this reading of Sophocles, is the moment when Heidegger translates the *deinotaton* of *deinon* — the most terrible, the most violent, or the most disquieting of the disquieting, there where Antigone (332–75) says that there is nothing more *deinon* than man — by *das Unheimlichste des Unheimlichen* which resides, he will say (p. 124 German, p. 162 English tr.), in the conflict, in the antagonistic relation (*im gegenwendigen Bezug*) between justice (*dikē*) and *tekhnē*. Heidegger asks, "Why do we translate *deinon* by *un-heimlich*?" The principle of his answer is that the saying (*Spruch*) that says, "Der Mensch ist das Unheimlichste [*deinotaton*]," "Man is the most *unheimlich*," gives the authentic, proper, Greek definition of man ("gibt die eigentliche *griechische* Definition des Menschen").

Why? Why translate thus? Not in order to add, afterward, a sense to the word *deinon* (which is often translated "violent" or "terrible"), nor because we understand the *Unheimliche* to be a sense impression, as an affect or as what makes an impression on our states of feeling, but because there is in the *Unheimliche* something that casts us out of the *heimliche*, of the peaceful calm of the "homely," of the *heimisch*, of the customary (*Gewohnten*), of the common and the familiar (*Geläufigen*). Man is the most *unheimlich* because he departs from the familiar, from the customary limits (*Grenze*) of habitude. When the chorus says of man that he is *to deinotaton* or *das Unheimlichste*, it is not a matter, according to Heidegger, of saying that man is this or that, and, in addition, *unheimlichste*; it is a matter of saying, rather, rather earlier [*bien plutôt, bien plus tôt*], that the essence of man, the proper of man (his basic trait, his *Grundzug*) is to be a stranger to everything that can be identified as familiar, recognizable, and so forth. The proper of man would be, in short, this manner of not being securely at home [*chez soi*] (*heimisch*), even if this means being close to oneself as to one's proper essence. It is as if Heidegger said, following a now somewhat traditional motif, that the proper of man is this experience that consists in exceeding the proper, the proper in the sense of what is appropriated in the familiar. On this issue Heidegger will not go so far as to say "there is no proper of man," but rather that this proper has as its basic trait, if not a certain impropriety or ex-propriation, at least the property of being apprehended qua [*en tant que*] property, as [*comme*] uncanny, non-appropriated, even non-appropriable, stranger to *heimisch*, to the reassuring proximity of the identifiable and the similar, to the familiar, to the interiority of home—beyond, in particular, all the "zoological" definitions, as Heidegger calls them, of man as *zōon logon ekhōn*.

Leaving there, for lack of time, everything that in those pages and beyond them resonates in Heidegger around this claim, "Der Mensch ist *to deinotaton*, das Unheimlichste des Unheimlichsten" (p. 114 German, p. 149 English tr.), I stress only, before returning to what in Celan seems to echo it uncannily, that the superlative (*das Unheimlichste*) counts as much as the equivocal and unstable sense (*das Unheimliche*), that it thus superlativizes, hyperbolizes, or extremizes. Man is not only *unheimlich*, an essence already as equivocal and uncanny as what *unheimlich* means (take a look at what Freud says in the essay that bears this title, "Das Unheimliche," about the contradictory significations of the German word, which designates both the most familiar and the most uncanny); man, what is called man, is not only *deinon* and *unheimlich* but *to deinotaton* and *das Unheimlichste*, the most *unheimlich* being, in other words, he excells sovereignly in this, he is more *unheimlich* than all and everyone, he attains, I will say, but this is not exactly Heidegger's language and word here, a sort of exceptional excellency, a sort of sovereignty among the *unheimlich* beings and the modalities of *Unheimlichkeit*. The superlative is the sign of the hyperbolic; it wears the crown of the sovereignty of human *Dasein*. And this sort of sovereignty, you have understood, concerns, under the trait of the *Unheimliche*, a certain experience of strangerness [*étrangèreté*]: not only of the uncanny [*étrange*], but of the strange [*étranger*] (a figure that is taken over later, in the texts on Trakl, in *On the Way to Language*, and that I have treated in previous seminars, a long time ago).

Keeping in mind this indissociable couple, the *sovereignly* and *super-latively unheimlich* and the strange or strangeness, we can now come back to the "Meridian" and to the moment of the itinerary where Celan has just evoked stepping outside the human ("ein Hinaus-treten aus dem Menschlichen") and the movement that consists in entering a realm that turns toward the human its uncanny face (the three appearances of art: the automata, the figure of the monkey, the Medusa's head); this moment of stepping outside the human must be set next to that which, previously, had let it be understood that, "perhaps" ("I believe," says Celan), poetry was this homage given to the majesty of the Absurd, insofar as it bears witness to the present or to the now of the human ("für die Gegenwart des Menschlichen zeugenden Majestät des Absurden"). Celan wonders also, as we have seen, whether or not poetry must take the path of art, a path that would also be that of the Medusa and of automata. From this mo-ment on, the value of the *unheimliche* is no longer separate from that of the strange [*étranger, fremd*], not only of the uncanny [*étrange*] but of the strange, and all the—multiple—approaches to what poetry would be are all approaches, not to an essence, but to a movement, to a path and a step, to a direction, to a turning in the direction of a step, as to a turning in the breath itself (*Atemwende*).

We will find an example of this in almost every line, at least starting from p. 178/70. I will cite only some of them, in order to suggest that this insistence on the step that sets free, that steps across, that comes and goes in such and such a direction, commands us to think of poetry as a path (*Weg*, a word Celan uses so often that we, rightly or wrongly, find it difficult not to associate it with an incessant and insistent medi-tation on the path, on the *Bewegung* of the path, on the movement of *Weg*, in Heidegger), as a path, according to Celan, for that which comes or goes, and thus is less something that *is* than an event, the coming of an event that arrives. I will stress very quickly this privilege accorded to the path, to the coming and going, to the step. In reading these lines, I will not only point out the step, but, for reasons I will explain in a moment, I will also slow down my step around three other words, namely, the *I*, *the strange* (*l'Etranger, das Fremde*), and the *abyss* (*Abgrund*).

In that case art would be the path traveled by poetry—nothing more and nothing less.

I know, there are other, shorter paths. But after all poetry, too, often shoots ahead for us. *La poésie, elle aussi, brûle nos etapes.* . . .

Can we now, perhaps, find the place where the strange was, the place where a person succeeded in setting himself free, as an—estranged—I? Can we find such a place, such a step?

". . . but now and then he experienced a sense of uneasiness because he was not able to walk on his head."—That is Lenz. That is, I am convinced, Lenz and his step, Lenz and his "Long live the king!"

". . . but now and then he experienced a sense of uneasiness because he was not able to walk on his head."

Whoever walks on his head, ladies and gentlemen, whoever walks on his head has heaven beneath him as an abyss. (178–79/70–72)

On this subject, see Heidegger at the beginning of the *Introduction to Metaphysics* (p. 2 German, pp. 2–3 English tr.), on the subject of "Why is there being? What is the ground of being?" Heidegger asks himself whether this ground is an originary ground (*Urgrund*) or whether this originary ground refuses all grounding and becomes *Abgrund*, or a grounding that is not one, an appearance of ground, *Schein von Gründung, Ungrund*.

Here occurs, then, in the path or in the poetic speech of Celan— but, as with all decisive events, under the category or the reservation of "perhaps" (*vielleicht*), in truth between two "perhapses" and even three "perhapses," even four, five, six, seven, eight "perhapses," (in some twenty-odd lines and two paragraphs)—here occurs then, between two and three and four, five, six, seven, eight "perhapses," the event of an unprecedented turning of which, with you, I would like to test the hazards and size up the slope, so to speak. Celan has just evoked the obscurity proper to poetry as the place of an encounter to come from the horizon of distance and of the strange. Here is a first *perhaps*: "That is, I believe, if not the inherent obscurity of poetry, the obscurity attributed to it for the sake of an encounter— from a great distance or sense of strangeness possibly of its own making (179/72). And there is then, under the reservation of a second *perhaps*, an uncanny division of the strange itself, there are perhaps two kinds of strangeness, side by side: "But there are perhaps two kinds of strangeness, in one and the same direction—side by side" (179/72). And then, to make even more precise this duality at the very heart of the strange, a sort of revolution within the revolution. You will recall that Lucile's "Long live the King!" had been greeted as a counter-word (*Gegenwort*) that was perhaps ("I believe," said Celan) poetry, an homage given, far from the political code of the reactionary counter-manifestation, to the (non-political) majesty of the absurd, which bears witness to the present or to the now of the human. Here another "Long live the King!," the "Long live the King!" of Lenz, that is, of Büchner, is supposed to go one step beyond that of Lucile. And it is no longer, this time, a word, or even a counter-word (*Gegenwort* bearing witness to a *Gegenwart*), it is, above all, no longer a majesty; it is a terrifying silence, it is a halt that leaves speech dumbstruck, that robs one of breath and of speech.

> Lenz—that is, Büchner—has here gone one step further than Lucile. His "Long live the King" no longer consists of words. It has become a terrible silence. It robs him—and us—of breath and speech.
>   Poetry: that can signify a turn-of-breath. Who knows, perhaps poetry travels its path—which is also the path of art—for the sake of such a breath turning? (179–80/72)

Still privileging, since it has been our concern throughout, a thinking of sovereignty, of its majesty in the figure of a present and self-present *ipseity*, sometimes self-present in the form of the ego, in the living present of the ego, of the "I," this "I," this power to say "I" that, from Descartes to Kant and to Heidegger, has always been literally, explicitly reserved for human being (only man can, according to these three, say or mean "I," "I, myself," only man can refer to himself in an auto-deictic fashion), what I would like to make apparent, if possible, is how Celan signals toward an alterity that, in the inside of the "I" as the punctual living present, as the very point of the self-present living present, an alterity of the wholly other, comes not to include and modalize another living present (as in the Husserlian analysis of temporalization, where, in the protention and the retention of another living present in the now living present, the ego comprises in itself, in its present, another present), but—and this is a wholly other matter—lets appear something of the present *of the other*, this "letting the most proper of the time of the other," of which we spoke last time.

Let me first read this long passage riddled with who knows how many "perhapses," which all have the purpose, in the end, of withdrawing these poetic statements on the event of the poem from the dimension and from the authority of knowledge.

Perhaps it succeeds, since strangeness [*l'Etranger, das Fremde*], that is, the abyss *and* the Medusa's head, the abyss *and* the automata, seem to lie in the same direction—perhaps it succeeds here in distinguishing between two kinds of strangeness [*deux sortes d'Etranger, Fremd und Fremd*], perhaps at precisely this point the Medusa's head shrivels, perhaps the automata cease to function—for this unique, fleeting moment? Is perhaps at this point, along with the I—with the estranged I, set free *at this point* and *in a similar manner*—is perhaps at this point an Other set free?

Perhaps the poem assumes its own identity as a result . . . and is accordingly able to travel other paths, that is, the paths of art, again and again—in this art-less, art-free manner?

Perhaps.

Perhaps one can say that every poem has its "20th of January"? Perhaps the novelty of poems that are written today is to be found in precisely this point: that here the attempt is most clearly made to remain mindful of such dates?

But are we all not descended from such dates? And to which dates do we attribute ourselves?

But the poem does speak! It remains mindful of its dates, but—it speaks, to be sure, it speaks only in its own, its own, individual cause.

But I think—and this thought can scarcely come as a surprise to you—I think that it has always belonged to the expectations of the poem, in precisely this manner to speak in the cause of the strange [*l'Etranger, fremder*]—no, I can no longer use this word—in precisely this manner to speak *in the cause of an Other*—who knows, perhaps in the cause of a *wholly Other*.

This "who knows," at which I see I have arrived, is the only thing I can add—on my own—here, today—to the old expectations.

Perhaps, I must now say to myself—and at this point I am making use of a well-known term—perhaps it is now possible to conceive a meeting of this "wholly Other" and an "other" which is not far removed, which is very near. (180/73–74)

Of course, I can only let you now read and reread the entire "Meridian." But perhaps we are beginning here to think this subtle, *unheimlich* difference between the two kinds of the strange, a difference that is like the place for the narrow passage of poetry of which Celan soon will speak. It is the difference, in the punctuality of the now, in the very point of the present instant, of *my* present, between, *on the one hand*, my other living present (retained or anticipated by an indispensable movement of retention or protention) and, *on the other hand*, the wholly other, the present of the other whose temporality cannot be reduced, included, assimilated, introjected, appropriated within mine, cannot even resemble it or be like it, the present or proper time of the other, which I must no doubt forgo, giving it up radically, but whose very possibility (the *perhaps* beyond all knowledge) is also at the same time the chance of the encounter (*Begegnung*) and of this event, of this coming, of this step that is called poetry. An improbable poetry ("who knows?"), but a poetry that robs and turns the breath, that is to say, also life and path, which can still be a path of art at the same time larger and narrower.

Let me read a final passage . . .

Elargissez l'Art! This question comes to us with its *Unheimlichkeit*, new and old. I approached Büchner in its company—I believed I would once again find it there.

I also had an answer ready, a "Lucilean" counter-word; I wanted to establish something in opposition, I wanted to be there with my contradiction.

Expand art?

No. But accompany art into your own unique place of narrow passage. And set yourself free.

Here, too, in your presence, I have traveled this path.

It was a circle.

Art—and one must also include the Medusa's head, mechanization, automata; *das unheimliche*, indistinguishable, and in the end perhaps the only strangeness [*l'unique et même Etranger; nur eine Fremde*] — art lives on.

Twice, in Lucile's "Long live the King" and as heaven opened up under Lenz as an abyss, the breath turning seemed to be there. Perhaps also, when I attempted to make for that distant but occupiable realm which became visible only in the form of Lucile. (183/80)

As you have well understood, in this division between the two kinds of the strange, two ways of thinking the other and time, in this very division between the two "Long live the Kings!" of which only the first calls itself *majestic*, of which only the first one, that of Lucile, calls for the word *majesty*, *poetic* and not *political* majesty, we have now passed (perhaps) beyond *all majesty, hence all sovereignty*. It is as if, after the poetic revolution that reaffirmed a poetic majesty beyond or outside political majesty, a second revolution, which robs one of breath or turns breath in the encounter with the wholly other, came to attempt or to recognize, to attempt to recognize, even, knowing [*connaître*] or recognizing [*reconnaître*] nothing, to attempt to *think* a revolution within revolution, a revolution in the very life of time, in the life of the living present. This discreet, even non-apparent, even minuscule, even microscopic dethroning of majesty exceeds knowledge [*savoir*]. Not in order to pay homage to some obscurantism of non-knowledge, but so as to prepare, perhaps, some poetic revolution within the political revolution, and perhaps also some revolution in the knowledge of knowledge, precisely between the beast, the marionette, the head, the Medusa's head, and the head of his majesty the sovereign. This is no doubt what is signed by the repetition of the "perhapses" and of the "who knows?" (*wer weiss*).

5

Rams

Uninterrupted Dialogue—Between Two Infinities, the Poem

Will I be able to bear witness, in a just and faithful fashion, to my admiration for Hans-Georg Gadamer?

Mingled with the gratitude and affection that have for so long characterized this feeling, I sense, somewhat obscurely, an ageless melancholy.

This melancholy, I dare say, is not only historical. Even if, thanks to some event still difficult to decipher, it had a historical reference, this would be in a manner that is singular, intimate, nearly private, secret, and still in reserve. For its first movement does not always orient it toward the epicenters of seisms that my generation will have perceived most often in their effects rather than their causes, only belatedly, indirectly, and in a mediated fashion, unlike Gadamer, who was their great witness, even their thinker. And not only in Germany. Every time we spoke together, always, it's true, in French, more than once here in Heidelberg, often in Paris or in Italy, through everything he confided to me, with a friendliness whose warmth always honored, moved, and encouraged me, I had the feeling of understanding better a century of German thought, philosophy, and politics—and not only German.

Death will no doubt have changed this melancholy—and infinitely aggravated it. Death will have sealed it. Forever. But underneath the petrified immobility of this seal, in this difficult to read but in some way blessed signature, I have a hard time distinguishing what dates from the death of the friend and what will have preceded it for such a long time.[1] The same melancholy, different but also the same, must have overcome me already in of our first encounter, in Paris in 1981. Our discussion must have begun by a strange interruption — something other than a misunderstanding — by a sort of prohibition, the inhibition of a suspension. And by the patience of indefinite expectation, of an *epochē* that made one hold one's breath, withhold judgment or conclusion. As for me, I remained there with my mouth open. I spoke very little to him, and what I said then was addressed only indirectly to him. But I was sure that a strange and intense sharing [*partage*] had begun. A partnership, perhaps. I had a feeling that what he would no doubt have called an "interior dialogue" would continue in both of us, sometimes wordlessly, immediately in us or indirectly, as was confirmed in the years that followed, this time in a very studious and eloquent, often fecund, fashion, through a large number of philosophers the world over and in Europe, but above all in the United States, who attempted to take charge of and reconstitute this still virtual or suspended exchange, to prolong it or to interpret its strange caesura.

I

In speaking of *dialogue*, I use a word that I confess will remain, for a thousand reasons, good or bad (which I will spare you), foreign to my lexicon, as if belonging to a foreign language, whose use would provoke translations a bit off, requiring precautions. By specifying above all "*interior* dialogue," I am delighted to have already let Gadamer speak in me. I inherit, literally, what he said in 1985, shortly after our first encounter, in the conclusion to his text "*Destruktion* and Deconstruction":

> Finally, that dialogue, which we pursue *in our own thought* and which is perhaps enriching itself in our own day with great new partners who are drawn from a heritage of humanity that is extending across our planet, should seek its partner everywhere — just because this partner is other, and especially if the other is completely different. Whoever wants me to take deconstruction to heart and insists upon difference stands at *the beginning of a dialogue*, and not at its end.[2]

What is it that remains, even today, so *unheimlich* about this encounter, which was, to my mind, all the more fortunate, if not successful, precisely for having been, in the eyes of many, a missed encounter? It succeeded so well at being missed that it left an active and provocative trace, a promising trace, with more of a future ahead than if it had been a harmonious and consensual dialogue.

I call this experience, in German, *unheimlich*. I have no French equivalent to describe in one word this affect: in the course of a unique and therefore irreplaceable encounter, a peculiar strangeness came to mingle indissociably with a familiarity at once intimate and unsettling, sometimes disquieting, vaguely spectral. I also use this untranslatable German word, *unheimlich*, to revive, even as I speak in French and you can read me in German,[3] our common sensitivity to the limits of translation. I also use it in memory of Gadamer's diagnostic concerning what many of our friends hastily interpreted as an originary misunderstanding. According to him, errors in translation had been one of the essential causes of that surprising interruption in 1981. At the opening of *Deconstruction and Hermeneutics*, in 1988, not long, I assume, after our second public debate—right here in Heidelberg, with Philippe Lacoue-Labarthe and Reiner Wiehl, about Heidegger's political commitments—Gadamer situated in these terms the test of translation and the always-threatening risk of misunderstanding at the border of languages: "My encounter with Derrida in Paris three years ago, which I had looked forward to as a dialogue between two totally independent developers of Heideggerian initiatives in thought, involved special difficulties. First of all, there was the language barrier. This is always a great difficulty when *thought or poetry* strives to leave traditional forms behind, trying to hear new orientations drawn from within their own mother tongue."[4]

The fact that Gadamer names "thought or poetry," rather than science or philosophy, is not fortuitous. That is a thread we ought not to lose track of today. Moreover, in "The Boundaries of Language" (1984), which came before the essay I just quoted from 1988, but which is closer to our meeting in 1981, Gadamer dwells at length on what links the question of translation to poetic experience. The poem is not only the best example of untranslatability. It also gives to the test of translation its most proper, its least improper, place. The poem no doubt is the only place propitious to the experience of language, that is to say, of an idiom that forever defies translation and therefore demands a translation that will do the impossible, make the impossible possible in an unheard-of event. In "The Boundaries of Language," Gadamer writes, "this [he has been speaking of the "phenomenon of foreign language"] is valid especially when it is a question of translation [a note refers to his essay "Reading Is like

Translating"⁵]. And in that case, poetry, the lyrical poem, is the great instance for the experience of the ownness and the foreignness of language."⁶

Supposing that all of poetry belongs *directly and simply* to what we call art or the fine arts, let us also recall what Gadamer specifies more than once, notably in his *Selbstdarstellung*.⁷ He underlines the essential role of what he calls "the experience of art" in his concept of philosophical hermeneutics, next to all the sciences of comprehension that serve him as a starting point. Let us never forget that *Truth and Method* opens with a chapter devoted to "the experience of art," to an "experience of the work of art" that "always fundamentally surpasses any subjective horizon of interpretation, whether that of the artist or that of the recipient."⁸ Concerning this horizon of subjectivity, the work of art never stands there like an object facing a subject. What constitutes its being a work is that it affects and transforms the subject, beginning with its signatory. In a paradoxical formula, Gadamer proposes reversing the presumed order: "The 'subject' of the experience of art, that which remains and endures, is not the subjectivity of the person who experiences it, but the work itself."⁹

But this sovereign authority of the work—for example, what makes the poem (*Gedicht*) a given order and the dict of a dictation—this sovereign authority of the work is also a call for a responsible answer and for dialogue (*Gespräch*). You will have recognized the title of a work Gadamer published in 1990, *Gedicht und Gespräch*.

I do not know if I have the right, without presumption, to speak of a dialogue between Gadamer and me. But should I aspire to it at all, I would repeat that this dialogue was first of all interior and *unheimlich*. The secret of what sustains [*entretient*] this *Unheimlichkeit*, here, at this very instant, is that this interior dialogue has probably kept [*gardé*] alive, active, and auspicious the tradition of that which seemed to suspend it outside, by which I mean, in particular, in the public sphere. I want to believe that, in a heart of hearts that can never be closed, this conversation [*entretien*] kept [*a gardé*] the memory of the misunderstanding with a remarkable constancy. This conversation cultivated and saved the hidden sense of this interruption uninterruptedly, whether silently or not—and for me, more often than not, in an interior and apparently mute way.

One speaks often and too easily of interior monologue. Yet an interior dialogue precedes it and makes it possible. Dividing and enriching the monologue, such dialogue commands and orients it. My interior dialogue with Gadamer, with Gadamer himself, with Gadamer alive, still alive, if I dare say, will not have ceased since our meeting in Paris.

No doubt this melancholy stems, as always with friendship, at least this is how I experience it each time, from a sad and invasive certainty: one day death will necessarily separate us. A fatal and inflexible law: one of two friends will always see the other die. The dialogue, virtual though it may be, will forever be wounded by an ultimate interruption. Comparable to no other, a separation between life and death will defy thought right from a first enigmatic seal, which we will endlessly seek to decipher. No doubt the dialogue continues, following its course in the survivor. He believes he is keeping the other in himself—he did so already while the other was alive— but now the survivor lets the other speak inside himself. He does so perhaps better than ever, and that is a terrifying hypothesis. But survival carries within itself the trace of an ineffaceable incision. Interruption multiplies itself, one interruption affecting another, in abyssal repetition, more *unheimlich* than ever.

Why insist so much on interruption already? What is the remembrance that most vividly disturbs my memory today? Well, it is what was said, what was done or what happened, after the last of the three questions that, in 1981 in Paris, I had dared to ask Gadamer. This question marked at once the test, if not the confirmation, of the misunderstanding, the apparent interruption of the dialogue, but also the beginning of an interior dialogue in each of us, a dialogue virtually without end and nearly continuous. At that time, indeed, I called for a certain *interruption*. Far from signifying the failure of the dialogue, such an interruption could become the condition of comprehension and understanding. Allow me just once to recall my question, the third and last of a series, about goodwill in the desire for consensus and about the problematic integration of psychoanalytic hermeneutics into a general hermeneutics.

Third question: bearing still on this axiomatics of goodwill. Whether with or without psychoanalytic afterthoughts, one can still raise questions about this axiomatic precondition of interpretative discourse that Professor Gadamer calls *Verstehen*, "understanding the other" and "understanding one another." Whether one speaks of consensus or of misunderstanding (as in Schleiermacher), one needs to ask whether the precondition for *Verstehen*, far from being the continuity of "rapport," as was said last night, is not rather the interruption of rapport, a certain rapport of interruption, the suspension of all mediation.[10]

The melancholic certainty of which I am speaking thus begins, as always, in the friends' lifetime Not only by an interruption but by a speaking of interruption. A *cogito* of adieu, this salut without return signs the very breathing of the dialogue, of dialogue in the world or of the most interior dialogue. Hence mourning no longer waits. From this first encounter, interruption anticipates death, precedes death. Interruption casts over each the pall of an implacable future anterior. One of us two *will have* had to remain alone. Both of us knew this in advance. And right from the start. One of the two *will have* been doomed, from the beginning, to carry alone, in himself, both the dialogue, which he must pursue beyond the interruption, and the memory of the first interruption.

And carry the world of the other, which I say without the facility of a hyperbole. The world after the end of the world.

For each time, and each time singularly, each time irreplaceably, each time infinitely, death is nothing less than an end of *the* world. Not *only one* end among others, the end of someone or of something *in the world*, the end of a life or of a living being. Death puts an end neither to someone in the world nor to *one* world among others. Death marks each time, each time in defiance of arithmetic, the absolute end of the one and only world, of that which each opens as a one and only world, the end of the unique world, the end of the totality of what is or can be presented as the origin of the world for any unique living being, be it human or not.

The survivor, then, remains alone. Beyond the world of the other, he is also in some fashion beyond or before the world itself. In the world outside the world and deprived of the world. At the least, he feels solely responsible, assigned to carry both the other and *his* world, the other and *the* world that have disappeared, responsible without world (*weltlos*), without the ground of any world, thenceforth, in a world without world, as if without earth beyond the end of the world.

II

That would be one of the first ways, doubtless not the only one, to let resound within us, before or beyond verifiable interpretation, a line [*vers*] of poetry by Paul Celan: "Die Welt ist fort, ich muß dich tragen."

Pronounced like a sentence, in the form of a sigh or a verdict, so goes the last line of a poem that we can read in the collection *Atemwende*. Shortly before his death, Celan gave me a copy of it at the École Normale Supérieure, where he was my colleague for several years. Another split, another interruption.

If I make his voice be heard [*entendre*] here, if I hear it in me now, that is above all because I share Gadamer's admiration for this other friend, Paul Celan. Like Gadamer, I have often attempted, in the night, to read Paul Celan and to think with him. With him toward [*vers*] him. If, once again, I wish to encounter this poem, it is, in fact, in order to attempt to address, or at least to make as if I am addressing, Gadamer himself, himself in me outside myself. It is in order to speak to him. Today I would like to pay homage to him in a reading that will also be an uneasy interpretation, quavered or quavering, perhaps even something wholly other than an interpretation. In any case, on a path that would cross his.

GROSSE, GLÜHENDE WÖLBUNG
mit dem sich
hinaus- und hinweg-
wühlenden Schwarzgestirn-
              Schwarm:

der verkieselten Stirn eines Widders
brenn ich dies Bild ein, zwischen
die Hörner, darin,
im Gesang der Windungen, das
Mark der geronnenen
Herzmeere schwillt.

Wo-
gegen
rennt er nicht an?

Die Welt ist fort, ich muß dich
              tragen.

VAST, GLOWING VAULT
with the swarm of
black stars pushing them-
selves out and away:

onto a ram's silicified forehead
I brand this image, between
the horns, in which,
in the song of the whorls, the
marrow of melted
heart-oceans swells.

In-
to what
does he not charge?

The world is gone, I must carry you.[11]

We will re-read this poem. We will attempt to listen to it, and then respond in a responsible fashion to what Gadamer often called the *Anspruch* of the work, the claim it makes upon us, the demanding call a poem sets up, the obstinate but justified reminder of its right to stand up for its rights. But why do I get ahead of myself? And why have I quoted first a last line, all alone, before any other, isolating it in a no doubt violent and artificial fashion: "Die Welt ist fort, ich muß dich tragen"?

No doubt, so as to acknowledge its charge. I will try to weigh [*peser*] the import [*la portée*][12] of this charge in a moment, in order to evaluate [*soupeser*] it, in order to endure its gravity, if not to think [*penser*] it. What is called weighing [*peser*]? An operation of weighing [*Une pesée*]? To *think* [penser] is also, in Latin as in French, to *weigh* [peser], to *compensate*, to *counterbalance*, to *compare*, to *examine*. In order to do that, in order to think and weigh, it is thus necessary to carry (*tragen*, perhaps), to carry in oneself and carry upon oneself. Supposing that we could wager everything on etymology, something I would never do, it appears that we in French are without the luck of having this proximity between *Denken* and *Danken*. We have a hard time translating questions like those that Heidegger raises in *What Is Called Thinking?*: "That which is thought, the thought [*Gedanc*], implies the thanks [*Dank*]. But perhaps these assonances between thought and thanks or gratitude are superficial and contrived. . . . Is thinking a giving of thanks? What do thanks mean here? Or do thanks consist in thinking?"[13]

But if we are not lucky enough to have this collusion or this play between thought and gratitude, and if the commerce of thanking always risks remaining a compensation, we do have in our Latin languages the friendship between thinking and weighing (*pensare*), between thought and gravity. And between thought [*pensée*] and the reach or grasp [*portée*] of someone. Whence the *examination*. The weight of a thought calls for and is always called the *examination*, and you know that *examen* is, in Latin, the hand of a scale. We count on this hand to measure the accuracy [*justesse*] and perhaps the justice of a judgment concerning what we give it to bear.

Another reason why I believed I had to begin by quoting, and then by repeating, the last line of this poem, "Die Welt is fort, ich muß dich tragen," was so as to follow faithfully, indeed, even to attempt to imitate, up to a certain point and as far as possible, a gesture that Gadamer repeats twice in his book on Celan, *Who Am I and Who Are You?: A Commentary on Celan's 'Atemkristall.'*[14]

Gadamer had announced that "following the hermeneutical principle," he would begin with the final line, which bears the stress of a poem that he was in the process of interpreting: "wühl ich mir den / versteinerten Segen."[15] As he explains: "For it contains evidently the core of this short poem."[16]

We are here today between two breaths or two inspirations, *Atemwende* and *Atemkristall*. Gadamer accompanies with a commentary this little poem by Celan:

WEGE IM SCHATTEN-GEBRÄCH	PATHS IN THE SHADOW-ROCK
deiner Hand.	of your hand
Aus der Vier-Finger-Furche	Out of the four-finger-furrow
wühl ich mir den	I grub for myself the
versteinerten Segen	petrified blessing[17]

No doubt this poem says something about the chance for a benediction or blessing (*Segen*), for a petrified blessing, like the seal that fascinated me an instant ago, and for a blessing under whose sign I would like to inscribe this moment. This sign is written by the same hand, by the same fingers, as so many other blessings of Celan. For example, "Benedicta":

Ge-	Be —
segnet seist du, von weit her, von	be thou blessed, from afar, from
jenseits meiner	beyond my
erloschenen Finger.	guttering fingers.[18]

As you will have noticed, the *wühlen* of the other poem, the one from *Atemwende* ("mit dem sich / hinaus-und hinweg- / wühlenden Schwarzgestirn-Schwarm") seems to echo the *wühlen* of this poem, collected in *Atemkristall* ("Wühl ich mir den / Versteinerten Segen").

Wühlen: isn't that the same unsettled burrowing, every time the movement of a pushing that is subversive and seeking, curious and pressed to know? Gadamer insists upon this word more than once. The blessing is not given, it is sought for; it seems to be extracted by hand. It exerts a questioning pressure. It strives to open the hand clenched into a fist and closed upon its meaning. A hand would keep hidden the message of blessing. The hand that blesses thus makes reading available, but it also calls for a reading of what it conceals from reading. The hand both gives and withdraws the meaning of the message. It retains the blessing itself, as if a blessing acquired in advance, a blessing that you can count upon, a verifiable, calculable, and decidable blessing, were not a blessing at all. Shouldn't a blessing, mustn't a blessing always remain improbable?

This poem, therefore, poses a first problem of interpretation. Gadamer proposes a hypothesis: "The closeness and charity of the benefactor is foregone to such an extent that the blessing is present only in petrifaction. Now, the poem says: This blessing of the benefactory hand is sought after with the grubbing and despairing fervor of an indigent."[19]

He then takes a bold, adventurous step. Through this vision, he proposes a reading of the scene of reading as one of subversion and reversal. What this poem gives to be read might also be the scene of reading, that is, the provocation that calls for a reading of what the poem itself gives to be read: "Accordingly, the benefacting hand is inverted boldly into the hand where palm-reading can reveal a message of beneficient hope."[20]

The blessing *of* the poem: this double genitive says well the gift of a poem that both blesses the other and lets itself be blessed by the other, by the receiver or the reader. But this address to the other does not exclude self-referential reflection, for it is always possible to say that the poem speaks *of itself*, of the scene of writing, of the signature and of the reading that it inaugurates. This specular and autotelic reflection does not close upon itself. Without any possible return, it is simultaneously a blessing granted to the other, the giving of a hand, *at once open and folded shut.*

What is the hand? What is *this* hand here, the hand of *this* poem? How could its openness and its being folded be represented at once, here, in an image or a tableau (*Bild*)? Already in his first sentence, Gadamer announces, I repeat, that "following the hermeneutical principle," he will begin with the last line of the poem, the one that bears the accent, where, in his view, "the core of this short poem is contained." Let us accept, at least provisionally and without question, that this would be the hermeneutical principle, and this its evidence. Let us postulate that the last line carries the meaning of the whole poem. In following these two axioms, Gadamer acknowledges very quickly, and explicitly, that his interpretive reading must take more than one interruption into account. His reading must also leave in suspense a series of questions that are so many interruptions in the decipherment of meaning.

These first interruptions initially follow folds that are also furrows for reading. As Gadamer writes:

> The context tells us what "shadow-rock" means. When the hand is clenched a little and the creases cast shadows, then, in the "strata" of the hand, that is, in the lattice of interrupted and folded lines, the breaks [the ruptures] interpreted by the palm-reader become visible. The palm-reader reads from them the language of destiny or of character. The "four-finger-furrow" is thus the continuous transverse crease which, without the thumb, joins the four fingers into a unity.[21]

Gadamer first describes, it seems, a sort of interruption that is multiple but wholly interior, that which, inside the hand, is both given and refused to reading: "in the lattice of interrupted and folded lines, the breaks interpreted by the palm-reader become visible. The palm-reader reads from them the language of destiny or of character." These lines of rupture are already situated *in* a text that is stretched out and given up. Here, the text is a hand that blesses. But it is one that, along these *internal* lines, threatens to deny itself, to conceal itself, to disappear. Without this threat, this risk, without this improbability, without this impossibility of proving—which must remain infinitely, and which must not be saturated or closed by any certainty—there would be neither reading nor giving nor blessing.

Further on, there is the sudden *interruption* of an edge, one that this time does not traverse the inside of the text. Rather, it surrounds the text. An *external* border delineates a suspensive interruption. After a series of sketched-out readings and venturesome questions, notably on the subject of the "I"—the "I" of the poet or of the reader in search of a blessing or a blessed reading—Gadamer leaves a series of questions undecided, undecidable, on the threshold. Far from stopping interpretive reading, these questions open and liberate the very experience of such reading. This time, it will concern the "you" no less than the "I." Placed under the question mark, these many affirmations link the possibility of blessing and the future of interpretation to a pensive and suspensive interruption. In order to underline the firm decision to leave the undecidable undecided, allow me to quote the entire paragraph, which concludes without concluding. The right to leave things undecided is recognized as belonging to the poem itself, not to the poet or the reader.

> Whose hand is it? It is difficult to see in this benefactory hand that no longer blesses anything but the hand of the hidden God, whose abundance of blessedness has become indiscernible, and only accessible to us as if in petrifaction, albeit in the reified ceremony of religion or the reified power of human faith. But, once again, the poem *does not decide* who "You" is. Its only message is the urgent need of the person who seeks a blessing from "your" hand, regardless of whose it is. What he finds is a "petrified" blessing. Is that still a blessing? An ultimate blessing? From your hand?[22]

I want to tell you now what, rightly or wrongly, I most want to keep alive in the echo of these last questions. More than the indecision itself, I admire the respect Gadamer shows for the indecision. This indecision seems to interrupt or suspend the decipherment of reading, though in truth it ensures its future. Indecision keeps attention forever in suspense, breathless, that is to say, keeps it alive, alert, vigilant, ready to embark on a wholly other path, to open itself up to whatever may come, listening faithfully, giving ear, to that other speech. Such indecision hangs upon the breath of the other speech and of the speech of the other—right where this speech might still seem unintelligible, inaudible, and untranslatable. Interruption is indecisive, it undecides. It gives its breath to a question that, far from paralyzing, sets in motion. Interruption even releases an infinite movement. In *Truth and Method*, Gadamer feels a need to underline what he calls the "boundlessness of the dialogue."[23] In "The Boundaries of Language,"[24] he names at least twice the "infinite process." *On the one hand*, the infinite process characterizes dialogue in general: from "the hermeneutical standpoint," dialogue "is never finished until it has led to a real agreement." If "no dialogue has ever really been finished," that is because a "real" agreement, a "perfect agreement between two people contradicts the very essence of individuality," a situation wherein Gadamer recognizes the sign of finitude itself. I would even say that interruptive finitude is what calls for the infinite process. *On the other hand*, the "infinite process" is named again, two pages further on, in order this time to characterize the interminable dialogue of the translator with himself.

In these last questions about what the poem leaves undecided, what I am determined to keep alive is the singular and no doubt intentional way in which Gadamer's rhetoric turns things. In truth, it is something other than rhetoric or a turn. Beyond any trope, Gadamer literally says that the poem *itself* will decide nothing. The poem is indeed here the "*subjectum*" we evoked a little while ago. If the poem retains an apparently sovereign, unpredictable, untranslatable, almost unreadable initiative, that is also because it remains an abandoned trace, suddenly independent of the intentional and conscious meaning of the signatory. It wanders, but in a secretly regulated fashion, from one referent to another—destined to outlive, in an "infinite process," the decipherments of any reader to come. If, like any trace, the poem is thus destinally abandoned, cut off from its origin and from its end, this double interruption makes of the poem not just the unfortunate orphan Plato speaks of in the *Phaedrus* when he discusses writing. This abandonment—which appears to deprive the poem of a father, to separate and emancipate it from a father who would expose

calculation to the incalculability of interrupted filiation—this immediate unreadability is also the resource that permits the poem to bless
(perhaps, only perhaps), to give, to give to think, to give cause to
think, to give the possibility of weighing the charge or the import, to
give rise to reading, to speaking (perhaps, only perhaps).

From the heart of its solitude and through its immediate unreadability, the poem can always speak—itself of itself, sometimes in a
transparent fashion, sometimes resorting to esoteric tropes that require an initiation and a reading technique. This self-reference always remains an appeal (*Anspruch*) to the other, even if only to the
inaccessible other in oneself. This self-reference in no way suspends
the reference to the inappropriable.

Even where the poem names unreadability, its own unreadability,
it also declares the unreadability of the world. Another poem of Celan's thus begins: "UNLESBARKEIT dieser / Welt. *Alles doppelt*"; "UN-
READABILITY of this world. All things twice over."[25] And, just a bit
further on, one hesitates to identify the "you" whom this poem apostrophizes: no matter whom, more than one, the poem itself, the poet,
the reader, the abyssal profundity of this or that other singularity forever encrypted, any or an entirely other, God, you or me ("Du, in
dein Tiefstes geklemmt").

III

Will we know how to read, will we have the ability to translate the
succession or substitution of definite articles (masculine, feminine, or
neuter) and, above all, of personal pronouns (*ich, er, dich*), so as to
attempt to respond to them or to answer for them? Articles and pronouns that name the living as well as the dead, animals, humans or
gods, and that so skillfully punctuate this poem, which ends:

Die Welt ist fort, ich muß dich tragen.

I will re-read it one more time. It would be necessary to do so
endlessly. I'll underline now the personal pronouns in it, as if to suggest that the *Anspruch* of this poem also evokes Gadamer's book on
Celan: *Who Am I and Who Are You?* It is as if I were permitting myself
timidly to slip in a postscript. Over every stanza, and this will not
have escaped either your eyes or your ears, stands guard, as it were,
the sentry of a different personal pronoun: in the first three stanzas,
sich, ich, er; in the last line, *ich* and *dich*. The last line says something
about the import (*tragen*), which we are going to attempt to think

through. It will run the risk of finding itself charged with carrying all the meaning of a poem that one might be quick to believe is there only to prepare for or to illustrate the meaning of the last line. The last line happens, however, to be dissociated and separated by the abyssal duration of a blank silence, like a disjointed aphorism, the sentence or verdict of another time, after a perceptible interruption, longer than any other, which we might be tempted to saturate, indeed, to overburden endlessly with virtual discourses, significations, or meditations.

> GROSSE, GLÜHENDE WÖLBUNG
> mit dem *sich*
> hinaus- und hinweg-
> wühlenden Schwarzgestirn-Schwarm:
>
> der verkieselten Stirn eines Widders
> brenn *ich* dies Bild ein, zwischen
> die Hörner, darin,
> im Gesang der Windungen, das
> Mark der geronnenen
> Herzmeere schwillt.
>
> Wo-
> gegen
> rennt *er* nicht an?
>
> Die Welt ist fort, *ich* muß *dich* tragen.

Throughout what I will now have the temerity to venture, listen only to the calls for help.[26] I am not sure of anything, even if I am also sure—but I draw no advantage from it—that no one has the right to be sure of anything here. The certainty of a guaranteed reading would be the first inanity or the worst betrayal. This poem remains for me the place of a unique experience. The calculable and the incalculable are allied there not only in the language of another but in the foreign language of another who gives me (what a fearsome present!) the occasion to countersign the future as much as the past: the unreadable is no longer opposed to the readable. Remaining unreadable, it secretes and keeps secret, in the same body, the chances of infinite, unfinished readings.

When I first discovered the poem—I confess this as a possible misdeed—my fascinated reading pounced right away on the last line. By hypotheses that I will tell you later, I avidly appropriated for myself a number of significations like so many scenes, stagings, and possible worlds, like so many addresses in which the *I* and the *you* were able to alight upon anyone and anything in the world, beginning with the poet, the poem, or their receiver, either in the history of literature or in life, between the world of the poem and the world of life, even beyond the world that is no more.[27] I thus tried first to translate the last line into French. Its grammatical present carries within it more than one time or tense. "Die Welt ist fort": the world has gone, already, the world has left us, the world is no more, the world is far off, the world is lost, the world is lost from sight, the world is out of sight, the world has departed, farewell to the world, the world has died, and so on.

But what world, what is *the* world? And, sooner or later: what is *this* world? So many inevitable and far-reaching questions. Of course, I will come back to these first steps, and to the "ich muß dich tragen" (I must carry you; it is necessary for me to carry you), which is in appearance easier to translate, but just as difficult to interpret.

I will not unfold here—I would not have the time to do so, and I have attempted to do so elsewhere—protocols of an apparently theoretical or methodological nature. I will say nothing, directly, of the insurmountable but always abusively surmounted border between, *on the one hand*, indispensable formal approaches, thematic, polythematic approaches that are attentive, as any hermeneutic must be, to the explicit and implicit folds of meaning [*sens*], to ambiguities and overdeterminations, to the rhetoric and to the intentional meaning [*vouloir-dire*] of the author, to all the idiomatic resources of the poet, of the language, and so forth, and, *on the other hand*, a disseminal reading-writing that, endeavoring to take all this into account, to account for all this, to respect its necessity, also directs itself [*se porte*] toward an irreducible remainder or excess. The excess of this remainder escapes any gathering in a hermeneutic. This hermeneutic is made necessary, and also possible, by the excess. Likewise, excess here makes possible, among other things, the trace of the poetic work, its abandonment or its survival, beyond any signatory and any specific reader. Without this remainder, there wouldn't even be the *Anspruch*, the injunction, the call, the provocation that sings or makes one sing in any poem, in what one could, with Celan, name "Singbarer Rest," "Singable Remnant," the title or the *incipit* of another poem from *Atemwende*.[28]

Of course, we must do everything to attempt to know the determinable meaning of this poem that ends or is signed in this way: "Die Welt ist fort, ich muß dich tragen." But even supposing that we knew how to comprehend and identify what Celan *meant to say*, supposing that we knew what dated event, in the world or in his life, he is bearing witness to, that we knew to whom he dedicates or addresses the poem, who the *I*, the *he*, or the *you* is for the poem as a whole and, for this may be different in each of its lines, well, even then we wouldn't exhaust the trace of this remainder, the very remaining of this remainder, which makes the poem both readable and unreadable to *us*. Besides, who is this "us"? What is its place, since it is certainly called but keeps silent, or, in any case, never presents itself *as such* in this poem, which always and only names *I*, *you*, and *he*. Its *shibboleth* is exposed to us and escapes from us, it awaits us; we are still awaiting one another, precisely where "Niemand / zeugt für den / Zeugen"; "No one / bears witness for the / witness."[29]

On the edge of an abyss, after the blank space of a pause of perhaps infinite duration, the last breath, the expiration of the poem, "Die Welt ist fort, ich muß dich tragen," is no doubt a line that appears disjoined. But it is also adjoined and conjoined by Celan, by the oeuvre that he bequeathed to us. For Celan fixed the form of this oeuvre in the public realm, even though this line disjoined from the poem could have appeared elsewhere, in which case it would not have lost its resources of meaning and would have called for other readings. The breath of this sigh, in *Atemwende*, is, certainly, the support, in the sense of the medium (Gadamer would perhaps say, and perhaps too quickly, the *subject* of the poem), but, in its very notation, in the music borne by it, it is sustained, supported, even prompted by what precedes, announces, and engenders it.

Now, to begin with the surest and simplest of observations, the formal arrangement of *thirteen* lines *plus one*—let us pay attention to this—seems remarkably skillful. In the orchestral architecture of its composition, I will pick out just four principal traits.

1. Grammatically, each of its verbs is conjugated in the *present* tense. Everything happens as if speech never left the presence of a present, even if—I'll get there in an instant—this grammatical appearance conceals the very heterogeneous temporalities it actually puts into operation.

2. Among these present tenses, but in a four-time rhythm, the punctuation marks the poem in a very visible fashion, visually differentiating it in its layout: (a) a *colon* [deux points] after the first stanza (so that, after a sort of implicit "that is to say," the second appears as the explanation or translation of the first); (b) a *period* [un point] after the second stanza, which comes to close a presentation; (c) a *question mark* [point d'interrogation] after the third stanza of three lines, the

poem's only question; (d) a *final period* [un point final], at the end, after the sentence, the *Spruch* of the *Anspruch*, the sentence, decision, or final appeal, the saying or the dict, indeed, the verdict of the poem, which looks like a *veridictum*, the truth of the *Dichtung*.

3. If, after the grammatical verb tense and the punctuation, we analyze the alternation of grammatical persons and personal pronouns, we will notice that, between the initial *sich* and the final *dich*, *er* follows *ich* ("brenn ich . . . Wo- / gegen / rennt er nicht?") in an interro-negative convolution. This interro-negative form or turn of phrase imprints upon the whole poem a torsion, I will even say a convulsive torment that leaves in advance its painful mark in the signature of the last line.

4. Finally, whether one analyzes them for the tense of their utterance or for the time of their statements, all of these grammatical present forms refer not only to different presents but, each time and for each one, to radically heterogeneous temporalities, to incommensurable chronological calendars or timetables that remain irreducibly anachronous to each other. And therefore untranslatable. Disproportioned. Untranslatable the one into the other, without analogy. In other words, one can only *attempt* to translate them, the one into the other. That is no doubt what this poem itself does, what it writes, what it signs and enjoins. Thus the poem happens by dint of translating itself—by pushing to the point of breathlessness the "infinite process" of translation we were talking about, if I can still say this in French, *tout à l'heure*, just now.[30] What comes to pass between its four disjoined and adjoined temporalities, which are attuned to their disadjoined writing?

A. First, without verb, the mute and silent presence of a *tableau* (image or painting):

GROSSE, GLÜHENDE WÖLBUNG
mit dem *sich*
hinaus- und hinweg-
wühlenden Schwarzgestirn-Schwarm:

B. Then, an *action*: the present performative of a first person:

der verkieselten Stirn eines Widders
brenn *ich* dies Bild ein, zwischen
die Hörner, darin,
im Gesang der Windungen, das
Mark der geronnenen
Herzmeere schwillt.

After the tableau, in the background of the *tableau*, but also in order to describe or explain the action of which it is like theatrical scenery, after the colon, an action presents itself as the duration of a narrative sequence.

C. After the tableau *and* the action, after the scenery and a sort of performative narrative, everything points to a negative question, distinguished by the question mark

Wo-
gegen
rennt *er* nicht an?

D. Finally, feigning, at the very least, to be the indirect response to a negative, worried, question, between the dread and the admiration before what appears so *unheimlich*, here is the present of responsibility, the sentence between the duty and the promise to carry the other, to carry *you*, the truth of the verdict on the edge of the end of the world

Die Welt ist fort, *ich* muß *dich* tragen.

One could pursue the analysis of this formal arrangement, and, to take one possible example among so many others, bend one's ear toward what could be called a syllabary put on the airwaves. Its letters are murmured, whispered, breathed out, sighing or whistling: between the *sch*—between (*zwischen*) schwa- and schwi (*Schwarzgestirn, Schwarm, zwischen, schwillt*)—the *w* (*Wölbung, weg, wühlenden, Welt*), and in still more determined fashion, the *wi* (*Widders, Windungen, schwillt*).

This formal analysis can be taken very far. It must, in fact. But it hardly seems risky. It belongs to the order of calculable guarantees and decidable evidence. It is not the same for the hermeneutical response to the *Anspruch* of the poem or the interior dialogue of the reader or counter-signatory. This response, this responsibility, can be pursued to infinity, in uninterrupted fashion, going from meaning to meaning, from truth to truth, with no calculable law other than that which the letter and the formal arrangement of the poem assign to it. But even though overseen by the same law, forever subjected to it, every bit as responsible, the experience that I call disseminal undergoes and takes on, in and through the hermeneutic moment itself, the test of an interruption, of a caesura or of an ellipsis, of an inaugural cut or opening. Such a gaping belongs neither to the meaning, nor to the phenomenon, nor to the truth, but, by making these possible in their remaining, it marks in the poem the hiatus of a wound whose lips will never close, will never draw together. These lips form around a speaking mouth that, even when it keeps silent, appeals to the other without condition, in the language of a hospitality that can no longer be subject to a decision. Because these lips will never again join, because the joining-together of what is to be joined no longer benefits from the assurance of a saturable context, the process remains forever infinite, certainly, but this time in discontinuous fashion. That is to say, differently finite and infinite. It is perhaps there that, alone in the distancing of the world, the poem hails or blesses, bears (*trägt*) the other, I mean "you"—as one might bear the grief of mourning or else bear a child, from conception through gestation to its delivery into the world. In gestation. This poem is the "you" and the "I" that is addressed to "you," but also to any other.

IV

Let's try now to be faithful, as much as is possible, to the hermeneutical demand itself, but also to this singular alterity that carries the demand itself beyond itself, in itself beyond itself. Let's timidly start out by reading the constellation of this poem, which is also the poem of a certain constellation, the configuration of stars in the sky, above the earth, even beyond the world. If this constellation never really gathers together, it seems promised or heralded in the first stanza, the one I have termed the tableau. Luminous, radiant, twinkling, incandescent, the arching of the celestial vault (*Grosse glühende Wölbung*) is animated with animal life. The black, star-spangled swarm carries the poem away in a hurried, hurrying, headlong movement of properly *planetary errancy*. The Greek noun leaves its trace there. Errancy is bound to be planetary. *Planētēs* means "wandering," "nomadic," and it is sometimes said of errant animals, as a matter of fact. *Planētikos* means unstable, turbulent, agitated, unpredictable, irregular; *planos* is used to describe an errant course but also a digression, for example, in the articulation of a discourse, of a written text, and so also of a poem. If this constellation appears animated, even animal, is it only because of the swarm? No. It is also because a ram (*Widder*) will soon bound into the poem: sacrificial animal, battering ram, the bellicose ram [*bélier*] whose rush breaks down the doors or breaks through the high walls of fortified castles (*Mauerbrecher*); the ram is, in addition, an animal whose name is a sign of the zodiac (21st of March, Ram or Aries). The zodiac (from *zōdion*, the diminutive of *zōon*, animal) makes it possible to read [*lire*] both the hour [*l'heure*] (according to the light [*lueur*] that appears on the ecliptic plane) and the date. In the astral conjunction of a birth, the horoscope *shows*. As its name indicates, *horoscopy* lets *the hours be seen* by announcing the destiny of an existence. One is thus witness to the becoming-calendar of a celestial vault, whose tableau is the very background of the poem. Elided here is an interminable meditation about what Heidegger named datability (*Datierbarkeit*). In this calendar, one can always seek, find or never find, along a path I explored in "Shibboleth,"[31] all the secret dates (anniversaries, the returns of singular and crypted events, birth, death, etc.). We are unable to do here what we really *ought to* do, to wit, listen to this poem in the echo-chamber of the whole of Celan's work, through what he inherits while reinventing it, in each of its themes, tropes, terms even, which are sometimes forged or coupled in the unique occurrence of a poem. That could extend to a syllabary. To limit myself to one example among so many possible others, the zodiacal vault recalls or announces many other horoscopic constellations. Thus, in *Die Niemandsrose*, the poem "Und mit dem Buch aus Tarussa" (following its epigraph taken from Tsvetaeva: "All poets are Jews") opens with "Of the / constellation of Canis [*Vom / Sternbild des Hundes*]."[32] This time, the star is light-colored (*vom Hellstern darin*). It is perhaps a yellow star (my yellow spot, my blind spot, my Jew's spot, *mein Judenfleck*, as another poem by Celan puts it[33]). The ghetto is not far away. After an allusion to the three stars of Orion's belt (*drei Gürtelsternen Orions*), Celan mentions again the "map of the sky [*auf der Himmelskarte*]." In "Hüttenfenster" ("Tabernacle Window"), here is how man would dwell as poet if all poets were Jews:

geht zu Ghetto und Eden, pflückt	goes to ghetto and Eden, gathers
das Sternbild zusammen, das er,	the constellation which they,
der Mensch, zum Wohnen	humankind, need for dwelling,
braucht, hier,	here,
unter Menschen	among humankind[34]

After the colon, as if to narrate the action that unfolds against the background or, rather, under the backdrop of this celestial vault teeming with animal life, here is the six-line stanza, the longest. Its plurivocity would demand hours and years of decipherment. It would be necessary to quote from one end to the other, among other things, both the Bible and Celan's corpus. The silicified forehead of the ram recalls, first, the black constellation (*Stirn, Schwartzgestirn*) of the celestial vault, then also the motif of petrification we saw earlier (*Versteinerten Segen*), a motif whose spectacular recurrence can be followed throughout Celan's work.

On the forehead of this enigmatic ram (because he could also be — this is one of the meanings of *Widder*—a sphinx-ram whose message remains to be deciphered), what is this image, this tableau (*Bild*) that "I" stamp, inscribe, and sign with fire ("brenn ich dies Bild ein"), between the horns? Surely, this inscription can always be a figure or a form (*Bild*) of the poem itself, which produces *itself* by *saying*, in an auto-deictic and performative fashion, as it were, its signature or its sealed secret, its seal. The allusion to song, indeed, to turns of phrase, to tropes and strophes or stanzas ("im Gesang der Windungen") cannot help but say something too about the poem in general, and singularly about *this* poem. There is no auto-telia closed upon itself in this hypothesis, certainly, but, while never forgetting it, let us not stop there for too long. Between the most animalistic life, which is named more than once, and the death or mourning that haunts the last line ("Die Welt ist fort, ich muß dich tragen"), the ram, its horns and the burning, recall and revive, no doubt, the moment of a sacrificial scene in the landscape of the Old Testament. More than one holocaust. Substitution of the ram. Burning. The binding of Isaac (Genesis 22). After having said a second time "Here I am," when the angel sent by God suspends the knife Abraham had raised to slit Isaac's throat, Abraham turns around and sees a ram caught by its horns in a bush. He offers it as a holocaust in the place of his son. God then promises to bless him and to multiply his seed like the stars of heaven, perhaps also like the stars of the first stanza. They can also become, in the poem, terrible yellow stars. And it is again a ram, in addition to a young bull, that God, speaking to Moses after the death of Aaron's two sons, commands Aaron to offer as holocaust in the course of a grand scene of atonement for the impurities, infamies, and sins of Israel (Leviticus 16). The ram was often sacrificed on other occasions (peace offerings, offerings for atonement, to ask forgiveness, etc.). We have many representations of this in stone sculptures. Very often you see the ram's horns seeming to coil in upon themselves, perhaps on the animal's silicified forehead ("der verkieselten Stirn eines Widders"). Throughout the whole culture of the Old Testament, the horns of the ram become the instrument with which music prolongs breath and carries voice. In what resembles a song punctuated like a sentence, the summons blown from the *shofar* rises to the sky: it recalls the holocausts and resounds in the memory of all the Jews of the world. This song of heartrending joy is inseparable from the visible form that secures its passage: the strange spires, twists and turns, torsions or contortions of the horn's form. "Im Gesang der Windungen" perhaps alludes to this turned form of breath, I dare not say *Atemwende*. The most famous rite, but by no means the only one, is repeated on the first date of the calendar, on the Jewish New Year's Day, when the tale of the binding of Isaac is read in all the synagogues of the world (Genesis 22). The *shofar* also announces the end of Yom Kippur. Consequently, it is associated, for all the Jews of the world, with confession, with atonement, with forgiveness requested, granted, or refused. To others or to oneself. Between these two charged dates, between New Year's Day and the Day of Atonement, the writing of God can, from one hour to the next, in the book of life, carry some and not carry others. Every Jew feels he is on the edge of every thing, on the edge of the whole, between life and death, as if between rebirth and the end, between the world and the end of the world, that is, between the world and the mournful annihilation of the other or of himself.

What happens after the punctuation of this second stanza? The stanza ends with the first period in the poem, placed after the action or dramaturgy of a sacrificial operation that is organized by a poet in the first person, who stamps and burns, in the same gesture, his image ("brenn ich dies Bild"). After this first period, here is the question, and the poem's only question mark: "Wo- / gegen / rennt er nicht an?" If the alliteration recalls the violence of the sacrifice ("das Mark der *geronnenen* Herzmeere schwillt"), the charge or battering of the ram could describe the movement of the animal just as well as that of the battering ram, the wooden beam, the tree trunk. Their stroke, their pushing, their rush, precipitates them, headlong, to attack or defend themselves, in order to weaken the adversaries' defenses. There is war, and the ram, the ram made of flesh or of wood, the ram on earth or in the sky, throws itself into the fray. It strikes out so as to strike down the adversary. It is a charge ("In- / to what / does he not charge?" to quote Michael Hamburger's judicious translation). Is not this *charge*—the ambiguity between languages here creates more than one opportunity—also an accusation or a price to pay ("charge," in English), and thus the discharge of a debt or the atonement of a sin? Doesn't the ram charge the adversary, a sacrificer or a wall, with every crime? For the question, as we noted earlier, is in the interro-negative form: Against what does he *not* strike? Against what does he *not* charge? Able to butt in order to attack or to seek revenge, the ram can declare war or respond to sacrifice by protesting in opposition against it. Its burst of indignant incomprehension would not spare anything or anyone in the world. No one in the world is innocent, not even the world itself. One imagines the anger of Abraham's and Aaron's ram, the infinite revolt of the ram of all holocausts. But also, figuratively, the violent rebellion of all scapegoats, all substitutes. Why me? Their adversity, their adversary, would be everywhere. The frontline, the forehead of this protest would hurl the ram against sacrifice itself, against men and God. The ram would, finally, want to put an end to their common world. It would charge against everything and against whomever, in all directions, as if blinded by pain. The rhythm of this stanza, "Wo- / gegen / rennt / er nicht an?," articulates the staccato movement of these blows. When you recall that Aaron included young bulls in the sacrifice of the ram, you might think of the last rush of the animal before it is put to death. The toreador also resembles a sacrificing priest.

That makes for many hypotheses, and for much indecision. That remains forever the very element of reading. Its "infinite process." Caesura, hiatus, ellipsis—all are interruptions that at once open and close. They keep access to the poem forever at the threshold of its crypts (one among them, only one, would refer to a singular and secret experience, wholly other, whose constellation is accessible only through the testimony of the poet and a few others). The interruptions also open, in a disseminal and non-saturable fashion, onto unforeseeable constellations, onto so many other stars, some of which would perhaps still resemble the seed that Yahweh told Abraham, after the interruption of the sacrifice, he would multiply like the stars: the abandon of traces left behind is also the gift of the poem to all readers and counter-signatories, who, always under the law of the *trace at work*, and *of the trace as work*, would lead to or get led along a wholly other reading or counter-reading. Such reading will also be, from one language to the other sometimes, through the abyssal risk of translation, an incommensurable writing.

Isn't what is valid for the lines we've just quoted also valid, *a fortiori*, for the last line? "Die Welt ist fort, ich muß dich tragen" is the sentence Celan chose (by what decision? whence was it dictated to him?) to leave the last word, as if it were an eschatological signature. We can *pronounce* it in our turn, rightly, only after the most pronounced interruption, the longest one marked in the poem. We need to hold a long time, the time of our breath, we need to catch our breath, the profound respiration of a wholly other breath (it's like another turn, a revolution, a reversal of breath, *Atemwende*), in order to sigh or expire: "Die Welt ist fort, ich muß dich tragen." A possible answer to the question "Wo- / gegen / rennt er nicht an?" is perhaps there, but one will never know, and no one has the power to decide.

The sentence is all alone. It stands, it supports itself, it carries itself all alone, on a line between two abysses. Isolated, islanded, separated like an aphorism, the sentence no doubt says something essential about absolute solitude. When the world is no more, when it is on the way to being no longer *here but over there*, when the world is no longer near, when it is no longer right *here* (*∂a*), but over there (*fort*), when it is no longer even present there (*∂a*) but gone far away (*fort*), perhaps infinitely inaccessible, then I must carry *you*, you alone, you alone in me or on me alone.

Unless one inverts, around the pivotal axis of an "I must" (*ich muß*), the order of the propositions or of the two verbs (*sein* and *tragen*), that is, inverts the consequence of *if, then*: if (where) there is necessity or duty toward you, if (where) *I* must, myself, carry you, yourself, well, then, the world tends to disappear. The world is no longer there or no longer here, "Die Welt ist fort." As soon as I am obliged, from the instant when I am obliged *to you*, when I *owe*, when I owe it *to you*, owe it *to myself* to carry *you*, as soon as I speak to you and am responsible for you, or before you, there can no longer, essentially, be any world. No world can any longer support us, serve as mediation, as ground, as earth, as foundation or as alibi. Perhaps there is no longer anything but the abyssal altitude of a sky. I am alone in the world right where there is no longer any world. Or again: I am alone in the world as soon as I owe myself to you, as soon as you depend on me, as soon as I bear, and must assume, head to head or face to face, without third, mediator, or go-between, without earthly or wordly ground, the responsibility for which I must re-spond in front of you for you, and for which I must answer in front of you for you. I am alone with you, alone to you alone; we are alone: this declaration is also an engagement. All the protagonists of the poem are also its virtual signatories or counter-signatories, whether they are named or not: *ich*, *er*, *∂u*, the ram, Abraham, Isaac, Aaron, and the infinite seed of their descendants, even God, each addressing him or herself, when the world is *fort*, to the absolute singularity of the other. All the protagonists hear themselves called, as does then the reader or the receiver of the poem, myself, ourselves here, as soon as the poem is entrusted, sole survivor, to our care, and as soon as we must, in our turn, carry it, save it at any price, be it beyond the world. The poem still speaks of itself, certainly, but with neither autotelia nor self-sufficiency. On the contrary, we hear it entrust itself to the care of the other, to our care, and put itself secretly within the range of the other. To bear this poem is to put oneself within its grasp, to put it within the other's grasp, to give it to the other to bear.

V

I wouldn't want to abuse your patience. So as not to make myself too unbearable, I will hasten, in my turn, toward a simulacrum of conclusion by situating, on a virtual map, the *five* obligatory points of passage on a potentially infinite course, in an "infinite process," as Gadamer would have said. Two of these points would halt us forever at the word *tragen*, the three others would halt us evermore at the word *Welt*.

1. *Tragen*, first. What does this verb *tragen* signify? And what is it made to *do* here, for example, by signing this poem? No one will decide with total certainty concerning the destination of the final sentence, the good-bye or the sending off to the other. On the one hand, the *dich* can designate a living being, a human or non-human animal, whether *present* or not, including the poet, to whom the poem could also be addressed through a return apostrophe, and including the reader and any receiver of this trace in general. The *dich* can also designate a living being *to come*. The *I must* (*ich muß*) must necessarily be turned toward the future. It orients itself in thought, as Kant would say, toward the orient of what comes, remains to come, of what rises or ascends in the sky. Above the earth. *Tragen*, in everyday usage, also refers to the experience of *carrying* a child prior to its birth. Between the mother and the child, the one in the other and the one for the other, in this singular couple of solitary beings, in the shared solitude between one and two bodies, the world disappears, it is far away, it remains a quasi-excluded third. For the mother who carries the child, "Die Welt ist fort."

2. But, to continue, if *tragen* speaks the language of birth, if it must address itself to a living being present or to come, it can also be addressed to the dead, to the survivor or to the specter, in an experience that consists in carrying the other in the self, as one bears mourning—and melancholy.

3. Consequently, these *two* potential senses of *tragen* exchange their diverse possibilities with at least *three* ways of thinking the

world, three thought-worlds of the world, three manners in which the world is *fort*, there rather than here, far away, departed, suspended, neutralized—or absent and annihilated. "Die Welt ist fort": that can remain an essential and permanent truth, but it can also happen a single time, singularly, in a history, and this occurrence would then be recorded in a narrative, like an event, and entrusted to someone. The present tense of the poem ("Die Welt *ist* fort") does not permit us to decide between these two hypotheses. Likewise, "the world" can designate the totality of beings or "all the others," "everybody" (*tout le monde, alle Welt*), the world of human beings or the world of living beings.

Here I must, at least by algebraic economy, pronounce three great proper names whose discourses would be both confirmed and contested, *countersigned*, in a paradoxical sense of this word, by the sending of this poem. In the first place, the name of Freud, both because of the allusion that we have just made to mourning and melancholy, and in order to remove the analysis, albeit interminable, from the order of consciousness, from self-presence and from the ego, from all egology. According to Freud, mourning consists in carrying the other in the self. There is no longer any world, it's the end of the world, for the other at his death. And so I welcome in me this end of the world, I must carry the other and his world, the world in me: introjection, interiorization of remembrance (*Erinnerung*), and idealization. Melancholy welcomes the failure and the pathology of this mourning.[35] But if *I must* (and this is ethics itself) carry the other in me in order to be faithful to him, in order to respect his singular alterity, a certain melancholy must still protest against normal mourning. This melancholy must never resign itself to idealizing introjection. It must rise up against what Freud says of it with such assurance, as if to confirm the norm of normality. The "norm" is nothing other than the good conscience of amnesia. It allows us to *forget* that to keep the other within the self, *as oneself*, is already to *forget* the other. Forgetting begins there. Melancholy is therefore *necessary*. At this point, the suffering of a certain pathology dictates the law—and the poem dedicated to the other.

4. Isn't this retreat of the world, this distancing by which the world retreats to the point of the possibility of its annihilation, the most necessary, the most logical, but also the most insane experience of a transcendental phenomenology? In the famous paragraph 49 of

Ideas I, doesn't Husserl explain to us, in the course of the most rigorous demonstration, that access to the absolute egological consciousness, in its purest phenomenological sense, requires that the existence of the transcendent world be suspended in a radical *epokhē*? The hypothesis of the annihilation of the world does not threaten, by right and in its meaning, the sphere of phenomenological and pure egological experience. On the contrary, it would open access to this sphere: it would make such access thinkable in its phenomenal purity. The sending of our poem repeats without weakening this phenomenological radicalization. It pushes to the limit this experience of the possible annihilation of the world and of what remains of the world or still survives it, to wit, its sense for "me," for a pure *ego*. But on the eschatological edge of this extreme limit, the sending of our poem encounters what was also the most worrisome test for Husserlian phenomenology—for what Husserl called its "principle of principles." In this absolute solitude of the pure *ego*, when the world has retreated, when "Die Welt ist fort," the *alter ego* that is constituted in the *ego* is no longer accessible in an originary and purely phenomenological intuition. Husserl must concede this in his *Cartesian Meditations*. The *alter ego* is constituted only *by analogy*, by *appresentation*, indirectly, inside of me, who then carries it there where there is no longer a transcendent world. I must then carry it, carry *you*, there where the world gives way: that is my responsibility. But I can no longer carry the other or you, if *to carry* means to include in oneself, in the intuition of one's own egological consciousness. It's a question of carrying without appropriating to oneself. *To carry* now no longer has the meaning of "to comprise" [*comporter*], to include, to comprehend in the self, but rather *to carry oneself for bear oneself toward* [se porter vers] the infinite inappropriability of the other, toward the encounter with its absolute transcendence in the very inside of me, that is to say, in me outside of me. And I only am, I can only be, I *must* only be starting from this strange, dislocated bearing of the infinitely other in me. I must carry the other, and carry *you*, the other must carry me (for *dich* can designate *me* or designate the poet-signatory, to whom this discourse is also addressed in return), even there where the world is no longer between us or beneath our feet, no longer ensuring mediation or reinforcing a foundation for us. I am alone with the other, alone to him and for him, only for you, that is, yours: without world. I am left with the immediacy of the abyss that engages me on behalf of the other wherever the "I must"—"I must carry you"—

forever prevails over the "I am," over the *sum* and over the *cogito*. Before *I am*, I *carry*. Before *being me*, *I carry the other*. I carry *you* and must do so, I owe it to you. I remain *before* [*devant*], owing, in debt and owing to you before you. I must keep myself in your reach, but I must also be your grasp. Always singular and irreplaceable, these laws or injunctions remain untranslatable from one to the other, from some to others, from one language to another, but that makes them no less universal. *I must* translate, transfer, transport (*übertragen*) the untranslatable in another turn even where, translated, it remains untranslatable. This is the violent sacrifice of the passage beyond— *Übertragen: übersetzen*.

5. This poem says the world, the origin and the history of the world, the archeology and eschatology of the concept, the very *conception* of the world: how the world was *conceived*, how it is born and straightaway is no longer, how it goes away and leaves us, how its end is announced. The other proper name I must pronounce here is the name of someone with whom Gadamer's interior dialogue was, I believe, always engaged, in uninterrupted fashion, as was Celan's, before and after the caesura of *Todtnauberg*: Heidegger, the thinker of Being-in-the-world (*In-der-Welt-sein*), not only put forward, more than once, an indispensable meditation upon the genealogy— Christian or not—of the concept of *cosmos* and of world or of its "regulative idea" in the Kantian sense. He not only said the *welten* of the world, its becoming-worldly [*mondanisation*], indeed, its worldization or globalization [*mondialisation*]. He also made us think the re-moval or de-severance (*Ent-fernung*) that distances and dis-distances what is near. Let us recall also the lexicon that gathers around *tragen* (*Übertragung*, *Auftrag*, and *Austrag*), which, in *Identity and Difference*, not far from an allusion to the *Ent-fernung* that distances and disdistances by bringing near, names the in-between (*Zwischen*): "in which the overwhelming and the arrival are held toward one another, are borne away from and toward each other. The difference between Being and beings, as the differentiation between overwhelming and arrival, is the perdurance [*Austrag*] of the two in *unconcealing keeping in concealment*. . . . On our way there we think of the perdurance of overwhelming and arrival."[36]

Above all, Heidegger attempted to distinguish among what is *weltlos*, what is *weltarm*, and what is *weltbildend*. This is the only series of propositions I can retain here. It concerns a group of three "theses" that Heidegger presents, shortly after *Being and Time*, in a seminar from 1929–30 on the world, finitude, and solitude (*Welt-Endlichkeit-Einsamkeit*): "der Stein ist weltlos, das Tier ist weltarm, der Mensch ist weltbildend"; "the stone is without world, the animal is poor in world, the human is a builder of worlds."[37]

For reasons I cannot develop here, nothing appears to me more problematic than these theses.

But what would happen if, in our poem, the departure, the *Fort-sein* of the world, in its proper instance, did not answer to any of these theses or categories? What if the *Fort-sein* exceeded them, from a wholly other place? What if it were everything save deprived of the world (*weltlos*), poor in world (*weltarm*), or world-forming (*weltbildend*)? Isn't it the very thought of the world that we would then have to rethink, from this *fort*, and this *fort* itself from the "ich muß dich tragen"?

This is one of the questions that, appealing to him for help, I would have liked to ask Gadamer in the course of an interminable conversation. In order to orient our thinking, in order to help us with this fearsome task, I would have begun by recalling how much we need the other and how much we will still need him, need to carry him, to be carried by him, there where he speaks, in us before us.

Perhaps I should have, for all these reasons, begun by quoting Hölderlin, from "Die Titanen": "Denn keiner trägt das Leben allein"; "For no one bears this life alone."

6

The Truth That Wounds

From an Interview

Évelyne Grossman: I would like to talk now about the question of the secret and of the undecidable, of which you have often spoken, particularly in two recent texts, "Rams: Uninterrupted Dialogue — Between Two Infinities, the Poem" and the one to which I referred a moment ago, about Hélène Cixous, "Geneses, Genealogies, Genres, and Genius." In "Rams," you write this wonderful sentence about Gadamer's interpretation of a poem by Celan: "Without this threat, this risk, without this improbability, without this impossibility of proving—which must remain infinitely, and which must not be saturated or closed by any certainty—there would be neither reading nor giving nor blessing," and you add a little further on, "the future of interpretation [is bound] to a pensive and suspensive interruption." This resonates with what you were saying a moment ago: we do not provide the proof of what we interpret but, at the same time, there is a great force of certainty.

Jacques Derrida: I say this in a text about Celan, but I believe that it can, analogously, be extended to any reading, to the reading of any poet, of any poetic writing. There is in every poetic text, just as in every utterance, in every manifestation outside of literature, an inaccessible secret to which no proof will ever be adequate. In everyday life, for example, I know that I have often surprised my students when I tell them: "One will never be able to prove that someone has lied." One will never be able to prove it, neither in everyday life nor in court. Testimony that is given may be *false*, but one can never prove that there has been *false testimony*. Why? Because, on the other side, on the side of the witness, as on the side of the poet, there is always the recourse that consists in saying: What I said is perhaps false, I was mistaken, but I did so in good faith. If that is so, then there is no perjury, no false testimony, and no lie. If I say something false but without the intention of deceiving, I am not lying. One will never be able to prove in an objectivable[1] way that someone has lied. This someone will always be able to say: I was in good faith. One will never be able to *prove* — what we call "prove" — that someone is in bad faith. This stems from the fact that the other is secret. I cannot be in the other's place, in the head of the other. I will never be equal to the secret of otherness. The secret is the very essence of otherness.

Coming back to the poetico-hermeneutic question, there is in all texts, especially in those of Celan, who is exemplary in this regard, a secret, that is to say, an overabundance of meaning, which I will never be able to claim to have exhausted. In the case of Celan, there may be an allusion to a referent from his life that is hidden or encrypted through numerous layers of hidden literary references. I received a letter about "Rams" a few days ago from the translator of Nelly Sachs. She says many generous things about the book but also that in all the elements I analyze there are echoes, affinities, and consonances with Nelly Sachs's poems. She was one of the friends and poets closest to Celan. So, behind this or that word, there may possibly be a greeting to Nelly Sachs or maybe a reference to a personal experience about which Celan never said anything to anyone, or to some trip or to some proper name. This neither discourages nor prevent interpretation. On the contrary, it gets interpretation going. This is the distinction I have been trying to make, for quite a long time now, going back to "The Double Session," between dissemination and thematic plurivocity.[2] One can inventory a multiplicity of meanings in a text, in a poem, in a word, but there will always be an excess that is not of the order of meaning, that is not just another meaning. There is, first off, spacing, since we were talking of space, spacing that does not pertain to meaning. The way in which Celan spaces his poem — What is it? What does it mean? Rhythm, caesura, hiatus, interruption: how is one to *read* them? There is therefore a dissemination irreducible to hermeneutics in Gadamer's sense. At this point, in "Rams," I play a game of approbation with Gadamer (I "agree" that he is "right") and *at the same time* there are perspectives that open up toward interruption. There, too, as we were saying a moment ago, not only does this not discourage reading but, for me, it is the condition of reading. If I could prove something concerning a Celan poem, could say, as many people do, "See, here is what it means"—for example, it is about Auschwitz, or Celan is about the Shoah (all obviously true!)—if I could prove it is that and only that, I would have destroyed Celan's poem. The poem would be of limited interest if all it amounted to was what it meant, what one believes it means. I try therefore to make myself listen for something that I cannot hear or understand, attentive to marking the limits of my reading in my reading. This comes down to saying: Here is what I believe one can reconstitute, what that could mean, why it is captivating and beautiful and strong, while leaving the unsaid intact, inaudible. That will, moreover, authorize other readings. My reading is modest and does not exclude many other readings of this poem. It is an ethics or a politics of reading, also.

ÉG: Still regarding Celan and "Rams," you evoke at one moment the wound one inflicts on a poem by reading according to this "experience that I call disseminal" of interpretive reading, a wound that is metamorphosed into the "speaking mouth" of the poem: "Such a gaping belongs neither to the meaning, nor to the phenomenon, nor to the truth, but, by making them possible in their remaining, it marks in the poem the hiatus of a wound whose lips will never close, will never draw together. These lips form around a speaking mouth that, even when it keeps silent, appeals to the other without condition, in the language of a hospitality that can no longer be subject to a decision." Is this mouth-wound for you a simple metaphor, or do you want really to suggest that the poem speaks to us through this mouth we have opened in it?

JD: The signature of a poem, like that of any text, is a wound. What opens, what does not heal, the hiatus, is indeed a mouth that speaks there where *it is wounded*. In the place of the lesion. In each poem by Celan, there is at least one wound, his or that of another (this is also why in "Shibboleth: For Paul Celan" I carefully followed the themes of circumcision, the mark, the incision). When one reads the poem, when one attempts to explain it, to discuss it, to interpret it, one speaks in one's own turn, one forges other phrases, poetic or not. Even when one recognizes—and this is my case—that on the side of the poem there is a wounded mouth, speaking, one still always risks suturing it, closing it. Hence the duty of the reader-interpreter is to write while letting the other speak, or so as to let the other speak. It is this that I also call, as I was saying a moment ago, *counter-signing*. That is a word Ponge also put to beautiful use, one that I remarked on, I believe, in *Signsponge*. One writes some other thing, but that is in order to try to let the other sign: it is the other who writes, the other who signs.

ÉG: But for that one must first of all wound it . . .

JD: The wound consists precisely in claiming to discover and to master meaning, in claiming to suture or to saturate, to fill this emptiness, to close the mouth. Imagine that someone claimed to have said everything that needed to be said on the subject of this poem or that line of Celan, that someone claimed to have exhausted the subject. That would be terrifying; it would be the destruction of the poem. In order *not* to destroy the poem, one must—and this is what I would like to do—try to speak of it in such a way, as Celan himself says, that the poem still speaks. It still speaks. One must speak in such a way as to give it the chance to speak. We are talking about this in reference to interpretive reading and the hermeneutics of the poem, but this also holds for life in general. One speaks, trying to listen to the other. One *should* speak while leaving to the other the chance to speak, while giving the floor to the other. It is a question of rhythm, of time: not to speak too much, thereby imposing silence on the other, and not to remain too silent. All this has to be negotiated.

ÉG: There is, nonetheless, something violent in the act of interpretation. Here you are telling me: it is about leaving speech [to the other]. However, the wound you describe in "Rams" also presupposes, it seems to me, a gesture of perforation, of opening that wounds: you evoke the lips of a wound that give to the poem this mouth through which it speaks.

JD: That is another dimension of violence, different from the one I was just speaking of: the risk of saturating, of suturing. One can also take the risk, and it is sometimes an interesting risk, of writing about a poem something of which the signatory was, at bottom, unaware, did not mean, did not master—in any case, would have been surprised to hear said of his own poem. I do not know what Celan would have thought of my reading. I have no idea, but the desire to surprise him with the gesture of my reading is not foreign to me. If I do something, it must be something that apprises or surprises, teaches something to the reader but also to the *I* who signs the text.

You saw that the position of the *I* and of the *You* is very complicated in this poem. Who is *I*? Who signs this poem? What is the literary signature and what is the non-literary signature of this poem? It is very difficult to say. Even impossible. Hence, an interpretation that surprises presupposes violence with regard to the conscious signatory of the poem: you meant what you did not know you wanted to say; you will have said more than you think or something other than you think. That is what analysis is, be it deconstructive or not. You said something you did not think you said or that you did not mean to say. It is violent, that's true.

ÉG: But is it also, I imagine, a physical wounding of the words of the poem? Is the wound brought to bear on the very body of writing that makes up the poem?

JD: There is already a "physical" wound, for example, in the fact of writing (in) another language. For example, I write in French about a German poem that is very difficult to translate. In this sense, the body of Celan's words is violently taken to task and exiled in another language—one he knew very well but which in the end is another language than that of the poem. It is a body, yes, thus there is love and violence there. I do not know if this is what you understand by "body of writing," but it is what makes the poem above all unique. Like anyone's body, it is unique. Once published, the poem must be respected as unique. It takes place only once. Even if one can connect certain of its elements with the rest of the Celan corpus, the Hölderlin corpus, the Nelly Sachs corpus, and so many others, the poem itself is unique. What I call here "the body of the poem" is this uniqueness incorporated, incarnated, in what one used to call the "signifiers," in the graphemes, which in themselves cannot be translated. To translate is to lose the body. The most faithful translation is violent: one loses the body of the poem, which exists only in German and once only. It is a hand-to-hand, bodily struggle. It is an attack. Translation is desired by the poet—he wants to be read, to be translated—but I recognize that there is aggression and hand-to-hand struggle. I too try to write a text that, without wanting to take this too far, ought to remain unique, in a certain manner. It is a certain reading, it happened to me once, I did it once, it is a text by me. To which I will add, it being a matter of the body, that when I say "the poem of Celan belongs to the German language," this is already a simplification. Celan's language is itself a bodily struggle with the German language, which he deforms, transforms, which he assaults, and which he incises. He wrestles with the body of the German language. In my own modest way, I do likewise in French. The struggle is not just between two languages, but between two languages each of which is caught up in its own civil war. There is a hand-to-hand, bodily struggle "within" every national language. Each time there is writing. No writing opens a passage without this bodily violence. How otherwise does one explain the charge — others would say the investment — the libidinal, even narcissistic charge that everyone brings to his own texts? It is my body, this is my body. Every poem says, "This is my body," and the rest: drink it, eat it, keep it in memory of me. There is a Last Supper in every poem, which says: This is my body, here and now. And you know what comes next: passions, crucifixions, executions. Others would also say resurrections . . .

December 12, 2003

Reference Matter

Appendix: The Meridian

PAUL CELAN
Translated by Jerry Glenn

Ladies and gentlemen!

Art, you will remember, has the qualities of the marionette and the iambic pentameter. Furthermore —and this characteristic is attested in mythology, in the story of Pygmalion and his creature —it is incapable of producing offspring.

In this form art constitutes the subject of a conversation which takes place in a room, and not in the Conciergerie, a conversation which, as we see, could be indefinitely prolonged if nothing were to intervene.

But something does intervene.

Art reappears. It is found in another work by Georg Büchner, in *Wozzek*, where it appears as one of many nameless characters, and "in the more livid light of a thunderstorm" —if I might be permitted to convey a phrase coined by Moritz Heiman in reference to *Danton's Death*. Art makes another appearance, unchanged, although the times are totally different, introduced by a barker. Here it has no connection with a "glowing," "surging," and "shining" creation as it did in the conversation mentioned above. This time art appears with a member of the animal kingdom and the "nothin'" that this creature "has on." This time art appears in the form of a monkey. It is, however, one and the same—we are immediately able to recognize it by the "coat and trousers." And art is also introduced to us in a third work by Büchner, *Leonce and Lena*. Time and light are here no longer recognized. We find ourselves "in flight to Paradise"; "all clocks and calendars" are soon to be "destroyed" or "proscribed." But first "two persons, one of each sex" are presented, "two world-famous robots have arrived," and a person who announces that he is "perhaps the third and most remarkable of the two" challenges us in a raspy tone to gaze with astonishment at what is before our eyes: "Nothing but art and mechanism, nothing but cardboard and watch springs."

Art appears here with a larger retinue than before, but we immediately see that it is in the company of its own kind; it is the same art, the same art we have seen before. Valerio is but another name for the hawker.

Art, ladies and gentlemen, with all that pertains to it and remains to be applied to it, is indeed a problem, as one sees, a problem which is hardy, long-lived, and transformable—that is to say, eternal.

A problem which allows a mortal, Camille, and a person who can be understood only in the context of his death, Danton, to string words together at great length. It is easy enough to talk about art.

But when art is being talked about there is always someone present who doesn't listen very carefully.

More precisely: someone who hears and listens and looks . . . and then doesn't know what the conversation was all about. But who hears the speaker, who "sees him speak," who has perceived language and form, and at the same time—what doubt could there be in the world of this drama?—at the same time has perceived breath, that is, direction and fate.

This person is—as you have guessed, since she, who is so often quoted, and rightly so, makes her appearance before you every year—this person is Lucile.

That which intervened during the conversation relentlessly presses on. It arrives with us at the Place de la Révolution, "the carts are driven up and stop."

Those who made the ride are there, Danton, Camille, the others. Even here they are not at a loss for words, words rich in artistry, which are effectively disposed, and here Büchner is often able to rely on direct quotations. There is talk of going-to-our-deaths-together,

Fabre even wants to be able to die "twice over." Everyone is in top form. Only a couple of voices, "a few"—nameless—"voices" observe that they've seen it all before and find it rather boring.

And here, as the end approaches, in the long drawn-out moments, Camille—no, not he, not he himself, but merely one who rode along—this Camille is dying a theatrical—one is almost tempted to say iambic—death, which only two scenes later, on the basis of a dictum so foreign, yet so appropriate, to him, we recognize as his own death. As pathos and bathos surround Camille and confirm the triumph of "puppet" and "wire," Lucile appears, the one who is blind to art, this same Lucile, for whom language is something personal, something perceptible. She appears once again, with her sudden "Long live the king!"

After all the words spoken on the platform (the scaffold)—what a statement!

It is a counterstatement, a statement that severs the "wire," that refuses to bow before the "loiterers and parade horses of history." It is an act of freedom. It is a step.

To be sure, it sounds like an expression of allegiance to the ancien régime—and that might not be a coincidence, in view of what I am venturing to say about the subject now, today. But these words—please allow one who also grew up with the writings of Peter Kropotkin and Gustav Landauer expressly to emphasize the point—these words are not a celebration of the monarchy and a past which should be preserved.

They are a tribute to the majesty of the absurd, which bears witness to mankind's here and now.

That, ladies and gentlemen, has no universally recognized name, but it is, I believe . . . literature.

"Alas, art." As you see, I remain entangled in these words of Camille.

I am well aware that it is possible to read these words in various ways, one can insert different accents: the acute of the present, the gravis of the historical (including the literary historical), the circumflex—a mark indicating length—of the eternal.

I insert—I have no choice—I insert the acute.

Art—"alas, art": it possesses, aside from its ability to transform, the gift of ubiquity; it is also found in "Lenz," and here—I must emphasize this point—as in *Danton's Death*, it is an episode in nature.

At table Lenz recaptured his good mood; literature was the topic of conversation and he was in his element. . . .

". . . The feeling that there is life in the thing that has been created is more important than these two factors. Indeed, it is the sole criterion in matters of art."

My guilty conscience with regard to the gravis forces me to make you aware of the passages I have just quoted. Above all, these lines have significance for literary history. They must be read in conjunction with the conversation from *Danton's Death* which I have already cited. In them one finds a concise formulation of Büchner's conception of aesthetics. When one leaves them and Büchner's "Lenz" fragment behind, it is but a short distance to Reinhold Lenz, the author of the "Notes on the Theater," and by way of him, the historical Lenz, still further back to Mercier's "Élargissez l'Art," which is of great significance in the history of literature. This maxim opens vistas. It is naturalism, it anticipates Gerhart Hauptmann. And in it are contained the social and political roots of Büchner's thought.

Ladies and gentlemen, I have appeased my conscience, if only temporarily, by making this point. But at the same time it disquiets my conscience anew—it also shows you that something continues to concern me, something that seems to be related to art.

I am also seeking it here, in "Lenz"—I am taking the liberty of calling this to your attention.

Lenz, that is, Büchner, has—"alas, art"—disdainful words for "Idealism" and its "wooden puppets." He contrasts them—and they are followed by the unforgettable lines about the "life of the most humble," the "movements," the "suggestions," the "subtle, scarcely perceptible play of their facial expressions"—he contrasts them with that which is natural, with all living creatures. And he illustrates this conception of art by relating a recent experience:

Yesterday, as I was walking along the edge of the valley, I saw two girls sitting on a rock; one was putting up her hair and the other was helping; and the golden hair was hanging down, and the face, pale and serious, and yet so young, and the black dress, and the other one so absorbed in helping her. The most beautiful, the most intimate pictures of the Old German School can convey but the vaguest impression of such a scene. At times one might wish to be a Medusa's head so as to be able to transform such a group into stone, and call out to the people.

Ladies and gentlemen, please take note: "One would like to be a Medusa's head," in order to . . . comprehend that which is natural as that which is natural, by means of art!

One would like to, not: *I* would like to.

Here we have stepped beyond human nature, gone outward, and entered a mysterious realm, yet one turned toward that which is human, the same realm in which the monkey, the robots, and, accordingly . . . alas, art, too, seem to be at home.

This is not the historical Lenz speaking, it is Büchner's Lenz. We hear Büchner's voice: even here art preserves something mysterious for him.

Ladies and gentlemen, I have inserted the acute. But we must not deceive ourselves. I have approached Büchner, consciously, if not voluntarily, with my question about art and literature—one question among many—in order to identify his question.

But as you see, whenever art makes an appearance Valerio's raspy tone cannot be ignored.

Büchner's voice leads me to the suspicion that these are the most ancient mysteries. The reason for my persistent lingering over this subject today is probably to be found in the air—in the air which we have to breathe.

And I must now ask if the works of Georg Büchner, the poet of all living beings, do not contain a perhaps muted, perhaps only half conscious, but on that account no less radical—or for precisely that reason in the most basic sense a radical calling-into-question of art, a calling-into-question from this direction? A calling-into-question, to which all contemporary literature must return if it is to continue posing questions? To rephrase and anticipate myself somewhat: may we proceed from art as something given, something to be taken for granted, as is now often done; should we, in concrete terms, above all—let's say—follow Mallarmé to his logical conclusion?

I have gotten ahead of myself (not far enough, I know), and now I will return to Büchner's "Lenz," specifically to that—episodic— conversation held "at table," during which Lenz re-captured his "good mood."

Lenz spoke for a long time, "smiling one minute, serious the next." And now, when the conversation is over, a statement is made about him, about the person who is concerned with problems of art, but also about the artist Lenz: "He had completely forgotten himself."

As I read that, I find myself thinking of Lucile; I read: *He*, he himself. Whoever has art before his eyes and on his mind—I am now referring to the story about Lenz—has forgotten himself. Art produces a distance from the I. Art demands here a certain distance, a certain path, in a certain direction.

And literature? Literature, which, after all, must travel the path of art? In that case we would in fact be shown here the path to the Medusa's head and the robot!

At this point I am not searching for a way out, I am just asking, along the same line, and also, I believe, in the line suggested in the Lenz fragment.

Perhaps—I'm just asking—perhaps literature, in the company of the I which has forgotten itself, travels the same path as art, toward that which is mysterious and alien. And once again—but where? but in what place? but how? but as what?—it sets itself free.

In that case art would be the path traveled by literature—nothing more and nothing less.

I know, there are other, shorter paths. But after all literature, too, often shoots ahead of us. *La poésie, elle aussi, brûle nos étapes.*

I will take leave of the one who has forgotten himself, the one concerned with art, the artist. I think that I have encountered poetry in Lucile, and Lucile perceives language as form and direction and breath. Here, too, in this work of Büchner, I am searching for the very same thing. I am searching for Lenz himself, I am searching for him, as a person, I am searching for his form: for the sake of the location of literature, the setting free, the step.

Büchner's "Lenz," ladies and gentlemen, remained a fragment. Would it be proper for us to search out the historical Lenz, in order to learn which direction his existence took?

"His existence was an inescapable burden.—So his life went on." Here the story breaks off.

But literature, like Lucile, attempts to see form in its direction; literature shoots ahead. We know *where* his life went, and how it *went on.*

"Death"—one reads in a work about Jakob Michael Reinhold Lenz by the Moscow academician M. N. Rosanow which appeared in Leipzig in 1909—"Death the redeemer was not slow in coming. Lenz was found dead on one of the streets of Moscow during the night of May 23–24, 1792. A nobleman paid for his burial expenses. His final resting place is unknown."

So *his* life had *gone on*.

This person Lenz: the true Lenz, Büchner's Lenz, the one we were able to recognize on the first page of the story, the Lenz who "walked through the mountains on the 20th of January"—this person, and not the artist and the one concerned with questions about art—this person as an I.

Can we now, perhaps, find the place where strangeness was present, the place where a person succeeded in setting himself free, as an—estranged—I? Can we find such a place, such a step?

". . . but now and then he experienced a sense of uneasiness because he was not able to walk on his head."—That is Lenz. That is, I am convinced, Lenz and his step, Lenz and his "Long live the king!"

". . . but now and then he experienced a sense of uneasiness because he was not able to walk on his head."

Whoever walks on his head, ladies and gentlemen, whoever walks on his head has heaven beneath him as an abyss.

Ladies and gentlemen, nowadays it is fashionable to reproach literature with its "obscurity." Permit me now, abruptly—but hasn't something suddenly appeared on the horizon?—permit me now to quote a maxim by Pascal, a maxim that I read some time ago in Leo Schestow: "Ne nous reprochez pas le manque de clarté puisque nous en faisons profession!" That is, I believe, if not the inherent obscurity of poetry, the obscurity attributed to it for the sake of an encounter—from a great distance or sense of strangeness possibly of its own making.

But there are perhaps two kinds of strangeness, in one and the same direction—side by side.

Lenz—that is, Büchner—has here gone one step further than Lucile. His "Long live the king" no longer consists of words. It has become a terrible silence. It robs him—and us—of breath and speech.

Literature: that can signify a turn-of-breath. Who knows, perhaps literature travels its path—which is also the path of art—for the sake of such a breath turning? Perhaps it succeeds, since strangeness, that is, the abyss *and* the Medusa's head, the abyss *and* the robots, seem to lie in the same direction—perhaps it succeeds here in distinguishing between strangeness and strangeness, perhaps at precisely this point the Medusa's head shrivels, perhaps the robots cease to function— for this unique, fleeting moment? Is perhaps at this point, along with the I—with the estranged I, set free *at this point* and *in a similar manner*—is perhaps at this point an Other set free?

Perhaps the poem assumes its own identity as a result . . . and is accordingly able to travel other paths, that is, the paths of art, again and again—in this art-less, art-free manner?

Perhaps.

Perhaps one can say that every poem has its "20th of January"? Perhaps the novelty of poems that are written today is to be found in precisely this point: that here the attempt is most clearly made to re- main mindful of such dates?

But are we all not descended from such dates? And to which dates do we attribute ourselves?

But the poem does speak! It remains mindful of its dates, but—it speaks, to be sure, it speaks only in its own, its own, individual cause.

But I think—and this thought can scarcely come as a surprise to you—I think that it has always belonged to the expectations of the poem, in precisely this manner, to speak in the cause of the strange— no, I can no longer use this word—in precisely this manner to speak *in the cause of an Other*—who knows, perhaps in the cause of a *wholly Other*.

This "who knows," at which I see I have arrived, is the only thing I can add—on my own, here, today—to the old expectations.

Perhaps, I must now say to myself—and at this point I am making use of a well-known term—perhaps it is now possible to conceive a meeting of this "wholly Other" and an "other" which is not far re- moved, which is very near.

The poem tarries, stops to catch a scent—like a creature when confronted with such thoughts.

No one can say hqw long the pause in breath—the thought and the stopping to catch the scent—will last. The "Something quick," which has always been "outside," has gained speed; the poem knows this; but it continues to make for that "Other," which it considers to be attainable, capable of being set free, and, perhaps, unoccupied—and, accordingly, attuned—like Lucile, one might say—attuned to it, to the poem.

To be sure, there can be no doubt that the poem—the poem today—shows a strong inclination toward falling silent. And this, I believe, has only an indirect relationship to the difficulties of word selection (which should not be underestimated), the more pronounced vagrancies of syntax, or the more finely tuned sense of ellipsis.

It takes its position—after so many radical formulations, permit me to use one more—the poem takes its position at the edge of itself; in order to be able to exist, it without interruption calls and fetches itself from its now-no-longer back into its as-always.

But this as-always can be nothing more than verbal communication—not, then, the abstract concept of speech—and presumably a "correspondence to," and not only because this is suggested by another form of communication, a "correspondence with."

But language become reality, language set free under the sign of an individuation which is radical, yet at the same time remains mindful of the boundaries established for it by language, of the possibilities laid open for it by language.

This as-always of the poem can, to be sure, only be found in the poem of that person who does not forget that he speaks from under the angle of inclination of his existence, the angle of inclination of his position among all living creatures.

Then the poem would be—even more clearly than before—the language of an individual which has taken on form; and, in keeping with its innermost nature, it would also be the present, the here and now.

The poem is alone. It is alone and underway. Whoever writes it must remain in its company.

But doesn't the poem, for precisely that reason, at this point participate in an encounter—*in the mystery of an encounter*?

The poem wants to reach the Other, it needs this Other, it needs a vis á vis. It searches it out and addresses it.

Each thing, each person is a form of the Other for the poem, as it makes for this Other.

The poem attempts to pay careful attention to everything it encounters; it has a finer sense of detail, of outline, of structure, of color, and also of the "movements" and the "suggestions." These are, I believe, not qualities gained by an eye competing (or cooperating) with mechanical devices which are continually being brought to a higher degree of perfection. No, it is a concentration which remains aware of all of our dates.

"Attention"—permit me at this point to quote a maxim of Malebranche which occurs in Walter Benjamin's essay on Kafka: "Attention is the natural prayer of the soul."

The poem becomes—and under what conditions!—a poem of one who—as before—perceives, who faces that which appears. Who questions this appearing and addresses it. It becomes dialogue—it is often despairing dialogue.

Only in the realm of this dialogue does that which is addressed take form and gather around the I who is addressing and naming it. But the one who has been addressed and who, by virtue of having been named, has, as it were, become a thou, also brings its otherness along into the present, into this present. In the here and now of the poem it is still possible—the poem itself, after all, has only this one, unique, limited present—only in this immediacy and proximity does it allow the most idiosyncratic quality of the Other, its time, to participate in the dialogue.

When we speak with things in this manner we always find ourselves faced with the question of their whence and whither: a question which "remains open" and "does not come to an end," which points into openness, emptiness, freedom—we are outside, at a considerable distance.

The poem, I believe, also seeks this place.

The poem?
The poem with its images and tropes?

Ladies and gentlemen, what am I really speaking of, when, from *this* direction, in *this* direction, with *these* words, I speak of the poem—no, of *the* poem?
I am speaking of the poem which doesn't exist!
The absolute poem—no, it doesn't exist, it cannot exist.
But each real poem, even the least pretentious, contains this inescapable question, this incredible demand.

And what, then, would the images be?

That which is perceived and to be perceived one time, one time over and over again, and only now and only here. And the poem would then be the place where all tropes and metaphors are developed ad absurdum.

Topos study?

Certainly! But in light of that which is to be studied: in light of utopia.

And human beings? And all living creatures?

In this light.

Such questions! Such demands!

It is time to turn back.

Ladies and gentlemen, I have reached the conclusion — I have returned to the beginning.

Elargissez l'Art! This question comes to us with its mysteries, new and old. I approached Büchner in its company — I believed I would once again find it there.

I also had an answer ready, a "Lucilean" counterstatement; I wanted to establish something in opposition, I wanted to be there with my contradiction.

Expand art?

No. But accompany art into your own unique place of no escape. And set yourself free.

Here, too, in your presence, I have traveled this path.

It was a circle.

Art — and one must also include the Medusa's head, mechanization, robots; the mysterious, indistinguishable, and in the end perhaps the only strangeness — art lives on.

Twice, in Lucile's "Long live the king" and as heaven opened up under Lenz as an abyss, the breath turning seemed to be there. Perhaps also, when I attempted to make for that distant but occupiable realm which became visible only in the form of Lucile. And once, proceeding from the attention devoted to things and all living creatures, we even reached the vicinity of something open and free. And finally the vicinity of utopia.

Poetry, ladies and gentlemen —: this pronouncement of the infinitude of mere mortality and futility.

Ladies and gentlemen, now that I am again at the beginning, permit me once more—briefly, and from a different direction—to pose my old question.

Ladies and gentlemen, a few years ago I wrote a little quatrain which reads:

> Voices from the path of the nettles:
> *come on your hands to us.*
> Whoever is alone with the lamp
> has only his palm to read from.

And last year, in commemoration of a proposed encounter in Engadine which came to naught, I composed a little story in which I had a person walk, "like Lenz," through the mountains.

In each instance I started to write from a "20th of January," from my "20th of January."

I encountered . . . myself.

Does one, when one thinks of poems—does one travel such paths with poems? Are these paths but circuitous paths, circuitous paths from thou to thou? There are, however, among possible paths, paths on which language acquires a voice; these are encounters, a voice's paths to a perceiving thou, creaturely paths, sketches of existence perhaps, a sending oneself ahead to oneself, in the process of searching for oneself . . . A kind of homecoming.

Ladies and gentlemen, I am approaching the conclusion. With the acute, which I inserted, I am approaching the conclusion of . . . *Leonce and Lena.*

And here, with the final two words of the drama, I must pay careful attention, lest, like Karl Emil Franzos, the editor of that *First Complete Critical Edition of Georg Büchner's Collected Works and Posthumous Papers*, which the Sauerländer Press published in Frankfurt am Main eighty-one years ago—I must pay careful attention, lest, like *my countryman Karl Emil Franzos, whom I have here found again*, I read "coming" for "accommodating," which is now the accepted variant.

But on second thought: aren't there quotation marks present in *Leonce and Lena*, quotation marks with an invisible smile in the direction of the words? And perhaps these are to be understood not as mere punctuation scratches, but rather as rabbit ears, listening in, somewhat timidly, on themselves and the words?

From this point, that is, from "accommodating," but also in light of utopia, I will now embark upon the study of topoi:

I will search for the region from which Reinhold Lenz and Karl Emil Franzos came, they who encountered me on the path I have taken today, as well as in Georg Büchner's works. I am also seeking the place of my own origin, since I have once again arrived at my point of departure.

I am seeking all of that on the map with a finger which is uncertain, because it is restless—on a child's map, as I readily confess.

None of these places is to be found, they do not exist, but I know where they would have to exist—above all at the present time—and . . . I find something!

Ladies and gentlemen, I find something which offers me some consolation for having traveled the impossible path, this path of the impossible, in your presence.

I find something which binds and which, like the poem, leads to an encounter.

I find something, like language, abstract, yet earthly, terrestrial, something circular, which traverses both poles and returns to itself, thereby—I am happy to report—even crossing the tropics and tropes. I find . . . *a meridian.*

With you and Georg Büchner and the state of Hesse I believe that I have just now touched it again.

Ladies and gentlemen, a great honor has been bestowed upon me today, an honor I will remember. Together with people whose personal contact and works constitute an encounter for me, I am the recipient of a prize which commemorates Georg Büchner.

I extend my sincerest thanks to you for this honor, for this moment, and for this encounter.

I extend my thanks to the state of Hesse, the city of Darmstadt, and the German Academy of Language and Literature.

I extend my thanks to the president of the German Academy of Language and Literature, to you, my dear Hermann Kasack.

Thank you, my dear Marie Luise Kaschnitz.

Ladies and gentlemen, I thank you for your presence.

Notes

1. Shibboleth

NOTE: The initial version of this text was delivered as a lecture at the International Paul Celan Symposium at the University of Washington, Seattle, in October 1984. Despite certain revisions and some new developments, the plan of exposition, the rhythm, and the tone of the lecture have been preserved as far as possible.

[The present translation offers an approximation, insofar as possible within the context of the overall volume, of the original layout of *Schibboleth: Pour Paul Celan*. Notably, asterisks are used to indicate Derrida's own endnotes, and Celan's German original has been placed in parallel with a translation. In this essay about a poet in whose poetry constellations and stars figure significantly, author's notes are marked by six-pointed asterisks. These notes attempt to preserve in spirit Derrida's own notes—the bulk of which trace variants in existing French translations—by doing the same for English variants. They also, of course, translate his other annotation. English translations have occasionally been modified to capture what Derrida's argument highlights in the French translations or the German original. When Derrida insists on details of the French translations, these are given.

On account of the marked importance in "Shibboleth" of numbers, translators' notes are keyed to alphabetic letters rather than to numbers.

The German original of Celan's writings is from *Gesammelte Werke*, ed. Beda Allemann and Stefan Reichert, in collaboration with Rolf Bücher (Frankfurt a. M.: Suhrkamp, 1983), 5 vols. Abbreviated hereafter as *GW*.

The French translations used by Derrida are "Le Méridien," trans. André du Bouchet, in *Strette* (Paris: Mercure de France, 1971), and "Le

Méridien," trans. Jean Launay, in *Poé∂ie* 9 (1979): 68–82, revised and republished in *Le Méridien et autres proses* (Paris: Seuil, 2002), 59–84. Derrida usually gives du Bouchet in the text, with Launay's variants in the notes.

The translation of "The Meridian" by Jerry Glenn has been used, since it was the translation Derrida owned and used in teaching "Majesties" in English. It first appeared in *Chicago Review* 29, no. 3 (1978), 29–40, and is reprinted here as an appendix, 173–85. Page numbers refer to the publication in this volume. Additional English translations of Celan's writings used to indicate variants have been abbreviated as follows:

> Billeter. "Bremen Address" and "Conversation in the Mountain," trans. Walter Billeter, in *Prose Writings and Selected Poems*, trans. Walter Billeter and Jerry Glenn (Carlton, Vic.: Paper Castle, 1977).
>
> Felstiner. *Selected Poems and Prose of Paul Celan*, trans. John Felstiner (New York: W. W. Norton, 2001).
>
> Hamburger. *Poems by Paul Celan*, trans. Michael Hamburger (London: Anvil Press Poetry, 1995).
>
> Joris, *Breathturn*. *Breathturn*, trans. Pierre Joris (Los Angeles: Sun & Moon, 1995).
>
> Joris, *Lightduress*. *Lightduress*, trans. Pierre Joris (Copenhagen: Green Integer, 2005).
>
> Joris, *Selections*. *Paul Celan: Selections*, ed. Pierre Joris (Berkeley: University of California Press, 2005).
>
> Lynch and Jankowsky. *65 Poems*, trans. Brian Lynch and Peter Jankowsky (Dublin: Raven Arts Press, 1985).
>
> Neugroschel. *Speech-Grille and Selected Poems*, trans. Joachim Neugroschel (New York: Dutton, 1971).
>
> Popov and McHugh. *Glottal Stop: 101 Poems by Paul Celan*, trans. Nikolai Popov and Heather McHugh (Middleton, Conn.: Wesleyan University Press, 2000).
>
> Waldrop. "The Meridian," "Conversation in the Mountains," and "Speech on the Occasion of Receiving the Literature Prize of the Free Hanseatic City of Bremen" (the "Bremen Address"), trans. Rosemarie Waldrop, in *Collected Prose*, trans. Rosemarie Waldrop (Riverdale-on-Hudson, N.Y.: Sheep Meadow Press, 1986).
>
> Washburn and Guillemin. *Last Poems*, trans. Katherine Washburn and Margret Guillemin (San Francisco: North Point Press, 1986).
>
> Wilner. Jacques Derrida, "Shibboleth: For Paul Celan," trans. Joshua Wilner, in *Word Traces: Readings of Paul Celan*, ed. Aris Fioretos (Baltimore: The Johns Hopkins University Press, 1994), 3–72 — Ed.]

a. The French is: "Une seule fois: la circoncision n'a lieu qu'une fois."

b. As Derrida indicates, the word *fois* semantically involves spatial turning, having acquired a temporal value, as in "someone's turn." Translations of Derrida have customarily rendered *une fois* as "once" or *à la fois* as "at once" or as "both." "At the same time" is also understood in *à la fois*, but here it translates *en même temps*. In *Voyous* (*Rogues*), Derrida returns to this word *fois* and stresses its signification: "The Latin etymology of the word *fois*, namely, this strange word *vicis* . . . signif[ies] the turn, succession, alternation, or alternative (it turns by being inverted, by turns, alternatively or vice versa, as in *vice versa* or the 'vicious circle')." Derrida then refers back to the present passage in "Shibboleth," to "this lexicon of *fois*," adding that *à la fois* is a supplement for *tour à tour* or "by turns" (*Voyous: Deux essais sur la raison* [Paris: Galilée, 2003], 25–26; *Rogues: Two Essays on Reason*, trans. Pascale-Anne Brault and Michael Naas [Stanford: Stanford University Press, 2005], 6–7). When translating other words and expressions in French involving *fois*, such as *chaque fois* ("each time") or "parfois" ("sometimes"), the English language cannot avoid the word "time," even if "time" (*le temps*) is lexically absent from French *fois*.

    c. *Alliance* denotes a broader range of meanings in French than in English, including marriage and the biblical covenant.

    d. For "what *comes down to* to marking itself as the one-and-only time," the French is "ce qui *revient à* se marquer comme l'unique fois." *Revenir à* has two senses here: "what *amounts to*, *comes down to*, marking itself as the unique time" and "what *comes again* to mark itself as the unique time." Recurrent in "Shibboleth," the verb *revenir*, or *revenir à*, literally "to come again," "to come back," "to return," or "to come back to," has, depending on the different contexts in this translation, been rendered by either "to come down to" or "to amount to." The substantive, *revenant*, means "specter" or "ghost," a sense active later in "Shibboleth."

    Page 2. acérée*: "The title of the poem perhaps alludes to Baudelaire's "*Confiteor* de l'artiste": "et il n'est pas de pointe plus acérée que celle de l'Infini [and there is no point more piercing than that of the Infinite]" (*Oeuvres complètes*, ed. Claude Pichois [Paris: Gallimard, 1975], 1:278).

    As I correct the proofs of this essay, I receive confirmation of this hypothesis in Werner Hamacher's very beautiful text "The Second of Inversion: Movements of a Figure Through Celan's Poetry": "Celan reported in conversation that he borrowed this text's title from a note by Baudelaire, cited in Hofmannsthal's journal under the date June 29, 1917" (trans. William D. Jewett, in *Yale French Studies* 69 [1985]: 308; Werner Hamacher, "Die Sekunde der Inversion: Bewegungen einer Figur durch Celans Gedichte," in *Paul Celan: Materialien*, ed. Werner Hamacher and Winfried Menninghaus [Frankfurt a. M.: Suhrkamp, 1988], 117).

    Page 3. language*: *GW* 1:251. Hamburger, 199. I thus commit myself to citing bilingually. This commitment implies no evaluation, even less is it a critique or an invitation to suspicion of the translators, who themselves have often found it indispensable to place side by side the two versions, the original and the other. In citing existing translations, I want above all to express an immense debt and to render homage to those who have taken on the responsibility or the risk of translating texts whose every letter, as we know, and every blank space, breathing, and caesura, defies translation, but calls for and provokes it by the same token.

The enigma of the *shibboleth*, as will be confirmed, merges seamlessly with that of translation, in its essential dimension. I am therefore not going to treat it in a note, before having even started. Whoever has read Celan will have passed through the experience of translation, of its limits, its aporias, its exigencies—I mean those of the original poem, which also *demands* to be translated. In general, I have abstained from translating, above all from retranslating. I did not want to seem to want, however little, to amend a first attempt. In the approach to texts such as these, lessons and polemics have no place. It may happen, to be sure, that I more readily go along with one or another participant in the debate on this subject that is currently under way in France. One thinks, above all, of essays by Henri Meschonnic ("On appelle cela traduire Celan," in *Pour la poétique* [Paris: Gallimard, 1973], 2:367–405), by Jean Launay ("Une lecture de Paul Celan," *Poésie* 9 [1979], 3–8), and by Philippe Lacoue-Labarthe ("Two Poems by Paul Celan," in *Poetry as Experience* [Stanford: Stanford University Press, 1999], 1–38), especially where formidable qualities of tone—the Mallarméan, for example—are at issue. But, giving up the idea of myself proposing a new translation, I have, out of principle, avoided making a choice. The reader will have available the original text and the published translations. The juxtaposition, sometimes, of several translations is not intended to create the appearance of a competition. It seems to me to aid both a sharper reading of the original and access to the true difficulties.

Page 4. comes*: *GW* 1:251–52. Hamburger, 195, trans. modified.

e. *Partage* in French signifies a "separation" or "division," thus a "partition." The French expressions used throughout for "on the one hand" and "on the other hand," *d'une part* and *d'autre part*, participate in the meaning of the word *partage*. If *partage* here signifies separation, parting, or division, it also can signify participation through sharing in what is divided up, and the share apportioned, not to mention one's lot.

f. "Une mise en oeuvre poétique de la datation": *mise en oeuvre* ("implementation, enactment") can also be rendered "setting-to-work." In the idiom of the text, one could also hear "setting-(in)to-(the)-work," i.e., putting the operation of dating in place in the work. Subsequent occurrences simply retain the French phrase.

Page 4. know*: *GW* 3:187–202 ("die Kunst, die wir schon kennen," 3:188). Waldrop, 38. Glenn, 174.

eternal*: *GW* 3:188, "auch ein Problem, und zwar, wie man sieht, ein verwandlungsfähiges, zäh—und langebiges, will sagen ewiges." Waldrop: "a problem also, and, as we can see, one that is variable, tough, long lived, let us say, eternal" (38).

remember*: *GW* 3:187. Waldrop: "Art, you will remember" (37).

Page 5. *étapes**: *GW* 3:194, "Dann wäre die Kunst der von der Dichtung zurückzulegende Weg—nicht weniger, nicht mehr. // Ich weiß, es gibt andere, kürzere Wege. Aber auch die Dichtung eilt uns ja manchmal voraus. La poésie, elle aussi, brûle nos étapes." Glenn, 178. Waldrop: "This would mean art is the distance poetry must cover, no less and no more. I know that there are other, shorter, routes. But poetry, too, more than once, can be ahead. La poésie, elle aussi, brûle nos étapes" (41–45).

January*: *GW* 3:194, "den 20. Jänner durchs Gebirg ging." Waldrop: "the Lenz who 'on the 20th of January was walking through the mountains'" (46). We will later encounter again the archaic or Austrian usage of *Jänner* or of *Feber*, and we will come back to it then. How is one to translate it?

translation*: *GW* 3:194. Waldrop: "he as an 'I'" (46).

form*: *GW* 3:197–98. Waldrop: "one person's language become shape" (49).

Bouchet*: *GW* 3:198. Glenn, 181, trans. modified. Waldrop: "become shape, and, essentially, a presence in the present" (49).

encounter*: *GW* 3: 198, "*im Geheimnis der Begegnung.*" Glenn, 181, trans. modified. Waldrop: "*in the mystery of encounter*" (49). [Following du Bouchet and Launay, Derrida translates *Geheimnis* as "secret"—Trans.]

Page 6. inscribed*: *GW* 3:196. Glenn 180, trans. modified. Waldrop: "Perhaps we can say each poem is marked by its own '20th of January'?" (47).

bleiben*: *GW* 3:196. Glenn, 180. Waldrop: "Perhaps the newness of poems written today is that they try most plainly to be mindful of this kind of date?" (47).

g. Operating throughout "Shibboleth" (and others of Derrida's texts), the "future" in the sense of *avenir* carries the sense of "to-come" (*à venir*, structurally never present as such), to be distinguished from the "future" as *futur* (a future time that would become a present). As Peggy Kamuf notes in her translation of Derrida's *Specters of Marx*, "*avenir* has the sense of a coming, an advent" (*Specters of Marx* [New York: Routledge, 1994], 177).

Page 7. zu*: *GW* 3:196. [Translation by Wilner, following in part the translation of du Bouchet: "Mais, parties de telles dates, quel circuit, tous, ne nous est-il donné de décrire? Et, nous-mêmes, pour quelle date, à venir, nous transcrivons-nous?" (190)"—Trans.] Waldrop: "But do we not all write from and toward some such date? What else could we claim as our origin?" (47).

h. "Si le poème se rappelle une date, se rappelle à sa date": the latter part of this phrase could mean "calls itself back to its date," in the sense of someone or something calling him or itself back to order, but also can, with its resonance of a polite formula, mean, "the poem recalls itself to its date," i.e., "the poem reminds its date of itself, that is, of the poem."

Page 8. name*: *GW* 3:196. I am myself appropriating here the two translations, different as they are, and the difference goes beyond tonal connotations. Du Bouchet: "Mais le poème parle! De la date qui est la sienne, il

préserve mémoire, mais—il parle. Il parle, certes, toujours, de la circon-
stance unique qui, proprement, le concerne" (190). Launay: "Mais un
poème, cela parle! Il garde la mémoire de ses dates, mais enfin—il parle.
Certes: toujours et seulement en son nom propre, le plus authentiquement
propre" (*Poeßie*, 76). Waldrop: "But the poem speaks! It is mindful of its
dates, but it speaks. True, it speaks only on its own, its very own behalf"
(48).

i. The distinction Derrida develops is clearer in French, since the French
word for "encounter," *rencontre*, is also employed in the phrase *de rencontre*,
meaning "chance," "passing," "casual," etc. Thus, e.g., here *le secret d'une
rencontre* is "the secret of an encounter"; *un secret de rencontre* is "a chance
secret."

Page 10. hopes*: *GW* 3:196. Glenn 180, trans. modified. Waldrop: "But
I think—and this will hardly surprise you—that the poem has always
hoped, for this very reason, to speak also on behalf of the strange—no, I
can no longer use this word here—*on behalf of the* other, who knows, perhaps
of an *altogether other*. // This 'who knows' which I have reached is all I can
add here, today, to the old hopes" (48).

j. *De la fois* could also be translated "of the occurrence," "of the occasion," "of the one time," or "of the once." The phrase "chaque fois une seule
fois," "each time only one time," which echoes throughout this essay, repeats Jean Launay's translation of Celan's "einmal, immer wieder einmal"
in the "Meridian." Jerry Glenn translates the German as "one time, over
and over again one time."

Page 11. absurdum*: *GW* 3:199, "Und was wären dann die Bilder? //
Das einmal, das immer wieder einmal und nur jetzt und nur hier Wahrgen-
ommene und Wahrzunehmende. Und das Gedicht wäre somit der Ort, wo
alle Tropen und Metaphern ad absurdum geführt werden wollen." Glenn,
183. Waldrop: "Then what are images? // What has been, what can be perceived, again and again, and only here, only now. Hence the poem is the
place where all tropes and metaphors want to be led *ad absurdum*" (51).)

exist*: *GW* 3:199, "Ich spreche ja von dem Gedicht, das es nicht gibt! //
Das absolute Gedicht—nein, das gibt es gewiss nicht, das kann es nicht
geben!" Glenn, 182. Waldrop: "I speak of the poem which does not exist! //
The absolute poem—no, it certainly does not, cannot exist!" (51).

Page 12. myself*: *GW* 3:201, "Meine Damen und Herren, ich habe vor
einigen Jahren einen kleinen Vierzeiler geschrieben—diesen: 'Stimmen
vom Nesselweg her: / *Komm auf den Händen zu uns.* / Wer mit der Lampe allein ist, / hat nur die Hand, draus zu lesen.' Und vor einem Jahr, in Erinnerung an eine versäumte Begegnung im Engadin, brachte ich eine kleine
Geschichte zu Papier, in der ich einem Menschen 'wie Lenz' durchs Gebirg
gehen liess. // Ich hatte mich, das eine wie das andere Mal, von einem '20.
Jänner,' von meinem '20. Jänner,' hergeschrieben. // Ich bin . . . mir selbst
begegnet." Glenn, 184, trans. modified. Waldrop: "Several years ago, I

wrote a little quatrain: 'Voices from the path through nettles: / *Come to us on your hands*. / Alone with your lamp. / Only your hand to read.' And a year ago, I commemorated a missed encounter in the Engadine valley by putting a little story on paper where I had a man 'like Lenz' walk through the mountains. // Both the one time and the other, I had transcribed myself from a '20th of January,' from my '20th of January.' // I had . . . encountered myself" (52–53).

*meridian**: *GW* 3:202, "Ich suche auch, denn ich bin ja wieder da, wo ich begonnen habe, den Ort meiner eigenen Herkunft. // Ich suche das alles mit wohl sehr ungenauem, weil unruhigem Finger auf der Landkarte—au einer Kinder-Landkarte, wie ich gleich gestehen muss. // Keiner dieser Orte ist zu finden, es gibt sie nicht, aber ich weiss, wo es sie, *zumal jetzt*, geben müsste, und . . . ich finde etwas! // Meine Damen und Herren, ich finde etwas, das mich auch ein wenig darüber hinwegtröstet, in Ihrer Gegenwart diesen unmöglichen Weg, diesen Weg des Unmöglichen gegangen zu sein. / Ich finde das Verbindende und wie das Gedicht zur Begegnung Führende. // Ich finde etwas—wie die Sprache—Immaterielles, aber Irdisches, Terrestrisches, etwas Kreisförmiges, über die beiden Pole in sich selbst Zurückkehrendes und dabei—heitererweise—sogar die Tropen Durchkreuzendes—ich finde . . . einen *Meridian*." Glenn 185, trans. modified. Waldrop: "I am also, since I am again at my point of departure, searching for my own place of origin. // I am looking for all this with my imprecise, because nervous, finger on a map—a child's map, I must admit. // None of these places can be found. They do not exist. But I know where they ought to exist, especially now, and . . . I find something else. // Ladies and gentlemen, I find something which consoles me a bit for having walked this impossible road in your presence, this road of the impossible. // I find the connective which, like the poem, leads to encounters. // I find something as immaterial as language, yet earthly, terrestrial, in the shape of a circle which, via both poles, rejoins itself and on the way serenely crosses even the tropics: I find . . . a *meridian*" (54–55). I italicize *zumal jetzt*: "especially now," says one translator, "at the present hour [*à cette heure*]," says the other. We will find a little later [*tout à l'heure*] this problem, that of the now just *like* that of the hour.

Page 13. time*: *GW* 3:198–99, "im Hier und Jetzt des Gedichts—das Gedicht selbst hat ja immer nur diese eine, *einmalige*, punktuelle Gegenwart—, noch in dieser Unmittelbarkeit und Nähe lässt es das ihm, dem Anderen, Eigenste mitsprechen: dessen Zeit." (I italicize *einmalige*: that which has the characteristic of a single, unique *time* [fois].) Glenn, 182, modified to follow the French translation by Launay. Waldrop: "in the here and now of the poem—and the poem has only this one, unique, momentary present—even in this immediacy and nearness, the otherness gives voice to what is most its own: its time" (50).

k. "Au gnomon de Paul Celan": cf. "au nom de Paul Celan," "in the name of Paul Celan."

Page 14. midnight*: *GW* 1:135. Hamburger, 99. Joris: "Speak— / But do not separate the no from the yes. / Give your saying also meaning: / give it its shadow. // Give it enough shadow, / give it as much / as you know to be parcelled out between / midnight and midday and midnight" (*Selections*, 54). We will return below to the question of that which binds the word, and the word as decree, aphorism, sentence, verdict, judgment (*Spruch*), to decision and circumcision, on the one hand, and to the date and the hour, on the other. Here, the imparting or distribution (*Verteilung*) and the gift of shade, that which gives meaning to the *Spruch*, to the word as judgment (*Urteil*), spreads or distributes the origin of meaning, that is, the shade, *between the hours*, between complete shade and the absence of shade, midnight and midday and midnight. The shade is imparted, spread out, or apportioned (*verteilt*) among the hours. And this imparting of shade *gives the meaning*.

Page 15. gift*: The date and the gift. The debt as well. Beyond etymology, this is the shade that would give meaning, here, to all our questions. This lecture had already been delivered, and the second version written, when I had the chance to read the manuscript of Jean Greisch's then unpublished text "Zeitgehöft et Anwesen (La dia-chronie du poème)," in *Contre jour*, ed. Martine Broda (Paris: Cerf, 1986), 167–83 [republished as "La dia-chronie du poème," in Greisch, *La parole heureuse: Martin Heidegger entre les choses et les mots* (Paris: Beauchesne, 1987), 300–404]. I would like to thank him here. I refer the reader to these rich analyses concerning Celan. Here I will have to be content with calling attention to two precious references, both of which I also owe to Greisch. First, he recalls and translates a text of Heidegger that "transforms the 'Datum' into a donation": "Moreover, poetic time is also different in each case, in accordance with the essential nature of the poetry and of the poets. For all essential poetry also poetizes 'anew' the essence of poetizing itself. This is true of Hölderlin's poetry in a special and singular sense. No calendrical time can be given for the 'Now' of his poetry. Nor is any date needed here at all. For this 'Now' that is called and is itself calling is, in a more originary sense, itself a date — that is to say, something given, a gift; namely, given via by the calling of this vocation [Derrida glosses *Berufung*, which is Heidegger's final phrase and means both "calling" and "vocation"]" (Martin Heidegger, *Hölderlin's Hymn "The Ister,"* trans. William McNeill and Julia Davis [Bloomington: Indiana University Press, 1996], 9). Greisch also recalls and analyzes the passage that Heidegger devotes to "datability" (*Datierbarkeit*) in *Die Grundprobleme der Phänomenologie*, ed Friedrich-Wilhelm von Herrmann (Frankfurt a. M.: Klostermann, 1975), vol. 24. I cite a few excerpts. They touch on a problem, that of the relationship between the calendrical and the noncalendrical date, which we will address directly a little further on: "By the term 'datability' we denote this relational structure of the now as now-when; of the at-the-time as at-the-time-when, and of the then as then-when. Every now dates itself as 'now, when such and such is occurring, happening, or in existence.'

. . . The date itself does not need to be calendrical in the narrower sense. The calendar date is only one particular mode of everyday dating. The indefiniteness of the date does not imply a shortcoming in datability as essential structure of the now, at-the-time, and then. . . . The time that is commonly conceived as a sequence of nows must be taken as this dating relation. This relation should not be overlooked and suppressed. Nevertheless, the common conception of time as a sequence of nows is just as little aware of the moment of pre-calendrical datability as that of significance. . . . Why could time-structures as elemental as those of significance and datability remain hidden from the traditional time concept? Why did it overlook them and why did it have to overlook them? We shall learn how to understand this from the structure of temporality itself" (Martin Heidegger, *The Basic Problems of Phenomenology*, trans. Albert Hofstadter [Bloomington: Indiana University Press, 1975], 262–63).

At the moment when the present work is in press in France, I become aware of the third volume of Paul Ricœur's great book *Temps et récit: Le temps raconté* (Paris: Seuil, 1985); *Time and Narrative*, vol. 3, trans. Kathleen Blamey and David Pellauer (Chicago: University of Chicago Press, 1988), page numbers are from the English. It includes, in particular, a rich analysis of calendar time and the institution of the calendar. This "institution constitutes the invention of a third form of time," between "lived time" and "cosmic time" (105). The "transcendental" analysis proposed (120 ff.), above and beyond the genetic and sociological approaches, is developed specifically by means of a critique of the Heideggerian concept of "ordinary time" and the elaboration of a philosophy of the trace, which is both close to and different from that of Levinas. They would deserve a more ample discussion as well as development, but I cannot commit myself to such in a note, at the moment of correcting these proofs. I hope to be able to return to this.

Page 16. 1967*: In Peter Szondi, *Schriften*, ed. Wolfgang Fietkau, foreword by Jean Bollack (Frankfurt a. M.: Suhrkamp, 1978), 2:390; *Celan Studies*, trans. Susan Bernofsky, with Harvey Mendelsohn (Stanford: Stanford University Press, 2003), 84. "Reading 'Engführung'" is also in *Celan Studies*, 27–82.

l. "Cut" translates the French noun *entaille*. Coming from the Latin sense of "pruning," as a tree, and meaning "to cut" in general, *entaille* is an "excision" that removes part of what is cut into, leaving an indentation (a "gauge" or "gash" into skin or flesh, a "tally" into leather, an "intaglio" into stone, etc.). Given the context throughout "Shibboleth" of sculpted scissions in language, in the tongue, and in the sex, we must therefore remember that *entaille* carries the sense of "shaping" or "reshaping": e.g., the penis is "reshaped" by circumcision, and language by the poem.

Page 18. name*: "Nächtlich Geschürzt," *GW* 1:125. Hamburger, 91.

m. French *revenance*, literally a "coming back" or "coming again," is formed from the present participle, *revenant*, which as a noun means "specter," "ghost" (as it also does in English).

Page 19. come*: *GW* 1:154. Hamburger, 109. Neugroschel: "Wax / to seal things unwritten, / divining / your name, / encoding your name. // Are you coming now, floating light? // Fingers, also waxen, / drawn through / alien, painful rings. / The fingertips, melted away. // Are you coming, floating light? // The clock's honeycombs, time-drained; / nuptial, the bee-myriad, / ready to travel. // Come, floating light" (89).

n. "Belonging," *appartenance* in French, loses the stem *-part-*, which is important throughout "Shibboleth" (as in "imparting," "partaking," or the partitive grammatical form). English *appurtenance* ("a thing forming a part of a whole, a belonging," *O.E.D.*) might suffice were the verb *to pertain* ("to belong as part of a whole, as possession, legal right or privilege, as one's care, as attribute, as appropriate to," *O.E.D.*) idiomatically able to replace the verb *to belong*. Because it cannot do so, "belong" and "belonging" have been used to translate *appartenir* and *appartenance*.

Page 20. on*: *GW* 1:282. Wilner's translation. Popov and McHugh: "Did the dove go astray, could her ankle-band / be deciphered? (All the / clouding around her—it was legible.) Did the covey countenance it? Did they understand, / and fly, when she did not return?" (15).

Page 21. One*: *GW* 1:270. Hamburger, 206.

doom*: *GW* 2:17. Lynch and Jankowsky, 49.

thousand*: "Die Silbe Schmerz," *GW* 1:280. Wilner's translation. Joris: "And numbers too / were woven into the uncountable. One and a thousand" (*Selections*, 91). Popov and McHugh: "And numbers were / interwoven with the / Innumerable. A one, a thousand" (13).

o. "Watchword" or "password," in French *mot d'ordre*, can also be "word of command."

Page 23. Aurora*: Martine Broda devotes "a long parenthesis" to this "shepherd-Spanish" in "Bouteilles, cailloux, schibboleths: Un nom dans la main," in *Dans la main de personne* (Paris: Cerf, 1986), 95–105.

Page 24. Schibboleth*: Published in *Von Schwelle zu Schwelle* (1955; in *GW* 1:131). Trans. Jerome Rothenburg in Joris, *Selections*, 52–53.

Page 27. Babel*: *GW* 1:272. Hamburger, 211. Neugroschel: "And there rises an earth, ours, / this one. / And we send none of us down / to you, / Babel" (205).

Page 28. lungs*: *GW* 1:284. Hamburger, 220.

Page 31. pasarán*: [Derrida gives his own translation of the Celan poem here, noting that, to his knowledge, no translation into French exists. For "in die Fremde," he gives "à l'étranger de la patrie"—Trans.] Neugroschel, 73, trans. modified to reflect Derrida's French version; Neugroschel gives "into the alien homeland." Jerome Rothenberg: "Heart: / let us see you here too, / here in the dust of this market. / Thunder your shibboleth here / into your alien homeland: / February. *No pasarán*" (Joris, *Selections*, 52–53).

Austrian*: *Feber* is Austrian dialect for *Februar*. *Jänner*, occurring in other poems, goes back (like *Jenner*) to the beginnings of Middle-High German and remains in use up through the nineteenth century. It does so even today in Austria, and here and there in Switzerland and Alsace.

p. Jean-Luc Nancy, *Le partage des voix* (Paris: Galilée, 1982); "Sharing Voices," trans. Gayle L. Ormiston, in *Transforming the Hermeneutic Context: From Nietzsche to Nancy*, ed. Gayle L. Ormiston and Alan D. Schrift (Albany: State University of New York Press, 1990), 211–59. Among its other meanings, *partage des voix* is the French idiom for a split, that is to say tied, vote.

Page 32. ring*: It would have been appropriate to do so everywhere, but I choose to recall Freud's *shibboleths* here, at the moment of this allusion to the ring, for example, the one symbolizing the alliance among the founders of psychoanalysis. Freud frequently used the word *shibboleth* to designate that which "distinguishes the followers of psychoanalysis from those who are opposed to it" ("Drei Abhandlungen zur Sexualtheorie," in *Gesammelte Werke* [London: Imago, 1940–68], 5:128; "Three Essays on the Theory of Sexuality," in Sigmund Freud, *The Standard Edition of the Complete Psychological Works*, ed. and trans. James Strachey [London: Hogarth, 1953–66], 7:226), or, in addition, "Dreams, the *shibboleth* of psychoanalysis" ("Zur Geschichte der psychoanalytischen Bewegung," in *Gesammelte Werke*, 10:102; "On the History of the Psycho-Analytic Movement," in *Standard Edition*, 14:57). See also "Das Ich und das Es," in *Gesammelte Werke*, 13:239 ("The Ego and the Id," in *Standard Edition*, 19:13) and "Neue Folge der Vorlesungen: Zur Einführung in die Psychoanalyse," in *Gesammelte Werke*, 15:6 ("New Introductory Lectures on Psychoanalysis," in *Standard Edition*, 22:7). The motif of the *shibboleth* was discussed in the course of a seminar organized with Wladimir Granoff, Marie Moscovici, Robert Pujol, and Jean-Michel Rey, as part of a symposium at Cerisy-la-Salle. See *Les fins de l'homme*, ed. Philippe Lacoue-Labarthe and Jean-Luc Nancy (Paris: Galilée, 1981), 185–86.

witness*: *GW* 2:72. Neugroschel, 241. Joris: "Noone / bears witness for the / witness" (*Selections*, 105).

Page 33. gulls*: *GW* 1:226. Hamburger, *177*. Joris: "Their—'a / riddle is pure / origin'—, their / remembrance of / swimming Hölderlin-towers, gull-/ blown" (*Selections*, 79). Neugroschel: "Their ('pure / origin is / an / enigma'), their / memory of / floating Hölderlin Towers, circled / by whirring gulls" (185). With regard to *Jänner*, Lacoue-Labarthe suggests an "allusion to Hölderlin's disconcerting manner of dating poems during his 'mad' period" (*Poetry as Experience*, 15). In this regard, one may also recall the title and first line of the poem "Eingejännert" (*GW* 2:351).

q. The translation of the poem cited in the French text renders *Novembersternen* as *Constellation de Novembre*, a rendering motivated by the allusion to Sagittarius in the poem's last line (*Schütze*).

Page 35. archer*: GW 2:22. Lynch and Jankowsky, 54, trans. modified. Joris: "NEXT TO THE HAILSTONE, in / the mildewed corn- / cob, home, / to the late, the hard / November stars obedient: // in the hearthread, the / knit of worm-talk—: // a bowstring, from which / your arrowscript whirrs, / archer" (*Breathturn*, 77).

Page 38. Rest*: "SINGBARER REST—der Umriß / dessen, der durch / die Sichelschrift lautlos hindurchbrach, / abseits, am Schneeort" (*GW* 2:36). Neugroschel: "Singable remainder—the outline / of him who mutely / broke through the sickle-script, / aside, at the snow-place" (231). Joris: "SINGABLE REMNANT—the outline / of him, who through / the sicklescript broke through unvoiced, / apart, at the snowplace" (*Breathturn*, 101). Popov and McHugh: "Singable remainder—trace / of one who—mute, / remote— broke out of bounds / through sicklescripts of snow" (20). Philippe Lacoue-Labarthe proposes "résidu chantable [singable residue]" for *Singbarer Rest* (*Aléa* 5, 79), R. M. Mason, "reliquat chantable [singable remainder]," in *La Revue de Belles-Lettres*, 2–3, 77.

more*: *GW* 2:76. Hamburger, 253, trans. modified. Joris: "all is less, than / it is, / all is more" (*Breathturn*, 187). Neugroschel: "All is less than / it is, / all is more" (243).

Page 39. brother*: *GW* 1:275. Wilner's translation.

r. *Annulation* is translated here as "annulment," but it can also be understood as "annulation," that is, "the forming of rings." In Derrida's French text, *annulation* carries both the senses of "annulment" and "annular movement."

s. See Friedrich Hölderlin, *Sämtliche Werke*, ed. Friedrich Beißner (Stuttgart: Kolhammer, 1951), 4: 226–72; "On the Difference of Poetic Modes," in Friedrich Hölderlin, *Essays and Letters on Theory*, ed. and trans. Thomas Pfau (Albany: State University of New York Press, 1988), 83–88.

Page 41. one*: *GW* 1:225. Hamburger, 175. Neugroschel: "Blessed art thou, No-one" (183). Cid Corman: "Praised be you, noone" (Joris, *Selections*, 78).

Salvation*: *GW* 2:107. Hamburger, 271. Joris: "One and unending, / annihilated, / I'ed. // Light was. Salvation" (*Breathturn*, 249). Neugroschel: "One and Infinity, / dieing, / were I'ing. // Light was. Salvation" (253). Felstiner: "One and infinite, / annihilated, / they I'ed. // Light was. Salvation" (281). With regard to *ichten*, Henri Meschonnic writes: "It seems that one should take this for the preterit of an infinitive *ichten* found in Grimm: 'to become I,' 'to create an I'—a genesis. In addition, *ichten* is between—*nicht* and *Licht*. Between the two, it partakes of both through its signifier—of nothingness and of light" ("On appelle cela traduire Celan," in *Pour la poétique* [Paris: Gallimard, 1973], 2:374.)

Page 42. rose*: *GW* 1:225. Hamburger, 175. Cid Corman: "Noone kneads us again from earth and loam, / noone evokes our dust. / Noone. // Praised be you, noone. / Because of you we wish / to bloom. / Against you. // A nothing / were we, are we, will / we be, blossoming: / the nothing's-, the noonesrose" (Joris, *Selections*, 78). Neugroschel: "No one kneads us again of earth and clay, / no one incants our dust. / No one. // Blessed art thou, No-one. / For thy sake we / will bloom. / Towards / thee. // We were, we are, we shall remain / a Nothing, / blooming: / the Nothing-, the / No-one's-Rose" (183).

Page 43. souls*: *GW* 1:227. Hamburger, 179. Joris: "Great, gray / close, like all that's lost, / sister figure: // All the Names, all the al- / names. So much / to be blessed ashes. So much / won land / above / the light, o so light / soul- / rings" (*Selections*, 81). Neugroschel: "Large, gray / sister-shape, / near as all that's lost: // All the names, all the / names cremated along. So many / ashes to bless. So much / land gained / above / the weightless, so weightless / soul- / rings" (187).

soapy*: *GW* 2:236. Washburn and Guillemin, 7, modified from "SERVED WITH THE ASH-LADLE / from the trough of being, silty." Joris: "SCOOPED WITH THE ASHLADLE / from the Beingtrough, / soapy" (*Lightduress*, 27).

Page 44. *Stunde**: *GW* 1:170. Hamburger, 123. Neugroschel: "as the hour's solace" (115). In Jean-Pierre Burgart's translation, "als Zuspruch der Stunde" is rendered as "l'heure s'adresse à toi [the hour addresses itself to you]," which does not exclude the hour from doing so in order to provide courage and consolation (*Zuspruch*). In Paul Celan, *Strette* (Mercure de France, 1971), 82–83.

Page 45. compliance*: *GW* 1:216. Wilner's translation. Popov and McHugh: "Mind this hour, it is your time, / mine the mouth and yours the rhyme. // Mine's the mouth, though it is still, / full of words that will not fill" (6). Felstiner: "Now's the time, and it's your time now, / time for chatting with my rhyme now. // Here's a mouth and here's its quelling, / here are words, hear them rebelling" (143). And "DEIN UHRENGESICHT, / . . . / verschenkt seine Ziffern," *GW* 3:88. Washburn and Guillemin: "YOUR CLOCK-FACE, / . . . gives away its numbers" (170).

Stundenzäsur*: "Und mit dem Buch aus Tarussa," *GW* 1:288. Neugroschel, 209, as revised in Joris, *Selections*, 94.

Page 46. it*: *GW* 3:185–86. Billeter, 21, trans. modified. Waldrop: "Only one thing remained reachable, close and secure amid all losses: language. . . . // In this language I tried, during those years and the years after, to write poems: in order to speak, to orient myself, to find out where I was, where I was going. . . . // It meant movement, you see, something happening, being en route, an attempt to find a direction. Whenever I ask about the sense of it, I remind myself that this implies *the question as to which sense of the clock hand is clockwise.* // For the poem does not stand outside time. True, it claims the infinite and tries to reach across time—but across, not above" (34).

shine*: *GW* 1:197–99. Hamburger, 137–41, trans. modified. Neugroschel: "Walk, your hour / has no sisters, you are— / are at home. A wheel, slow, / rolls on its own, the spokes / climb, / . . . / Years. / Years, years, a finger / gropes down and up, / . . . / Came, came. / Came a word, came, / came through the night, / wanted to glow, to glow" (155–59). Robert Kelly: "Go, your hour / has no sisters, you are— / are at home. A wheel, slowly, /

rolls by itself, the spokes / clamber, / . . . / Years. / Years, years, a finger / feels down and up, / . . . / Came, came. / Came a word, came, / came through the night, / wanted to shine, wanted to shine" (Joris, *Selections*, 67–69).

Page 47. Night-and-night*: *GW* 1:199. Hamburger, 141. [Neugroschel and Kelly are identical to Hamburger, except for all using "ashes" in the place of "ash"—Trans.]

t. "Donnant lieu, rappelant le lieu, donnant et rappelant le temps": The French idiom *donner lieu*, given the importance of "place" and "taking place" in the texts of Celan, has usually been translated here by variations such as "open the space of," "open a place for," and, where "space" or "place" is difficult to retain in English and in context, by "open onto," "occasion," or "make room for."

Page 50. returned*: "Conversation in the Mountain," Billeter, 51, trans. modified. Waldrop: "do you hear me, you do, it's me, me, me and whom you hear, whom you think you hear, me and the other . . . because the Jew, you know, what does he have that is really his own, that is not borrowed, taken and not returned?" (17).

name.*: Waldrop, 17. Billeter: "his name, the ineffable" (51).

u. "Comme 'un nom à coucher dehors'": i.e., a long, unpronounceable name.

Page 51. strangers*: *GW* 1:167. Hamburger: "(If I were like you. If you were like me. / Did we not stand / under *one* tradewind? / We are strangers.)" (119). Neugroschel: "(Were I like you. Were you like me. / Did we not stand / under *one* tradewind? / We are strangers)" (109).

him*: *GW* 1:214. Hamburger, 157. Neugroschel: "The talk was of too much, too / little. Of Thou / and thou again, of / the dimming through light, of / Jewishness, of / your God. // . . . // The talk was of your God, I spoke / against Him" (179). Cid Corman: "Of too much was the talk, of /too little. Of you / and again-you, of / the dimming through brightness, of /Jewishness, of / your God. // . . . // Of your God was the talk, I spoke /against him" (Joris, *Selections*, 76). Felstiner: "Our talk was of Too Much, of / Too Little. Of Thou / and Yet-Thou, of / clouding through brightness, of / Jewishness, of / your God. // . . . // Our talk was of your God, I spoke /against him" (141).

Page 52. yours*: *GW* 1:222. Hamburger, 169. Neugroschel: "all this / grief of yours" (181).

Kaddish: Neugroschel: "To a mouth, / for which it was a myriad-word, / I lost— / lost a word / left over for me: / sister. // To / many-godded-ness / I lost a word that sought me: *Kaddish*" (181). Felstiner: "To a mouth / for which it was a thousandword, / lost— / I lost a word / that was left to me: / Sister" (151).

Judenfleck*: *GW* 1:229. Felstiner, 161 trans. modified.

grau*: *GW* 1:244. Hamburger, 189. Joris is identical (*Selections*, 88). Felstiner: "Jewish curls" and "Human curls" (173).

Page 53. Worte*: *GW* 1:287. Neugroschel, 207.

Page 54. wound-read*: *GW* 2:24. Lynch and Jankowsky: "it carries across / the wound-read" (56). Joris: "It carries / sore readings over" (*Breathturn*, 81). [The two French translations given by Derrida especially inform his commentary: Jean-Pierre Burgart, "il passe / la plaie lisible (it crosses / the readable wound)," *Strette*, 98–99; Jean Launay and Michel Deguy: "il passe / ce qui a été lu jusqu'à blesser, de l'autre côté (it takes / what was read to the point of wounding, to the other side)," *Poésie*, 9 (1979): 42. — Trans.]

v. Jean Launay, "Une lecture de Paul Celan," *Poésie* 9 (1979): 4.

Page 56. ours*: *GW* 1:239. Hamburger, 187. Joris: "Who, / who was it, that / lineage, the murdered one, the one / standing black into the sky: / Rod and ball — ? // (Root. / Root of Abraham. Root of Jesse. No one's / root — oh / ours.)" (*Selections*, 83–84). Felstiner: "Who, / who was it, that / stock, that murdered one, that one / standing black into heaven: / rod and testis — ? // (Root. Root of Abraham. Root of Jesse. No One's / root — O / ours)" (167).

word*: *GW* 1:242–43. Felstiner, 171, trans. modified from "circumcise his word." Cid Corman: "Rabbi, I rasped, Rabbi / Loew: // From him remove the word" (Joris, *Selections*, 86).

Page 58. Ra*: Cid Corman: "TO ONE WHO STOOD AT THE DOOR, one / evening: // to him / I let my word out —:" and, further, "Throw eveningsdoor open too, Rabbi. //. . . / Rip the morningsdoor off, Ra—" (Joris, *Selections*, 86).

Page 61. one*: Felstiner, 171, trans. modified. Cid Corman: "to him / I let my word out —//. . . // From him remove the word, / for him / write the living / nothingness at heart, / to him / extend your two / brokenfingers in grace- / bestowing judgment. / To him" (86–87).

Page 62. Wort*: *GW* 1:201. Hamburger, 143. Neugroschel: "it / was hospitable, it / never abrupted" (161). Felstiner: "it / was welcoming, it / did not interrupt" (125). Robert Kelly: "it / was hospitable, it / didn't interrupt" (Joris, *Selections*, 71).

1967*: On the secret of this encounter, on that which came to pass there or not, Philippe Lacoue-Labarthe poses, it seems to me, the essential questions, the just one. See his *Poetry as Experience*.

w. *Le double trenchant*: a *trenchant* is also the fleshing knife for removing skin and hide.

2. Poetics and Politics of Witnessing

NOTE: This text was first published in English translation by Rachel Bowlby as "'A Self-Unsealing Poetic Text': Poetics and Politics of Witnessing," in *Revenge of the Aesthetic: The Place of Literature in Theory Today*, ed. Michael Clark (Berkeley: University of California Press, 2000), 180–207. It was subsequently published in an expanded French version in *Derrida*, Cahiers de l'Herne, ed. Marie-Louise Mallet and Ginette Michaud (Paris: Editions de l'Herne, 2004), 521–39. The text that appears here is a revised version of the English translation and is based on the augmented French version as published by l'Herne.

1. Paul Celan, "Aschenglorie," in *Atemwende* (Frankfurt a. M.: Suhrkamp, 1967), 68; English trans. by Joachim Neugroschel, in Celan, *Speechgrille and Selected Poems* (New York: Dutton, 1971), 240; French translations by, first, Andre du Bouchet, in Celan, *Strette* (Paris: Mercure de France, 1971), 50, and, second, by J. P. Lefebvre, in Celan, *Renverse du souffle* (Paris: Seuil, 2003), 78.

2. [In the section that follows, Derrida discusses the Latin etymology of *témoignage*, *témoin*, etc., an etymology that will soon be contrasted with the German family of *Zeugen*, *Zeugnis*, etc. with the English *witness*, *to bear witness*, as well as with the Greek *marturion*, etc. In order to maintain Derrida's intention of highlighting the Latin roots of the vocabulary at stake, *témoin*—i. e., witness—is in the following passages translated as "the one who testifies"—Ed.]

3. Emile Benveniste, *Indo-European Language and Society*, summaries, table, and index by Jean Lallot, trans. Elizabeth Palmer (London: Faber and Faber, 1973). See p. 526 for the passage under discussion (trans. slightly modified).

4. [Benveniste uses the term *institution* in the broadest possible sense, referring to all aspects of social organization. As he explains in the Preface, "The expression 'institution' is here understood in a wider sense: it includes not only the institutions proper, such as justice, government, religion, but also less obvious ones which are found in various techniques, ways of life, social relationships and the processes of speech and thought. The subject is truly boundless, the aim of our study being precisely to throw light on the genesis of the vocabulary which relates to it. Our starting point is usually one or the other of the Indo-European languages and the examples chosen come from the terms of pregnant value. Round the chosen datum, by an examination of its peculiarities of form and sense, its connexions and oppositions and, following this, by comparison with related forms, we reconstruct the context in which it became specialized, often at the cost of profound transformations. In this way we endeavour to restore a unity dissolved by processes of evolution, bringing buried structures to light and harmonizing the divergencies of technical usages. In so doing we shall also demonstrate how languages reorganize their systems of distinctions and renew their semantic apparatus" (*Indo-European Language and Society*, p. 11)—Ed.]

5. On occasion, Benveniste himself uses the word *témoin* to characterize a word or a text insofar as it attests to a use or an institution. See, e.g., the chapter on hospitality, where Benveniste writes, "*Témoin ce texte*."

6. Ibid. p. 526, trans. modified.

7. Jean-François Lyotard, *The Differend*, trans. Georges Van Den Abbeele (Minneapolis: University of Minnesota Press, 1988), 66, 102.

8. "We," meaning a traditional community—I would not, in fact, say an institutional one in Benveniste's sense. This community must have been constituted out of a heritage in which language, linguistic feeling, is neither dominant nor just one element among others, and in which the history of Greek, Roman, Germanic, and Saxon systems of meaning is inseparable from philosophy, Roman law, or the two Testaments (in fact, from all the testaments out of which this tradition of bearing witness is made).

9. I have tried to do so elsewhere, in particular, around questions of the animal, of the life of the living creature, of survival and death—especially in *Of Spirit*, trans. Geoffrey Bennington and Rachel Bowlby (Chicago: University of Chicago Press, 1989), and *Aporias*, trans. Thomas Dutoit (Stanford: Stanford University Press, 1993).

10. Martin Heidegger, *Sein und Zeit*, para. 54 and chap. 2 (Tübingen: Niemayer, 1979); *Being and Time*, trans. John Macquarrie and Edward Robinson (New York: Harper & Row, 1962).

11. [Etymologically, the French term for oath, *serment*, derives from the Latin *sacramentum*—Ed.]

12. Martin Heidegger, *Holzwege* (Frankfurt a. M.: Klostermann, 1950), 343; *Early Greek Thinking*, trans. David Farrell Krell and Frank Capuzzi (1975; rpt. San Francisco: Harper & Row, 1984), 57.

13. [Trans. modified—Ed.]

14. On this being-witness or, rather, on this becoming-witness of the judge or the arbiter and, conversely, on this being- or becoming-arbiter of the witness, which will lead to so many problems, obscurities, and tragic confusions, we should again appeal to Benveniste (*Indo-European Language and Society*, bk. 5, chap. 3, "*ius* and the Oath in Rome").

15. In 1990–91, in "Circumfession," thus some years before this text's publication in 2000, the syntaxes and the meanings of the term *pour*, "for," found themselves at play or at work, from one end of the 59 periods to the other. For example: "and which piercing the night replies to my question: 'I have a pain in my mother,' as though she were speaking *for* [pour] me, both in my direction and in my place" (Jacques Derrida, "Circumfession," trans. Geoffrey Bennington, in Geoffrey Bennington and Jacques Derrida, *Jacques Derrida* (Chicago: University of Chicago Press, 1993), 23). Also: "over the admission I owe the reader, in truth that I owe my mother herself for [car] the reader will have understood that I am writing *for* [pour] my mother, perhaps even for a dead woman . . . for [car] if I were here writing for [pour] my mother, it would be for a living mother who does not recognize her son, and I am periphrasing here for whomever no longer recognizes me, unless it be so that one should no longer recognize me, another way of saying, another version, so that people think they finally recognize me, but what credulity" (ibid., 25–26). Again, right at the question of witnessing, with which this text ends (cf. ibid., 314): "the witness I am seeking, for [pour], yes, for, without yet knowing what this vocable, *for*, means in so many languages, for already having found him, and you, no, according to you, for

having sought *to* find him around a trope or an ellipsis that we pretend to organize, and for [*pour*] years I have been going round in circles, trying to take as witness not to [*pour*] see myself but to [*pour*] re-member myself around a single event" (ibid., 59).

16. Maurice Blanchot, *The Step Not Beyond*, trans. Lycette Nelson (Albany: State University of New York Press, 1992), p. 107.

17. "Der Meridian," in Paul Celan, *Gesammelte Werke* (Frankfurt a. M.: Suhrkamp, 1983), 3:196; "The Meridian," trans. Jerry Glenn, *Chicago Review* 29 (1978): 35 and p. 180 of this volume. I interpret this passage in "Shibboleth."

3. Language Is Never Owned

1. [Jacques Derrida, *Monolingualism of the Other; or, The Prosthesis of the Origin*, trans. Patrick Mensah (Stanford: Stanford University Press, 1998), 57, trans. modified — Trans.]

2. [Derrida refers to a part of Évelyne Grossman's question that was cut from the final transcription of the interview — Trans.]

3. [Our translation reflects a correction of a transcription error in the original interview, which has been confirmed by the interviewer. The French for "by what [*par ce*]" there reads as "because [*parce que*]."

4. Majesties

[NOTE: This text is excerpted from Jacques Derrida's seminar "La bête et le souverain," delivered at the École des Hautes Études en Sciences Sociales, Paris, in 2001–3. It is extracted from the sessions of February 20 and March 6, 2002. At the time, Derrida's reading focused on Paul Valéry's "Monsieur Teste" and Paul Celan's "The Meridian." The excerpt commences at a moment when, as Derrida's handwritten note in the manuscript explains, "we had already started [in the previous sessions] to read the 'Meridian' and its references to the marionettes." For his reading of the "Meridian," Derrida uses the bilingual German-French edition edited and translated by Jean Launay (*Le Meridien et autres proses* [Paris: Seuil, 2002]). The English translation used by Derrida is that by Jerry Glenn ("The Meridian," *Chicago Review* 29 [1978]: 29–40), reproduced in this volume as an appendix; where necessary, it is modified here to agree with Launay's translation. Page references are to the German-French edition and to the English translation, and are given by Derrida in the manuscript. Here English page numbers refer to the Glenn translation in the appendix of this volume. All notes are by the translator — Ed.]

1. Jean Launay's translations of two central terms in the "Meridian," *unheimlich* and *fremd*, are *étrange* and *étranger* (by extension, *Etranger* for *das Fremde*). See *Le Meridian et autres proses*, 105, n. 41. In the present text, *étrange/unheimlich* is rendered as "uncanny," and *étranger/fremd* as "strange" (by extension, the adjectival noun *Etranger / das Fremde* as "the strange").

2. Braces {} indicate translator's interpolations beyond glosses from the original French.

3. Glenn's translation of the sentence as "in the mystery of the encounter" is noted by hand by Derrida in the manuscript.

4. English translation modified to agree with Launay's French translation. Glenn's translation, which Derrida notes in the margin of his manuscript, runs: "they are a tribute to the majesty of the absurd, which bears witness to mankind's here and now."

5. Launay draws on the German critical edition of the "Meridian"— Paul Celan, *Der Meridian: Endfassung—Entwürfe—Materialien*, ed. Bernhard Böschenstein and Heino Schmull (Frankfurt a. M.: Suhrkamp, 1999) for his translation and notes.

6. Trans. modified.

7. Glenn's translation of *unheimlich* as "mysterious" is noted by hand by Derrida in the manuscript.

8. The expression used here is "le terriblement inquiétant de l'étranger." An earlier French standard translation for the Freudian *unheimlich*, the "uncanny," was *l'inquiétante étrangeté*, whereas a more recent standard is *l'inquiétant*. Both of these expressions are alluded to here.

9. The English translation of Heidegger's *Einführung in die Metaphysik* used here is *An Introduction to Metaphysics*, trans. Ralph Manheim (New Haven: Yale University Press, 1959).

10. The French translation of Heidegger's *Einführung in die Metaphysik* to which Derrida refers is *Introduction à la métaphysique*, trans. Gilbert Kahn (Paris: Presses Universitaires de France, 1958); Manheim's translation has been modified to reflect the French version.

5. Rams

NOTE: [This text, under the title "Le Dialogue ininterrompu: Entre deux infinis, le poème" ("Uninterrupted Dialogue: Between Two Infinities, the Poem") was delivered as a public lecture in memory of Hans-Georg Gadamer on February 5, 2003, at the University of Heidelberg. The English translation was prepared for public delivery in Jerusalem, where parts 3, 4, and 5 were presented on June 20, 2003. After this lecture, Jacques Derrida changed the title to "Béliers" ("Rams"), keeping the original title as subtitle — Trans.]

1. [In French, this and the preceding sentence begin "À jamais. Mais." Derrida frequently associates the phonically and semantically similar *à jamais* ("forever"), *jamais* ("never"), and *mais* ("but") — Trans.]

2. Hans-Georg Gadamer, *Gesammelte Werke* (Tübingen: J. C. B. Mohr [Paul Siebeck], 1990–), 2:372; *"Destruktion* and Deconstruction," trans. Geoff Waite and Richard Palmer, in *Dialogue and Deconstruction: The Gadamer-Derrida Encounter*, ed. Diane P. Michelfelder and Richard E. Palmer (Albany: State University of New York Press, 1989), 113, trans. modified.

Emphasis mine [JD]. [Here "dialogue," not "conversation," translates Gadamer's *Gespräch*, since the French translation chooses *dialogue*—Trans.]

3. [Derrida delivered this lecture in French, and the audience had a German translation available.—Trans.]

4. Hans-Georg Gadamer, *Dekonstruction und Hermeneutik*, in *Gesammelte Werke*, 10:138–47; "Letter to Dallmayr," trans. Diane Michelfelder and Richard Palmer, in *Dialogue and Deconstruction: The Gadamer-Derrida Encounter*, 93, trans. modified. Emphasis mine [J.D.].

5. Hans-Georg Gadamer, "Lesen ist wie Übersetzen," *Gesammelte Werke*, 8:279–85.

6. Hans-Georg Gadamer, "Grenzen der Sprache," *Gesammelte Werke*, 8:350–61; "The Boundaries of Language," trans. Lawrence K. Schmidt, in *Language and Linguisticality in Gadamer's Hermeneutics*, ed. Lawrence K. Schmidt (Lanham: Lexington Books, 2000), 16, trans. modified. ["Ownness," *propriété* in the French translation, translates Gadamer's *Eigenheit*, from *eigen* as "own" or "proper"—Trans.]

7. Hans-Georg Gadamer, "Selbstdarstellung," *Gesammelte Werke*, 2:478–508; "Reflections on My Philosophical Journey," trans. Richard Palmer, in *The Philosophy of Hans-Georg Gadamer*, ed. Lewis Hahn, Library of Living Philosophers (Chicago: Open Court, 1997), 3–63.

8. Hans-Georg Gadamer, "Vorwort zur 2. Auflage" (1965), *Wahrheit und Methode*, in *Gesammelte Werke* 2:441; "Preface to the Second Edition [1965]," *Truth and Method*, trans. Garrett Barden and John Cumming (New York: Crossroad, 1985), xix.

9. Ibid., *Gesammelte Werke*, 1:108; *Truth and Method*, 92.

10. Jacques Derrida, "Three Questions to Hans-Georg Gadamer," trans. Diane Michelfelder and Richard Palmer, in *Dialogue and Deconstruction*, 53, trans. modified.

11. Paul Celan, *Atemwende* (Frankfurt a. M.: Suhrkamp, 1967), 93. As of the date when this speech was written and delivered, no French translation of *Atemwende* existed. Fortunately, a remarkable bilingual edition has since appeared: *Paul Celan: Renverse du souffle*, trans. Jean-Pierre Lefebvre (Paris: Seuil, 2003). Our poem can be found on p. 113. [For a complete English translation of *Atemwende*, see *Breathturn*, trans. Pierre Joris (Los Angeles: Sun & Moon, 1995); this poem appears on p. 233. The poem is also translated by Michael Hamburger in *Poems of Paul Celan* (New York: Persea Books, 1988), 267. A third English version is that by Walter Billeter, in Paul Celan, *Prose Writings and Selected Poems*, trans. Walter Billeter and Jerry Glenn (Carlton, Vic.: Paper Castle, 1977), 83. The Hamburger translation is given in the text—Trans.]

12. [The word Derrida uses, *portée*, has a wide range of meanings, including "carry" in the sense of "range," the "carrying distance" or "carrying capacity" of a projectile, the "import," "importance," "implications," "significance," or "meaning" of an idea or an action, but also the 'impact" or

"consequence" of words or of writings. It is also the "reach," "scope," or "capacity" of a mind to conceptualize or understand, someone's physical or intellectual "level." Depending on the context, *portée* may also be translated as "stave"—a word that, interestingly, refers both to music (the lines which *bear* musical notation) and poetry ("a verse or stanza of a song, poem, etc.," *O.E.D.*, s.v. "stave"). In architectural lingo, *portée* covers such ideas as "loading," "span," and "bearing." The word also describes a group of animals born to the same mother at the same time (a "litter"). In the French text of "Rams," a whole galaxy of verbs clusters around *portée*, including, for instance (and only for instance): *porter, importer, exporter, déporter, reporter, rapporter, emporter, transporter, supporter.* In this essay, *portée* is semantically connected to the German word *tragen.*—Trans.]

13. Martin Heidegger, *What Is Called Thinking?*, trans. J. Glenn Gray and F. Wieck (New York: Harper Torchbooks, 1968), 139, trans. modified. The German is: "Zum Gedachten und seinen Gedanken, zum 'Gedanc' gehört der Dank. Doch vielleicht sind diese Anklänge des Wortes 'Denken' an Gedächtnis und Dank nur äußerlich und künstlich ausgedacht. . . . Ist das Denken ein Danken? Was meint hier Danken? Oder beruht der Dank im Denken?" (*Was heißt Denken?* [Tübingen: Niemeyer, 1954], 91). [In the French translation cited by Derrida, *Qu'appelle-t-on penser?*, trans. A. Becket and G. Granel (Paris: Presses Universitaires de France, 1959) 144–45, *reconnaissance*, a word used in the French text of "Rams," translates Heidegger's *Dank*, "thanks" or "gratitude"—Trans.]

14. Hans-Georg Gadamer, *Wer bin ich und wer bist du? Kommentar zu Celans 'Atemkristall,'* rev. ed. (Frankfurt a. M.: Suhrkamp, 1986). [The title by Gadamer appears in English in *Gadamer on Celan: "Who Am I and Who Are You?" and Other Essays*, trans. and ed. Richard Heinemann and Bruce Krajewski, with introduction by Gerald L. Bruns (Albany: State University of New York Press, 1997). *Atemkristall* is translated there as *Breathcrystal*—Trans.]

If time and daring hadn't failed me, I would have attempted to read together, in order to give an account of the hands and the fingers, "Aus der Vier-Finger-Furche" and, in "Aschenglorie" (in *Atemwende*), "ASCHENGLORIE / hinter / deinen erschüttert-verknoteten / Händen am Dreiweg / . . . / Aschen- / glorie hinter / euch Dreiweg- / Händen" (68); "ASH-GLORY behind / your shaken-knotted / hands on the three-forked road / . . . / behind your three-forked hands" (*Speech-grille and Selected Poems*, trans. Joachim Neugroschel [New York: Dutton, 1971, 240). [Other English translations of this poem appear in: *Selected Poems and Prose of Paul Celan*, trans. John Felstiner (New York: W. W. Norton, 2001), 261; and *Breathturn*, trans. Pierre Joris (Los Angeles: Sun & Moon, 1995), 177—Trans.]

I have proposed a reading of this poem in "Poetics and Politics of Witnessing," pp. 65–96 of this volume.

15. [Celan, "WEGE IM SCHATTEN-GEBRÄCH," *Atemwende*, 14—Trans.]

16. [*Gadamer on Celan*, 95 — Trans.]

17. Celan, *Atemwende*, 14; trans. Michael Hamburger, quoted in *Gadamer on Celan*, 95. [For an alternative English version, see Joris, *Breathturn*, 69 — Trans.]

18. In Paul Celan, *Die Niemandsrose*, in *Gesammelte Werke* (Frankfurt a. M.: Suhrkamp, 1986), 1:249; hereafter *GW*. [Trans. Felstiner, *Selected Poems*, 175; another English version can be found in Neugroschel, *Speech-Grille and Selected Poems* — Trans.]

19. *Gadamer on Celan*, 95.

20. Ibid.

21. Ibid.

22. Ibid., 96.

23. Gadamer, *Truth and Method*, xxii.

24. From *Language and Linguisticality*, in *Gadamer's Hermeneutics*, 16, trans. modified.

25. Paul Celan, *Schneepart* (Frankfurt a. M.: S. Fischer, 1971), and *GW* 2:338; Hamburger, *Poems*, 321, trans. modified. [Also translated in Felstiner, *Selected Poems and Prose*, 333, and in *Paul Celan: Selections*, ed. Pierre Joris (Berkeley: University of California Press, 2005), 131 — Trans.]

26. These appeals no doubt began when I devoted a seminar to this poem a few months ago in New York (New York University, 2002). They occasioned exchanges with my friends Avital Ronell and Werner Hamacher, whom I thank here.

27. [*Voire au-delà du monde qui n'est plus*: Lost in any translation of *voire* is the homophone *voir*, "to see," implying the sense of "to see beyond the world that is no more" — Trans.]

28. ["Singable remnant" in *Breathturn*, trans. Joris, 101; "Singable remainder-trace" in *Glottal Stop: 101 Poems by Paul Celan*, trans. Nikolai Popov and Heather McHugh (Middleton, Conn.: Wesleyan University Press, 2000), 20; "Singable remainder" in Neugroschel, *Speech-Grille*, 231 — Trans.]

29. "ASCHENGLORIE," in *Atemwende*, 68; Neugroschel, *Speech-Grille*, 240. [Also translated in: Joris, *Breathturn*, 177; Joris, *Selections*, 105 (changed from from "Nobody" to "Noone" on the basis of Derrida's "Poetics and Politics of Witnessing"); and Felstiner, *Selected Poems*, 261 — Trans.] See above, n. 14.

30. [The expression *tout à l'heure*, disjoined from any context, refers in French both to the recent past and/or to the near future. One could use *tout à l'heure to* say in a "moment from now," but also a "moment ago." Furthermore, the expression can also be construed as meaning "right now" (*tout de suite*), thus conflicting with the idea of an "infinite process." All these senses seem to occur in the same moment: "all at once" or "all on time" — Trans.]

31. "Shibboleth: For Paul Celan," pp. 1–64 in this volume. On "datability," notably in reference to Heidegger, see pp. 194–95, note to p. 15, in this volume.

32. Celan, *Die Niemandɗrose, GW* 1:287. [Trans. Neugroschel, in Joris, *Selectionɗ*, 93 — Trans.]

33. "Eine Gauner- und Ganovenweise / Gesungen zu Paris emprès Pontoise / par Paul Celan / de Czernowitz près de Sadigore," in Celan, *Die Niemandɗrose, GW* 1:229–30. *Macula*, the word for the spot (yellow, at the back of the eye) clearly retains this connotation of a mark sullying the immaculate; this mark spots or charges the immaculate, like an original sin of sight.

34. [Hamburger, *Poemɗ*, 215. Also translated in Felstiner, *Selected Poemɗ*, 199 — Trans.]

35. [In the two previous sentences, the French verb is *accueillir*. It could also be translated "to receive," "to take in," "to accommodate" — Trans.]

36. Martin Heidegger, *Identität und Differenz* (Pfüllingen: Neske, 1957), 62–63; *Identity and Difference*, trans. Joan Stambaugh (1969; rpt. New York, Harper, 1974), 65.

37. Martin Heidegger, *Die Grundbegriffe der Metaphysik: Welt—Endlichkeit—Einɗamkeit, Geɗamtauɗgabe*, 29–30 (Frankfurt a. M.: Klostermann, 1983), 273 ff.; *The Fundamental Concepts of Metaphysicɗ: World, Finitude, Solitude*, trans. William McNeill and Nicholas Walker (Bloomington: Indiana University Press, 1995), 284 ff.

6. The Truth That Wounds

1. [JD's neologism, meaning "capable of being exhibited as an object" — Trans.]

2. "The Double Session," in *Diɗɗemination*, trans. Barbara Johnson (Chicago: University of Chicago Press, 1981). See especially Derrida's commentary on Jean-Pierre Richard's *L'univerɗ imaginaire de Mallarmé* (246–62) and his conclusion: "If there is thus no thematic unity or total meaning to reappropriate beyond the textual instances, no total message located in some imaginary order, intentionality, or lived experience, then the text is no longer the expression or representation (felicitous or otherwise) of any *truth* that would come to diffract or assemble itself in the polysemy of literature. It is this hermeneutic concept of *polyɗemy* that must be replaced by *diɗɗemination*" (262).

Printed in the USA
CPSIA information can be obtained
at www.ICGtesting.com
JSHW020159300524
64007JS00006B/550